Advances in Japanese Business and Economics 7

More information about this series at http://www.springer.com/series/11682

Advances in Japanese Business and Economics

Advances in Japanese Business and Economics showcases the research of Japanese scholars. Published in English, the series highlights for a global readership the unique perspectives of Japan's most distinguished and emerging scholars of business and economics. It covers research of either theoretical or empirical nature, in both authored and edited volumes, regardless of the sub-discipline or geographical coverage, including, but not limited to, such topics as macroeconomics, microeconomics, industrial relations, innovation, regional development, entrepreneurship, international trade, globalization, financial markets, technology management, and business strategy. At the same time, as a series of volumes written by Japanese scholars, it includes research on the issues of the Japanese economy, industry, management practice and policy, such as the economic policies and business innovations before and after the Japanese "bubble" burst in the 1990s.

Overseen by a panel of renowned scholars led by Editor-in-Chief Professor Ryuzo Sato, the series endeavors to overcome a historical deficit in the dissemination of Japanese economic theory, research methodology, and analysis. The volumes in the series contribute not only to a deeper understanding of Japanese business and economics but to revealing underlying universal principles.

Masayuki Otaki

Keynesian Economics and Price Theory

Re-Orientation of a Theory of Monetary Economy

Springer

Masayuki Otaki
Institute of Social Sciences
The University of Tokyo
Bunkyo-ku
Tokyo
Japan

ISSN 2197-8859 ISSN 2197-8867 (electronic)
Advances in Japanese Business and Economics
ISBN 978-4-431-55344-1 ISBN 978-4-431-55345-8 (eBook)
DOI 10.1007/978-4-431-55345-8

Library of Congress Control Number: 2015931950

Springer Tokyo Heidelberg New York Dordrecht London

Printed on acid-free paper

Springer is part of Springer Science+Business Media (www.springer.com)

Preface

The dichotomy between macroeconomics and microeconomics, despite both being branches of economics observing and studying the same economy, perplexes most students of economics, including professional researchers. It is therefore reasonable to investigate how these segregated theoretical approaches relate to each other, and to integrate them. That is the main aim of this book.

As Keynes suggested, there is an important economic element in macroeconomics that does not exist in microeconomics: money. Neoclassical microeconomics theory is concerned with describing a barter economy that does not include money. This is evident from the fact that attempts to integrate money into a neoclassical economic framework have never succeeded. A critical reason for such failures is that in a barter economy there is no serious difficulty with *double coincidence of wants*. Market participants are assumed to find their transaction counterparts without any difficulty. In such scenarios, the economy operates efficiently without money as a medium of exchange. In reality, however, there is no guarantee that the transaction counterpart, whose goods a market participant wants, also needs the goods that may be offered in exchange. Therefore, a barter economy is inefficient whenever there is the difficulty of the double coincidence of wants.

Money can be regarded as a kind of implicit social contract for overcoming such difficulties. Once money is introduced into the economy as a medium of exchange and a store of value (the distinction between these two concepts is almost meaningless because money is hoarded for the future exchange of goods), the function of goods markets or their prices differs completely from that in the barter economy. As elementary microeconomics tells us, prices are determined to equilibrate demand and supply in the barter economy. Such an adjustment towards equilibrium does not, however, work in the monetary economy. The value of money, tentatively defined as the inverse of a price index, is mainly determined by rational expectations concerning future value. This is partially because money does not have economic value in itself when hoarded for future consumption. This prominent characteristic of money implies that the price index sequence forms a nested structure. The current price index is a function of the future price index that is determined beforehand. Similarly, the future price index is affected by the price index in the immediately succeeding future period, and so on. Thus, the values of each price index sequence depend on their own future levels; they do not depend on demand and supply conditions in goods markets or on nominal money supply levels.

Accordingly, in the monetary economy, the current price level does not necessarily equilibrate goods markets even if price movements are flexible to goods market adjustments. If money is insufficiently supplied through fiscal and monetary policy mechanisms, purchasing power contracts in the economy as a whole, resulting in an excess supply of labor and involuntary unemployment. This is a peculiarity of the theory of effective demand with flexible prices, which is developed by this book, when applied to the monetary economy.

Besides incorporating the crucial role of money in the market economy, the unification of macro and microeconomic theory is a substantial contribution made by this book to economic theory as a whole. It enables the use of the most popular value judgment in economics to evaluate macroeconomic policies, the concept of *Pareto efficiency*, which addresses the efficient allocation of scarce resources. In general, however, it is difficult to infer any value judgments in the discussion of macroeconomic policies by professional economists. Such an arbitrary attitude endangers the establishment of social justice parameters in the discipline and practice of economics.

Pareto efficiency seems to be quite a narrow concept for evaluating the effects of macroeconomic policies. For example, it disengages from the problem of fairness of income distribution. However, there remain many macroeconomic problems that can be resolved by incorporating the concept of Pareto efficiency. One of these involves the problem of involuntary unemployment that is examined in this book. Involuntary unemployment is defined as the situation where workers are unemployed despite their willingness to work under prevalent wage rates. If effective demand expands such that these workers find employment, their lifetime utility will improve. Moreover, since profits will also increase together with production, the expansion of effective demand is beneficial for employers as well as for incumbent employees, and results in economic gains for every agent in the economy. Therefore, any policy that reduces involuntary unemployment improves resource allocation in a Pareto sense. This discussion implies that involuntary unemployment is a waste of scarce resources (i.e., labor), and that an expansionary fiscal-monetary policy contributes to improving socioeconomic welfare by absorbing idle resources for product activity.

To summarize, Keynesian theory is supported by two pillars. The first is the *bubble-like* property of money, where the price level is determined by its future expected value; essentially a self-fulfilling prophecy. However, it must be noted that, as opposed to the barter economy, the price level does not always clear the market in the monetary economy. The second is the strict dynamic microeconomic foundation underpinning this theory that allows for the evaluation of macroeconomic policy impacts. This is because the legitimacy of policies should be judged from the viewpoint of Pareto efficiency and exclude the irrational behavior of economic agents.

Acknowledgments

Our esteemed teacher Hirofumi Uzawa delivered the Lucas paper at his seminar for undergraduate students. Although I had neither knowledge nor skills enough to manipulate functional analysis and probability theory in advance of this event, and I have never believed in the omnipotence of the market mechanism, I acutely felt that this paper had a decisive effect on macroeconomic theory. This was because it was the first time that I found a utility function in macroeconomic analysis.

Until that time, the controversy between Keynesian and monetarist macroeconomists was almost always concerned with the shape of the IS/LM and the Phillips curve. As such, the established theories contained much arbitrariness. Looking back on this memory, Professor Uzawa, who is one of the pioneers of optimal growth theory, found a reformulation of macroeconomic theory in the Lucas paper beyond the grievous chasm of other theorists' economic thoughts.

It took me about 10 years to understand the Lucas paper properly. However, this experience defined the origins of my career as a researcher of macroeconomic theory, in conjunction with Professor Uzawa's stringent education for theorists as artisans, and my many other good memories of him.

I am also deeply thankful for my association with Professor Akiyoshi Horiuchi and my old friend Masaharu Hanazaki. My adolescence was not smooth and, as many a graduate school student does, I sometimes became desperate about my future. Both of them not merely enlightened me about economics, but were also generous enough to share my difficulties. In line with these important relationships, I am grateful to the Research Institute of the Capital Formation Development Bank of Japan. Specifically, Mitsuhiro Usui and Hiroaki Jindo have been very kind to me and have allowed me to give many seminars. The institute also provided opportunities for intensive and incisive discussions with my friends Morio Kuninori, Susumu Cato, and Masaoki Tamura. Additionally, I am sincerely grateful for the warm-heartedness of Professor Michio Nitta and the late Professors Masuo Tomioka and Juro Hashimoto.

Special thanks should be given to Professor Ryuzo Sato, who so kindly gave me the opportunity to publish this book, and encouraged me in the process of writing it. Professors Hajime Hori, Kazuo Mino, and Hiroshi Yoshikawa also spared much time to discuss the contents of this work. Their suggestions have improved the transparency of the logic used. In addition, I thank the anonymous referees for their constructive comments.

Last but not least, I must also acknowledge my family. I wish to express inexhaustible love and gratitude to my wife Midori and sons Haruaki and Toshiaki; without their support this book could not have been completed.

Contents

About the Author

Masayuki Otaki is a professor of economics at the Institute of Social Sciences at the University of Tokyo. His main areas of research are macroeconomic theory, environmental economics, educational economics, and economic thought. Born in 1957, Prof. Otaki received a Bachelor's degree in economics at the University of Tokyo in 1981 and a Ph.D. in economics at the University of Tokyo in 1990. He was appointed professor of economics at the Institute of Social Sciences at the University of Tokyo in 2001.

Chapter 1
Introduction

1.1 Introduction to Part 1

Keynes (1936, Chap. 2) argues:

> For it is far from being consistent with *the general tenor of the classic theory, which has taught us to believe that prices are governed by marginal prime cost in terms of money and that money-wages largely govern marginal prime cost.* Thus if money-wages change, one would have expected the classical school to argue that prices would change in almost the same proportion, leaving the real wage and the level of unemployment practically the same as before, any small gain or loss to labour being at the expense of profit of other elements of marginal cost which have been left unaltered. They seem, however, to have been diverted from this line of thought, partly by the settled conviction that labour is in a position to determine its own real wage and partly perhaps, by preoccupation with the idea that the prices depend on the quantity of money.

Thus, it is quite unnatural that the quantity of money appears in the aggregate price determination of many models without any discussion, if prices are assumed to be mainly governed by their nominal marginal costs in microeconomic theory. This indicates that there is still a chasm between macroeconomics and microeconomics, which cannot be easily reconciled. Contemporary economists (including the "New Keynesians" and the "Real-business School"—ironically, the only exception is Lucas (1972), who will be rigorously reconsidered in Chap. 14) avoid or neglect this serious concern, and continue introducing real cash balances into the utility function without hesitation. This is a curious assumption when the actual functions of money are considered. After excluding the exceptionally acquisitive people who are fascinated only with the accumulation of wealth, most ordinary people demand money to prepare for future consumption. This implies that the monetary economy is inherently a *dynamic economy*, in contrast to the assumptions of new Keynesian economics. Although the models belonging to new Keynesian economics resemble dynamic models, their structures are essentially static, and artificial lag structures rule (e.g. Gali (2008) introduced by Calvo (1983)). Intertemporal substitution of consumption streams never change the properties of the static model formatted by Blanchard and Kiyotaki (1987).

M. Otaki, *Keynesian Economics and Price Theory*,
Advances in Japanese Business and Economics 7, DOI 10.1007/978-4-431-55345-8_1

The *dynamic economy* has two prominent characteristics:

i. The economy is assumed to be infinitely viable; that is, the economy has no end period; and
ii. Economic decisions are decentralized across generations.

These two characteristics, which can be well described by the overlapping generation (OLG) model in the production economy, enable fiat money to circulate. Money never circulates if there is an end period within this dynamic economy. At the end period T, money becomes valueless by definition because exchanging money for goods is not feasible after this point. As a result, people born in period $T-1$ never receive money from their nearest ascendants; that is, generation $T-2$. By iterating the backward induction to the current period 0, it is possible to ascertain that fiat money never circulates if there is an end period of the economy.

Price theory can be reconstructed on the basis of the model of the dynamic monetary economy by referring to the above assertion of Keynes. The vital principle is that price is equalized to marginal cost, and is not directly affected by the quantity of money. Although such a principle is self-evident and seems incapable of adding any useful results, on considering that all *dynamic* transactions are settled in *monetary* terms, it can be seen that there exists a genetic nested structure in the monetary economy. This nested structure renovates price theory in the monetary economy, which is entirely different from that in the barter economy. Using a heuristic method, this can be outlined as follows:

Denote the price level, the nominal wage, and the labor productivity as p, W, γ, respectively. Unit labor cost then becomes $\frac{W}{\gamma}$. If firms are price takers, neither fixed production nor entry-exit costs exist, and in equilibrium the zero-profit condition prevails, thus:

$$p_t = \frac{W(p_t, p_{t+1})}{\gamma} \tag{1.1}$$

holds. Henceforth, this type of equation is referred to as the *fundamental equation* in the monetary economy. This equation is developed and furnished by Otaki (2007, 2011a, b). Also, in this model the current nominal wage, W, which provides sufficient incentives to individuals, is a function of the current and the future price vector (p_t, p_{t+1}), because individuals never decide on whether to work without considering their lifetime utility.

The fundamental Eq. (1.1) satisfies the condition that price is equalized to its marginal cost, as emphasized by microeconomics. This implies that Eq. (1.1) is applicable to the standard theory on the barter economy. However, Eq. (1.1) also has deeper implications for the prominent characteristics of the monetary economy. Since there is no endogenous variable except the equilibrium price sequence, this difference equation represents the determination of the price level. The prominent and fundamental characteristics of the fundamental Eq. (1.1) are as follows:

i. ***The nested theory of value***: the value of money, which is defined as the inverse of the current price, is determined by the rational expectation of the future value of money itself; and

ii. ***The irrelevance of the quantity of money to value***: the fundamental Eq. (1.1) does not contain the quantity of money. This implies that, except for the case in which an extraneous belief in the value of money prevails, the equilibrium price level is independent of the quantity of money. That is, money becomes non-neutral, even excluding some ad-hoc price stickiness.

These properties of the model are fully used for the analyses throughout this book.

Usually, according to price theory in the barter economy, the price level is determined to equalize supply to demand. However, such conventional wisdom is not applicable to the monetary economy, since the current price p_t is determined to satisfy the fundamental Eq. (1.1) for an arbitrarily fixed rational expectation concerning the future price p_{t+1}. There is no need to equilibrate the market at this price. Accordingly, quantity adjustment takes place instead of price adjustment.

Barro and Grossman (1971) succeed in representing the underemployment equilibrium in their static model. However, they are unable to show why price levels are fixed and located out of the Walrasian equilibrium. On the contrary, the fundamental equation developed here and based on the simple dynamic marginal principle provides the required microeconomic foundation for the quantity adjustment process and the endogenously determined fixed price.

To summarize: on the one hand, price theory in the barter economy shows that price levels are determined so that markets are cleared, and that the price adjustment process dominates the economy. On the other hand, price theory in the monetary economy reveals that the price level is determined by rational expectations of the future value of money. This is unrelated to whether the markets are cleared, and thus the quantity adjustment process becomes a natural consequence. This intrinsic characteristic provides a rigorous microeconomic foundation for the Kahn (1931)–Keynes (1936) fiscal multiplier as Otaki (2007, 2011a, b) proved.

1.2 Introduction to Part 2

In this part, the fundamental theory constructed in Part 1 is applied to labor economics and inflation theory. In Chap. 3, based on Otaki (2009), the existence of involuntary unemployment is rigorously proved in the sense that curtailing nominal wages never improves employment levels, and that such nominal wage negotiation systems are efficient. In the previous part, it was assumed that the equilibrium nominal wage is equal to the nominal reservation wage since there are always unemployed workers in equilibrium, and workers do not have bargaining power in nominal wage negotiations. However, to prove the existence of involuntary unemployment, it is necessary to introduce the bargaining power of workers.

The order of the game is crucial for efficient wage bargaining. It is assumed that employment and output-level decisions are in advance of nominal wage negotiations. The order of the game provides an unintentional coordination motive to both employer and employees. They can agree on maximizing the total surplus (profits plus the surplus from working) and thereafter divide the maximized surplus. Thus, the employment/output level is equal to that where workers have no bargaining power, and hence the bargaining power of workers does not hinder improving the employment level. Since the equilibrium nominal wage is determined above the nominal reservation wage, involuntary unemployment owing to the shortage of effective demand emerges.

Chapter 4 proves the existence of the long-run downward Phillips curve without ad-hoc price friction, based on Otaki and Tamai (2011). The assumption of the fundamental theory on the point that labor productivity is fixed is relaxed. There is a prominent negative statistical correlation between Japanese labor productivity and the unemployment rate, for example. Although there might be various interpretations concerning this correlation, the following causality is assumed: a higher unemployment rate lowers labor productivity in the long run.

There is a persuasive reason that supports such causality. As Otaki (2014a, b) proves, income disparity caused by unemployment deprives workers of the opportunity of fundamental education. By the intrinsic nature of financial markets, asymmetric information concerning borrowers' quality is quite serious. Non-wealthy families are unable to finance educational investment for their children because their default cost is relatively low, and thus they are not creditworthy for financial intermediaries even if the children are of high ability. Deprivation of educational opportunity hinders the nurturing of various human resources for skills employed within the firm. As such, labor productivity possibly degenerates via a higher unemployment rate. Also, current goods become expensive relative to future goods when labor productivity is curtailed. This is because the slowdown in labor productivity implies that production cost for the current goods becomes higher relative to any fixed future price level. This means that disinflation progresses along with stagnant labor productivity.

The following flowchart summarizes this section:

Unemployment rate $\Uparrow \Rightarrow$ Labor productivity $\Downarrow \Rightarrow$ Inflation rate $\Downarrow$.

Thus, we obtain a downward long-run Phillips curve without ad-hoc price stickiness assumptions.

1.3 Introduction to Part 3

This part covers various applications of the fundamental theory developed in Chap. 2 to international economics. Throughout, variants of the fundamental equation play a crucial role because the equation is a critical formula that transforms a barter economy into the corresponding monetary economy.

In Chap. 5, a basic model that describes a flexible exchange rate regime under perfect capital mobility is developed. Unlike those of Fleming (1962) and Mundell (1963), this model is based on a rigorous dynamic microeconomic foundation. Also, unlike Obstfeld and Rogoff (1996) and their successors, this study, which is based on Otaki (2012a), is simple and analytical in the sense that definitive and qualitative results are obtained without depending on numerical analysis. The following results are presented: First, the business cycle diffuses internationally via inflation caused by an appreciation of the real exchange rate. In this sense, the employment isolation effect, which is intensively analyzed by Laursen and Metzler (1950), is imperfect even in a stationary state.

Chapter 6 deals with the role of key currency. Except for some European countries such as Germany, imbalances in the current account are not as prominent in many advanced economies as is suggested (e.g. around 1–2 % of GDP in Japan). However, these imbalances are persistent. For example, Japan and China continue to be creditors and the United States has been the largest debtor country in the world from the mid-1960s. Such sustainable (at least seemingly) and persistent current account imbalances cannot be explained without analyzing the roles of key currencies. That is, although the balance of payments of most advanced economies permit the exchange rate to fluctuate, and this can be regarded as being located around equilibrium as the model in Chap. 5 predicts, there remains a non-negligible imbalance between the key-currency country and its affiliates. Chapter 6 addresses this question based on Otaki (2013a, b).

Although the same currency may be circulated across borders as a key currency, other types of currency alignment can be considered. Chapter 7 deals with a theory of an optimum currency area with a rigorous microeconomic foundation. The optimum currency area theory developed by Mundell (1961) emphasizes that linked economies, between which the mobility of production resources such as capital and labor is quite high, should unite their central banks and use the same currency. However, this argument is ambiguous as to why such a proposition is upheld. Chapter 7, based on Otaki (2012c), explicitly introduces a policy game of twin economy central banks under perfect capital mobility. This captures one of the accomplishments of an optimum currency area; the transition from the non-cooperative game of the two central banks to a cooperative game regime.

A currency alignment such as the Eurozone might be founded on Mundell's optimum currency area. Nevertheless, imbalances on current accounts are serious between affiliates, and, in this situation, creditor countries such as Germany can never be benevolent enough, as the Euro crisis suggests. This problem is dealt with in Chap. 8. The Euro zone is far from an optimum currency area in the sense that most residents seem to adhere to the concept of the nation state, at least economically. It seems natural to regard the Euro as an unadjustable locally fixed exchange rate regime rather than an optimum currency area. Further, it is possible to show that *austere policies* that put much priority on the equilibrium of current accounts to achieve high employment are a necessary condition for sustaining such a regime. In addition, as the tax levying ability of a government improves, austere policies contribute to the economy's welfare. This is because fiscal abundance makes an economy more credible, and it can provide much liquidity in a domestic economy.

Chapter 9 is closely related to Chap. 7. Both chapters analyze how international factor movements affect a small open economy. However, in contrast to Chap. 7, the economy being discussed in Chap. 9 is located far from the rest of the world and there are non-tradable goods in both economies. There is thus no guarantee that nominal equilibrium wages will become equal between them. If physical capital moves freely beyond boundaries, all tradable goods firms will move to the cheap wage economy. Such a surge of foreign direct investment (FDI) implies that the high-wage economy experiences massive unemployment and a reduction of domestic demand. This phenomenon is called *industrial hollowing*. In Chap. 9, the mechanism and welfare implication of industrial hollowing is analyzed. It will be shown that industrial hollowing is a kind of *fallacy of composition* in the sense that although firms perceive the real exchange rate as an exogenous variable, it is an endogenous variable in the economy as a whole. That is, massive remittances of earnings overseas will result in the appreciation of the real exchange rate, and thus FDI is not so profitable when this appreciation effect is taken into consideration.

Chapter 10 relates to Chap. 5. A model of the gold standard is constructed, and the severity of international business cycle diffusion is compared. Unlike the flexible exchange rate system extended in Chap. 5, nominal money supply links directly to the imbalance of the current account under the gold standard. That is, since the autonomy of monetary policy is retained and the exchange rate partly absorbs exogenous shocks under a flexible exchange rate system, the diffusion in the foreign business cycle is indirect and mitigated compared with impacts under the gold standard, as historical evidence suggests.

1.4 Introduction to Part 4

This part extends the fundamental theory put forward in Part 1 into a Keynesian monetary growth model, in which, instead of aggregate saving, capital investment becomes the driving force of economic growth. The most prominent characteristic of this growth theory is to emphasize the role of human capital rather than that of physical capital because, in general, physical capital is mobile and can be rebuilt. As such, FDI immediately enriches any country unless human capital plays a crucial role in economic development and/or growth. Thus, microeconomic analysis concerning the role of human capital in economic growth is quite important for economic growth theory.

Since the accumulation of human and physical capital is almost directly related to firm behavior, it is indispensable for pursuing the actual source of economic growth to find and format how these two capitals interact within the firm. In Chap. 11, based on Otaki and Yaginuma (2012) and Otaki (2013b, d), the concept of dexterity is formulated, which is made up of the positive externalities from human capital to physical capital, and proves that its legitimate evaluation acutely sustains economic growth.

There are two theories about intangible assets accumulated within the firm. One is Arrow's (1962) *learning by doing* effect. Arrow assumed that average labor productivity increases with the cumulative volume of outputs. This implies that workers gradually accustom their production processes towards higher productivity. This theory of the firm also emphasizes the significant and intangible progress of quality of labor. However, it must be noted that Arrow assumes that no cost is incurred by such learning processes except for time. In reality, the learning by doing process can never be achieved without a "trial and error" process. This is because learning comprises structural reflections on unprecedented accidents partly caused by unintentional misbehaviors. This undeniable fact suggests that there is a substantive investment cost required for the education of stakeholders.

Arrow also neglects the interaction between human and physical capital. Almost all the skills embodied in workers are firm-specific. It is not difficult to imagine that the skills attached to blue-collar occupations are heavily dependent on the nature of the factories and machines that they use. However, the skills of white-collar workers are not circumscribed by the firm. These workers establish human networks and/or customer relationships inside and outside of their company, which not only builds up their own social credibility, but also heightens the credibility of their corporation and improves productivity. Thus, against Arrow's (1962) specification, it is plausible to assume that the contribution to production of labor and capital is genetically decomposable, and that progress in the skills of employees brings positive externality to physical capital in reality. This positive externality is named as *dexterity*.

The second existing theory about intangible assets within firms was proposed by Uzawa (1969) and Penrose (1959), and contains a famous model establishing a microeconomic foundation for Tobin's (1969) *q*. Although Uzawa (1969) succeeds in providing a rigorous economic growth theory including capital investment, differing from Arrow (1962) and the theory put forward in this book, the role of employees in economic growth is quite restrictive. He treats labor as a variable production resource even in the short run. This implies that a labor force is standardized and interchangeable through markets for the unskilled labor force. Employees are also not required to nourish intangible specific skills as such. Instead, he assumes that all the intangible assets deployed for the growth of the firm are contained within physical capital. This is rather a strange assumption. Physical capital comprises machines, factories, and buildings that will never think and actively learn from experience. Unlike the theory put forward in Chap. 11, the effective quality of physical capital can never be improved by employee skills development. In this sense, Uzawa's assumption implies that inorganic substances can automatically accumulate intangible assets. This is far from reality.

To summarize, the studies of Arrow and Uzawa pay little attention to the inseparability between employee skills (human capital) and physical capital. Since markets fail owing to such inseparability, the alternative theory in Chap. 11 succeeds in specifying the acute driving force of economic growth, but also in explaining the raison d'être of firms, which closely relates to Coase's (1937) assertion that a firm exists because it can achieve more efficient allocation of resources than markets in some circumstances.

Chapter 12 constructs a Keynesian economic growth model under perfect competition based on the previous chapter and the contribution of Otaki and Tamura (2013). Although, as aforementioned, Uzawa (1969) formulates a growth theory including investment function, his model deals with a real economy, which does not include the monetary factor. This implies that there is no unemployment due to the shortage of effective demand to which Keynes (1936) attaches so much importance. Based on the fundamental monetary theory outlined in Part 1, this section succeeds in showing that an imperfect employment equilibrium coexists with economic growth. In addition, the analysis determines whether steady economic growth is feasible without expanding the public debt ratio to the real NDP (the NY ratio). This is an important problem in the consideration of whether higher employment levels are sustainable or compatible with capital accumulation without the need for an excess fiscal intervention in the market economy. The discussion shows that the NY ratio is kept constant as long as the market is competitive. This theorem implies that a monetary economy can achieve a high employment equilibrium only by moderate fiscal intervention. In this sense, a monetary market economy is sustainable under perfect competition.

There are two economic reasons why such a harmonious result is obtained. One is that investment in human capital grows autonomously regardless of the level of effective demand. Since the specification of the human capital investment adjustment cost function follows Uzawa's (1969) "Penrose function", the average cost for achieving a given economic growth rate, which is equal to the progress rate in skills of employees, is kept constant regardless of the level of human capital accumulation. Such a property leads an economy to steady growth, since there are no obstacles to that growth. The other reason is the fact that, unlike the monopolistic competition case, firms never perceive demand constraints under perfect competition. When goods markets in an economy are under monopolistic competition, each firm faces a downward demand curve, in which location is conditional on effective demand, and a firm cannot sell its goods without limitation (i.e. a firm faces the demand constraint). Thus, human capital investment is constrained by the level of effective demand. In other words, unless perfect competition prevails in markets, there emerge obstacles for economic growth. As such, the penetration of perfect competition is a necessary condition for achieving steady growth in a monetary market economy.

Chapter 13 considers the sustainability of economic growth under monopolistic competition in a monetary market economy, based on Otaki (2013c). Sustainability is defined by the convergence of the abovementioned NY ratio. The NY ratio will diverge if a government pursues incessant growth in its monetary market economy. That is, steady economic growth is unsustainable and the scale of the government is enlarged without limitation under monopolistic competition. Such a phenomenon is often observed even in advanced countries. This devastating proposition is induced by the following logic. First, as aforementioned, investment is constrained by the level of effective demand and ceases to increase autonomously, and hence an economy loses the driving force of growth. This implies that whereas labor productivity is improved incessantly by investment, the equilibrium growth rate falls to zero. Second, if residents of the economy desire economic growth and reduction of unemployment caused by labor productivity progress, the government is forced to expand its expenditure artificially and stimulate effective demand. This enlarges the stock of public debt relative to real GDP. Third, because aggregate consumption and investment adjusts in line with such an expansion instantaneously, growth in the economy is in fact temporary. If the economy is to continue to grow, incessant additional government expenditure is necessary. As such, the accumulation of public debt is cumulative, and thus economic growth is unsustainable in a monetary market economy under monopolistic competition.

However, it must also be noted that labor productivity progress possibly improves economic welfare in an economy where the population is decreasing, even though monopolistic competition prevails. This is because real GDP per capita increases with labor productivity progress as long as its velocity does not exceed the rate of population decline, and unemployment does not increase.

1.5 Introduction to Part 5

This part reconsiders the consistency and relevance of existing monetary theories. Chapter 14 deals with the theory advanced by Lucas (1972), which has essentially the same structure as the theory advanced in this book. The focus is on why Lucas has been able to prove the neutrality of money despite the fact that it is possible to rigorously derive the non-neutrality of money and succeed in constructing Keynesian economic theory, which in turn can be broadly applied to labor economics, international economics, and economic growth theory as suggested above.

The prominent features of the Lucas model are twofold: (i) money injection by its own interest; and (ii) an extraneous rational belief based on the quantity theory of money. Both assumptions are necessary for the proof of the neutrality of money. Otani (1985) showed that this proposition is not upheld if condition (i) is violated. He added a lump-sum term to the money-supply rule, which is independent of money hoarding carried over from the previous period. This hinders the equilibrium price level from increasing proportionately to the additional money supply. Thus, if condition (i) is violated, money becomes non-neutral. Further, Otaki (2012b) considers the case that condition (ii) is not satisfied. Instead of the quantity-theoretic belief, it is presumed that *confidence* in money is as defined in Chap. 2. This construction succeeds in proving that such a belief constitutes a rational (or self-fulfilling) expectations equilibrium, and that money becomes non-neutral also in this case.

These two studies are based on a deterministic model, although the original paper by Lucas adopts a stochastic one. Accordingly, the following question must be asked: Even though the abovementioned two conditions can be accepted, is the Lucas model still valid as a stochastic monetarist model? There are two questions intrinsic to the stochastic model, which come from the fact that the Lucas model is a signal extraction problem in general equilibrium. The first relates to the transformation between conditional cumulative distribution functions. Since an individual infers the true state of an economy through the equilibrium price, the joint distribution of the price and other stochastic variables generally depends on the functional form of the equilibrium price function. Thus, the transformation of the joint distribution function, which contains the equilibrium price, into the joint distribution function, which comprises only exogenous stochastic shocks (i.e. from various environments), relies on the form of the equilibrium price function. This, in turn, is assumed to be a function of the environment. However, the proof advanced by Lucas (1972) pays little attention to this problem. It is therefore necessary to analyze whether his procedure retains legitimacy.

The other problem is the equivalence between the functional equations that are thought to represent market equilibrium. Lucas (1972) transforms the initially defined functional equation using a specific money-supply rule and the quantity-theoretic equilibrium price function, and proves that such an equilibrium price function satisfies the transformed functional equation. Nevertheless, there is an error in the transformation, and the proof-of-existence is incomplete. The discussion in Part 5 corrects this transformation, and provides a sufficient condition imposed on the utility function to complete the proof.

Chapter 15 critically analyzes Kiyotaki and Wright's (1989, 1991) monetary theory based on the search theory mainly developed by Diamond (1982). It is seen that the properties identified by Kiyotaki and Wright (1989) possess few distinctive features from the standard OLG model. This is because even though their model emphasizes the fact that the difficulty seen in the double coincidence of wants promotes the circulation of money, this is almost in common with the OLG model. That is, an OLG model with money, which is deployed in Lucas (1972) and this book, also incorporates such difficulties as the fact that younger individuals acutely need future goods. However, older individuals, who live within the same period, want current goods. Accordingly, the difficulty seen in the double coincidence of wants has already been embedded in existing monetary theory.

Kiyotaki and Wright (1991) tried to improve their theory. In the 1991 paper they advocate that money can circulate without the function of a store of value. In other words, they consider that the two functions of money (i.e. as a medium of exchange and store of value) can be seen as separable. However, it has long been overlooked that the Kiyotaki and Wright (1991) model has the same type of equilibrium solution as that of the Diamond model. That is, there is the equilibrium of a barter economy in their model. This is because they substantially fail to express the difficulty of the double coincidence of wants despite the fact that they introduce a variety of goods into their model. This is similar to the Diamond model, where all individuals, independent of their status, can potentially purchase any kind of goods if they wish, and thus there is no difficulty resulting from the double coincidence of wants. Here, the distinct features between a "commodity trader" and a "money trader" are twofold. One is that money is perishable because it serves only as a medium of exchange, and is assumed not to function as a store of value. The other is that differences may exist in the threshold values (distance) where these traders decide to purchase a good.[1]

Such a difference should be advantageous for a money trader if money can circulate within an economy. However, it is clear that the equilibrium threshold value in

[1] They assume a Hoteling-type circle model. As the distance from an individual, which corresponds to the variation of goods, becomes large, the good produced at such a location brings less utility.

a barter economy is the best response under the conditions of the storability of commodities and perishable money, because money hoarding provides scarce opportunities for exchange. Consequently, there is no change in the behavior of a commodity trader even though a government intends to inject money into the economy. This implies that the Kiyotaki and Wright (1991) model cannot succeed in establishing the reasons why a barter economy moves to a monetary economy, without the role of money as a store of value. This proposition is formally proved in Chap. 15.

References

Arrow KJ (1962) The economic implications of learning by doing. Rev Econ Stud 29:155–173

Barro RJ, Grossman HI (1971) A general disequilibrium model of income and employment. Am Econ Rev 61:82–93

Blanchard OJ, Kiyotaki N (1987) Monopolistic competition an the effects of aggregate demand. Am Econ Rev 77:647–666

Calvo GA (1883) Staggered prices in a utility-maximizing framework. J Monetary Econ 12:383–398

Coase RH (1937) The nature of the firm. Economica 4:386–405

Diamond P (1982) Aggregate-demand management in search equilibrium. J Polit Econ 90:927–954.

Fleming JM (1962) Domestic fiscal policies and floating exchange rates. IMF Staff Pap 9:369–380

Gali G (2008) Monetary policy, inflation, and the business cycle: an introduction to the new Keynesian framework. Princeton University Press, Princeton

Kahn RF (1931) The relation of home investment to unemployment. Econ J 41:173–198

Keynes JM (1936) The general theory of employment, interest and money. Macmillan, London

Kiyotaki N, Wright R (1989) On money as a medium of exchange. J Polit Econ 97:927–954

Kiyotaki N, Wright R (1991) A contribution to the pure theory of money. J Econ Theory 23:215–235

Laursen S, Metzler L (1950) Flexible exchange rates and the theory of employment Rev Econ Stat:281–299

Lucas RE Jr (1972) Expectations and the neutrality of money. J Econ Theory 4:103–124

Mundell RA (1961) A theory of optimum currency area. Am Econ Rev 51:657–665

Mundell RA (1963) Capital mobility and stabilization policy under fixed and flexible exchange rates. Can J Econ Polit Sci 29:475–485

Obstfeld M, Rogoff K (1996) Foundations of international economics. MIT Press, Massachusetts

Otaki M (2007) The dynamically extended Keynesian cross and the welfare-improving fiscal policy. Econ Lett 96:23–29

Otaki M (2009) A welfare economic foundation for the full-employment policy. Econ Lett 102:1–3

Otaki M (2011a) A pure theory of aggregate price determination. Theor Econ Lett 1:122–128

Otaki M (2011b) Kahei koyo riron no kiso (Fundamentals of the theory of money and employment). Keiso Shobo, Tokyo

Otaki M (2012a) A Keynesian model of a small open economy under a flexible exchange rate. Theor Econ Lett 2:278–282

Otaki M (2012b) The role of money: credible asset or nemeraire. Theor Econ Lett 2: 365–368

Otaki M (2012c) A microeconomic foundation for optimum currency area. Theor Econ Lett 2:395–399

Otaki M (2013a) How a key currency functions as an international liquidity provision and insurance system. Theor Econ Lett 3:43–47

Otaki M (2013b) Evaluation of dexterity and a theory the growth of a firm. Mod Econ 4:226–229

Otaki M (2013c) On the endogenous sustainability of economic growth: why is the scale of government enlarged? Theor Econ Lett 3:159–163

Otaki M (2013d) Kokuai Kinyu Keizai seicho riron no kiso (Fundamentals of the theory of international economics and economic growth). Keiso Shobo, Tokyo

Otaki M (2014a) Income disparity, uneven economic opportunity, and verifiability. Adv Soc Sci Res J 1:44–49
Otaki M (2014b) Efficacy in education and intergenerational wellbeing. Theor Econ Lett 4:183–189
Otaki M, Tamai Y (2011) On the dynamic role of monopolistic competition. Theor Econ Lett 1:114–117
Otaki M, Tamura M (2013) Monetary growth theory under perfect and monopolistic competitions. Theor Econ Lett 3:216–219
Otaki M, Yaginuma H (2012) Kigyo seicho to jinteki shihon no chikuseki: keieiken to kigyo seicho no conflict (The growth of a firm and accumulation of human capital: the conflict between the managerial right and the growth of a Firm). DBJ Discussion Paper Series No. 1208, Research Institute of Capital Formation, Development Bank of Japan. http://www.dbj.jp/ricf/research/discussion.html. Accessed 22 July 2014
Otani K (1985) Rational Expectations and non-neutrality of money. WeltwirtschaftlichesArch 121:207–216
Penrose E (1959) The theory of the growth of the firm. Oxford University Press, Oxford
Tobin J (1969) A general equilibrium approach to monetary theory. J Money Credit Bank 1:15–29
Uzawa H (1969) Time preference and Penrose effect in a two-class model of economic growth. J Polit Econ 77:628–652

Part I
Keynesian Economics and Price Theory

Chapter 2
Price Theory in a Monetary Economy

2.1 Introduction

As discussed in Chap. 1, a monetary economy is a nested structure. That is, the current price level is determined by a rational belief concerning the future price level, which is expressed by the fundamental equation:

$$p_t = \frac{W(p_t, p_{t+1})}{\gamma} \tag{2.1}$$

Where: p_t and p_{t+1} are the current and the future price level, respectively; W is the nominal wage, which depends on these prices; and γ denotes labor productivity.

In Sect. 2.2, the fundamental equation is derived from an individual's rational economic behavior. Based on this, basic Keynesian models under perfect and monopolistic competition are constructed. The perfect competition version aims to show that an imperfect employment equilibrium emerges even in the absence of monopolistic power. The new Keynesian theories entirely rely on this.[1] In addition, the Kahn (1931)–Keynes (1936) fiscal multiplier regarding the monetary economy is derived from developed price theory with rational expectations. The monopolistic competition version is provided to enable welfare analysis of the discretionary fiscal-monetary policy. Although the perfect competition model bears no surplus in the present model, and aggregate demand management policy is neutral from the viewpoint of welfare economics, an expansionary fiscal-monetary policy improves the Pareto efficiency of resource allocations in the monopolistic competition model.

[1] Although equilibrium in the new Keynesian model suggests that resource allocation is second best, and that leisure is excessively long and consumption levels below the optimum, such properties do not emerge from the shortage of effective demand, but from distorted pricing owing to monopolistic behavior. Thus, imperfect unemployment in the new Keynesian models is rooted in distortions found on the supply side, not on the demand side.

M. Otaki, *Keynesian Economics and Price Theory*,
Advances in Japanese Business and Economics 7, DOI 10.1007/978-4-431-55345-8_2

As discussed in detail in Sect. 2.5, the equilibrium of monopolistic competition achieves a relatively superior Pareto allocation compared with the perfect competition case, because of the emergence of an economic surplus derived from monopoly profits, although this seems to be counterintuitive. Such monopolistic profits proportionately increase with aggregate demand, which is enhanced by an expansionary fiscal-monetary policy through the multiplier process. Thus, such policies can improve resource allocation.

In Sect. 2.3, the legitimacy of the functional form of the lifetime utility function is discussed. The following assumptions are made:

I. The lifetime utility function is additively separable between the lifetime consumption stream and the labor supply;
II. The lifetime utility from the consumption stream is homothetic or linear homogenous; and
III. Working hours are assumed to be fixed, and labor demand and supply adjusted according to the number of employees.

Assumptions I and II are compatible with price index number theory, which has been most intensively developed by Dewert (2009). It is common for the consumer price index (CPI) not to contain the price of leisure; that is, the nominal wage. This implies that the disutility function of labor should be additively separable. Moreover, the CPI is an approximation of the true index, and the true index should be independent of an individual's utility level to nullify a change caused by the income effect. A sufficient condition that satisfies such a requirement is Assumption II.[2]

Assumption III is not as straightforward as the first two assumptions. This assumption relates to the concavity of the disutility function of working hours per capita. As discussed in Sect. 2.3, progressive hourly wages are accrued when an employer intends to increase working hours per capita. Thus, an employer would dilute working hours per capita, and instead increase the number of employees as far as possible when business upturns. Thus, in principle, there is no lower limit to working hours per capita. However, in practice, there is a limit on the number of employees, and hence working hours per capita reduce until full employment is automatically achieved, regardless of business condition. Accordingly, the familiar representative individual assumption only explains how working hours per capita vary, and cannot explain the more serious problem pertaining to loss of jobs by individuals.

In Sect. 4, the analysis turns to how Keynesian theory relates to the quantity theory of money (i.e. monetarism). The quantity theory of money is based on the extraneous belief that the equilibrium price during each period is proportionate to the quantity of money. That is, individuals *believe* the following formula:

$$p_t = \kappa^{-1} M_t, \tag{2.2}$$

Where: κ is some positive constant, and M_t is the current quantity of money.

[2] Although it is enough to define the true index by stating that the utility function from the consumption stream is homothetic, this assumption is too weak when the level of the incentivized wage is determined.

Since additional money is unable to purchase additional goods whenever the relationship described by Eq. (2.2) is upheld, the level of real GDP is unrelated to the quantity of money. This implies that the economy should be at its full capacity, and there should be no idle resources whenever this extraneous belief is self-fulfilling. In Sect. 2.4, a rigorous proof is advanced that the quantity theory of money, which is sustained by the baseless extraneous belief encapsulated in Eq. (2.2), becomes relevant only when full employment is kept intact throughout time.

In Sect. 2.5, the properties of the theories in Sect. 2.2 are reconsidered. These theories reveal that resource allocation under monopolistic competition dominates resource allocation under perfect competition. This assertion is counterintuitive from the point of view of the first fundamental theorem of welfare economics. However, the following presumptions and properties must be noted: (1) The first fundamental theorem is upheld only within the range of a finite number of individuals and goods. This is because the proof requires the feasibility of adding up budget constraints of individuals. As mentioned above, the *dynamic* economy comprises an infinite number of individuals and goods. Thus, the presumption of the first fundamental theorem is violated; and (2) While current prices become dearer under monopolistic competition, the required information, which the intertemporal decision needs, is the relative price of future goods to current goods (i.e. the inflation rate). Whenever individuals are confident of the future value of money, the inflation rate is lowered by monopolistic competition. Since inflation is a kind of tax incurred by money hoarding, monopolistic competition appeases such an excess burden intrinsic to the monetary economy. Relying on these intuitive points, this section rigorously proves the Pareto dominance of monopolistic competition over perfect competition. Section 2.6 summarizes and concludes this chapter.

2.2 The Fundamental Equation

In this section, the *fundamental equation* in the monetary economy is derived, and this governs the motion of the price level. This is used to develop a Keynesian economic model with: (i) optimization of economic agents, (ii) no exogenous price stickiness, and (iii) rational expectations excluding extraneous belief-like quantity theoretical expectations. The models are based on the same structure. This exposition basically adopts the overlapping generations (OLG) model in the production economy developed by Lucas (1972). An individual lives for two periods; deciding whether to work when young, and what to do after this. In this period, labor productivity is denoted by γ .

Since income-earning ability is concentrated in the years prior to 65 for most consumers, and goods are assumed to be perishable, an individual worker must save fiat money obtained from the older (post-65) generation in exchange for produced goods to prepare for future consumption. Thus, there is an incentive for the circulation of money as long as the economy is *dynamic*, as defined in Sect. 1.1.

2.2.1 The Keynes–Walras Model

In this model it is assumed that only one kind of good is produced and the goods market operates under perfect competition (i.e. every firm behaves as a price taker).

The Decisions of Individuals The lifetime utility function U_t is identified as follows:

$$U_t \equiv u(c_{1t}, c_{2t+1}) - \delta_t \cdot \alpha, \tag{2.3}$$

Where: c_{1t} and c_{2t+1} are the current and future consumptions of the individual born in period t; δ_t is a definition function that takes vale unity when the individual is employed and zero when unemployed; and α denotes the disutility of labor. In this case $u(\cdot)$ is a homothetic utility function concerning lifetime consumption and can be written as follows:

$$u(c_{1t}, c_{2t+1}) \equiv f(v(c_{1t}, c_{2t+1})),$$

Where: f is a monotonously increasing continuous function, and v is a linear homogenous function.

The budget constraint faced by the individual is therefore:

$$\delta_t \cdot W_t \geq p_t c_{1t} + M_t, M_t \geq p_{t+1} c_{2t+1}, \tag{2.4}$$

Where: W_t and M_t are the nominal wage and nominal money demand, respectively; and (p_t, p_{t+1}) is the vector of good prices. The constraint (2.4) is equivalent to:

$$\delta_t \cdot W_t \geq p_t \cdot c_{1t} + p_{t+1} \cdot c_{2t+1}. \tag{2.5}$$

An individual maximizes (2.3) subject to (2.5) on $(c_{1t}, c_{2t+1}, \delta_t)$. This problem decomposes into the following two-step problem:

i. Given the level of labor income, optimize lifetime utility from the consumption stream, and
ii. Decide whether to work by conferring the optimized utility from the lifetime consumption.

Since $u(\cdot)$ is homothetic, the first problem is solved as the following indirect utility function:

$$ID \equiv f\left(\frac{\delta_t \cdot W_t}{\psi(p_t, p_{t+1})}\right), \tag{2.6}$$

Where: ψ is a linear homogenous function.

Based on Eq. (2.6), it is possible to solve the second problem concerning the decisions made in relation to the labor supply of the individual. If $ID \geq \alpha$ holds, the lifetime utility from consumption exceeds the disutility of labor, and thus every individual wishes to work; that is, $\delta_t = 1$. Otherwise, no one wants to participate; that is, $\delta_t = 0$.

The following assumption about the equilibrium of the labor market can then be made:

Assumption 2.1
Equilibrium in the labor market is always interior. That is, there are some individuals who are unemployed.

The equilibrium nominal wage is determined by this assumption such that $ID = \alpha$. This is because if $ID > \alpha$, there are ceaseless applications to the lower wage offers, and as a result, the nominal wage falls to a level that satisfies $ID = \alpha$. That is, the equilibrium nominal wage W_t is determined as being equal to the reservation wage:

$$W_t = f^{-1}(\alpha)\cdot\psi(p_t, p_{t+1}). \tag{2.7}$$

It must be noted that Eq. (2.7) is the equilibrium condition for the labor market in this model.

The Decision of Firms: The Fundamental Equation We have assumed that firms are price takers and that no fixed costs prevent their entry/exit decisions. Consequently, at equilibrium, the zero-profit condition should be held, and:

$$p_t = \frac{W_t}{\gamma}. \tag{2.8}$$

Substituting Eq. (2.7) into Eq. (2.8) gives:

$$p_t = \frac{f^{-1}(\alpha)\cdot\psi(p_t, p_{t+1})}{\gamma}. \tag{2.9}$$

This is the exact form of the *fundamental equation* in the monetary economy, which was described as Eq. (2.1) in Sect. 1 under the situation of perfect competition; that is, the Walrasian equilibrium. The fundamental equation depicts the nested structure of the monetary economy, as outlined in Sect. 1.1. Individuals call for their nominal wage W_t by conferring the future price level p_{t+1}. The equilibrium current price p_t is determined to equalize the unit revenue p_t to the unit labor cost $\frac{f^{-1}(\alpha)\cdot\psi(p_t, p_{t+1})}{\gamma}$. This implies that since individuals *believe* and confer the future value of money (i.e. the inverse of p_{t+1} is not zero), the current value of money is determined by that value. This represents the nested structure of the monetary economy in that the current value of money is always affected by the future values of money. Accordingly, it is not necessary to determine a price level to equalize the demand for goods with supply. In this sense, price theory in the monetary economy is quite different from that in the barter economy.

The most prominent property of the fundamental equation is that it does not contain the stream of the nominal money supply $\{M_{t+j}\}_{j=0}^{\infty}$. This implies that price levels are determined, in principle, regardless of the quantity of money. Thus, the real cash balance $\left\{\frac{M_{t+j}}{p_{t+j}}\right\}_{k=0}^{\infty}$ can be manipulated by a change in the quantity of money, as long as there are idle resources for additional money to purchase additional goods; that is, Assumption 2.1 is satisfied. As shown below, this implies the non-neutrality of money without the assumption of any exogenous price stickiness.

Confidence in Money: An Exclusion Method of Extraneous Beliefs Since $\psi(\cdot)$ in Eq. (2.9) takes a linear homogenous form, it can be transformed into:

$$\gamma = f^{-1}(\alpha)\cdot\psi\left(1,\frac{p_{t+1}}{p_t}\right). \tag{2.10}$$

Accordingly, the equilibrium inflation rate $\frac{p_{t+1}}{p_t}$ is constant over time. Let this value be denoted as ρ^*. It is apparent from Eq. (2.10) that the fundamental equation by itself cannot determine price levels and only ρ^* is determined. This means that there is an arbitrary constant value for determination of the price sequence *per se*. Such arbitrariness or indeterminacy makes room for rational extraneous belief, which connects the price level with an intrinsically unrelated economic variable such as the quantity of money. This will be rigorously discussed in Sect. 2.4.

To eliminate this inconvenience, an assumption is made concerning *confidence* in money.

Definition 2.1
Money is confident if and only if:

$$\frac{dp_{t+1}}{dM_t} = 0. \tag{2.11}$$

Confidence in money implies that younger individuals believe in the intrinsic value of money, which is unrelated to the quantity of money. Although this seems to be a curious assumption for those who are captives in the quantity theory of money, the condition expressed in Eq. (2.11) is deeply rooted in our daily lives. For example, every individual deposits money in banks and funds consumer credits without any anxiety. This suggests that individuals believe in the future intrinsic value of money, and rationally anticipate that the future value of money will not be affected by monetary policy.

Equation (2.11) excludes extraneous beliefs in the following manner. Let us denote the historically given rational expectation concerning the future price as $\overline{p_{t+1}}$, which is not the function of the quantity of money M_t. Thereafter, the equilibrium prices are expressed as $\overline{p_{t+1}}\cdot[\rho]^{j-1}$. The current equilibrium price can be solved by backward induction as $\overline{p_{t+1}} \cdot [\rho]^{-1}$. Thus, the following theorem is obtained:

Theorem 2.1

If money is confident, according to the condition expressed in (2.9), the all-equilibrium price sequence $\{p_{t+j}\}_{j=0}^{\infty}$ *becomes independent of the quantity of money* M_t.

This theorem is presumed throughout this chapter.

The Role of the Government The government issues fiat money to finance wasteful public expenditure. The budget constraint of the government becomes:

$$p_t \cdot g \equiv M_t - M_{t-1}, \tag{2.12}$$

Where: g denotes real public expenditure. (2.12) is transformed into:

$$g + \frac{M_{t-1}}{p_t} \equiv \frac{M_t}{p_t}. \tag{2.13}$$

Equation (2.13) implies that the sum of real public expenditure and the consumption of the current older individuals are equal to the current real cash balance. Furthermore, it must be noted that the real cash balance $\frac{M_t}{p_t}$ can be manipulated by a change in the quantity of money M_t under Theorem 2.1.

The Dynamic Keynesian Cross: Market Equilibrium There are three markets in this model: the goods market, the labor market, and the money market. The labor market is in equilibrium when Eq. (2.10) is satisfied. The goods and money markets are mutually dependent, and if one of these markets is in equilibrium, so is the other. Here, the equilibrium condition for the goods market is analyzed. From the zero-profit condition of the firms as expressed by Eq. (2.9), real GDP y_t is equal to the total labor income. Thus, we obtain the following equilibrium condition:

$$y_t = c\left(\rho^*\right) \cdot y_t + \frac{M_t}{p_{t-1}} + g. \tag{2.14}$$

The first term on the right-hand side of Eq. (2.14) represents the consumption function of the younger generation, which is derived from the homothetic utility function $u(\cdot)$. The second term represents the consumption of the older generation, and the third term represents the real wasteful public expenditure. Substituting Eq. (2.13) into (2.14) gives:

$$y_t = c\left(\rho^*\right) \cdot y_t + \frac{M_t}{p_t}. \tag{2.15}$$

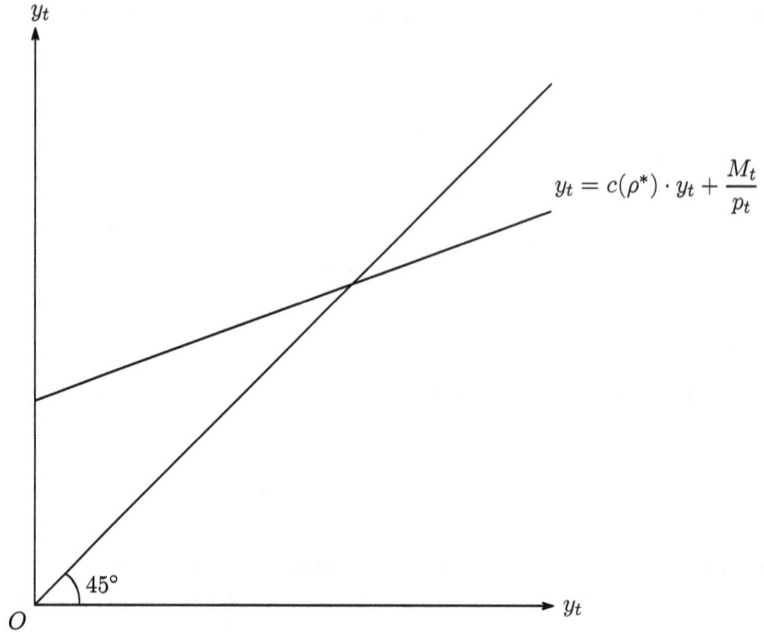

Fig. 2.1 The dynamic Keynesian cross

Equation (2.15) is illustrated in Fig. 2.1. This is the dynamic Keynesian cross in the sense that the intertemporal decision on the consumption stream is woven into it. Moreover, and differing from Mankiw (1988),[3] Eq. (2.14) represents the causality from effective demand to aggregate supply. That is, an increase in the real cash balance as a result of the fact that expansionary fiscal policy forces up real GDP and the multiplier $\frac{1}{1-c(\rho^*)}$ has the same value as that expressed in Kahn (1931) and Keynes (1936).

Finally, it must be noted that if the government keeps the real cash balance constant over time except for the initial period, the equilibrium becomes stationary, in the sense that real GDP and inflation rate do not depend on time. Hence, the Keynes–Walras equilibrium formulated here can become the long-run equilibrium. That is, the economic situation to which Keynesian economics can be applied is never limited to short-run analysis. Indeed, contrary to the new Keynesian and the

[3] The spurious multiplier of Mankiw (1988) is derived by the following economic causality. Since he assumes static monopolistic competition, the real wage is lower than the Walrasian equilibrium, and thus excess leisure (underemployment) occurs. When the government levies a lump-sum tax, the income effect reduces the leisure and people begin to work more. Thus, government expenditure is not essential for this model. However, it is apparent that such a policy reduces economic welfare unless the government expenditure brings about some additional utility, as shown by Startz (1994).

real business cycle schools, the prevalence of idle resources is the ordinal case for the market economy.

2.2.2 The Keynes–Chamberlin Model: The Welfare Economics Foundation of Aggregate Demand Management Policies

In the previous section, it was assumed that the same goods are produced and every firm behaves as a price taker. In such a setting, there is no surplus in terms of both employees and employers. Hence, although fiscal-monetary policy will affect real GDP and employment levels, this type of policy does not contribute to economic welfare. In this section, instead it is assumed that goods are differentiated and each firm monopolistically produces its intrinsic good. However, it is also assumed that its economic behavior does not directly affect macroeconomic variables such as real GDP and the aggregate price level. That is, macroeconomic variables are exogenous for each firm but endogenous for the economy as a whole. This equilibrium concept is known as monopolistic competition and was developed mainly by Chamberlin (1933).

By deploying the concept of monopolistic competition, monopolistic rent emerges for each firm. That is, an economic surplus, which does not exist in the Walrasian equilibrium, occurs as a reward for producing a good that no other firm can imitate. As such, the economy under monopolistic competition achieves a superior allocation to that in the Walrasian equilibrium (Otaki and Tamai 2011) when the economy is dynamic in the sense of the definition provided in Sect. 1.1.

It might be argued that monopolistic behavior lessens production. However, such excessively small production never occurs whenever the marginal cost is constant (this assumption will be justified in Sect. 2.3). This is because, as opposed to the pure monopoly case, the relevant price tied to the demand function of each firm is the *relative* price of the firm's goods to the price index, and always takes the value unity under the symmetric equilibrium assumption. The reason why shortages in production emerge in static monopolistic competition models (e.g. Blanchard and Kiyotaki 1987) is entirely due to the assumption that the marginal cost (the marginal disutility of labor) is an increasing function of working hours. Nonetheless, as shown in Sect. 2.3, unemployment cannot be explained under such an assumption.

Since monopolistic pricing establishes the following relationship between the price level and the nominal wage is:

$$p_t = \frac{W_t}{\gamma\left[1-\eta^{-1}\right]} \Rightarrow W_t = \gamma\left[1-\eta^{-1}\right]p_t,$$

The real profits that a firm can earn are:

$$\frac{1}{p_t}\left[p_t - \frac{W_t}{\gamma}\right]y_t \Rightarrow \eta^{-1}y_t, \tag{2.16}$$

Where: η is the price elasticity of demand and y_t is the real effective demand per firm, which is always equal to its production.

Equation (2.16) shows that the surplus (the monopoly rent) emerging within a firm is proportionate to the real effective demand that the firm faces. If the equilibrium is symmetric and the total effective demand is distributed to each firm equally, the total effective demand increases proportionately, y_t. Thus, whenever the total effective demand is stimulated by some expansionary fiscal-monetary policy, there is an increase in real profits per firm, which forms the only economic surplus within this economy. Equally, since there is no surplus from labor income as long as the economy is located at imperfect employment, as shown by Eq. (2.6) in Sect. 2.2, an upturn in the profits of each firm always improves economic welfare. To summarize, an expansionary fiscal-monetary policy improves economic welfare whenever the economy falls into imperfect employment equilibrium. This theorem, which will be proved below, can be regarded as a rigorous microeconomic foundation for the legitimacy of Keynesian aggregate demand management policies.

The Model Assume that goods are differentiated as far as the density of the interval $B \equiv [0,1]$. Each firm $z, z \in B$ monopolistically produces good z without fixed costs. The other settings of the model are the same as those in the previous section. Otaki (2007) reached the same conclusions, although this study was limited to a confined class of the utility function. The extension was completed by Otaki (2011).

The Decision of Individuals The instantaneous utility c_{it+j} is the continuous constant elasticity of substitution form. That is:

$$c_{1t} \equiv \left[\int_0^1 \left[c_{1t}(z)\right]^{1-\eta^{-1}} dz\right]^{\frac{1}{1-\eta^{-1}}}, c_{2t+1} \equiv \left[\int_0^1 \left[c_{2t+1}(z)\right]^{1-\eta^{-1}} dz\right]^{\frac{1}{1-\eta^{-1}}}. \tag{2.17}$$

Where: $c_{it+j}(z)$ is the demand for good z during period $t+j$ of an individual in the i th stage of life, who is born at the beginning period t. The lifetime utility function U_t is defined by:

$$U_t \equiv u(c_{1t}, c_{2t+1}) - \delta_t \cdot \alpha. \tag{2.18}$$

At this time, $u(\cdot)$ is a linear homogenous function. The optimization problem for each individual then comprises the following three-step backward induction:

i. For given $E_{i,t+j} \equiv \int_0^1 p_{t+j}(z) \cdot c_{i,t+j}(z) dz$, maximize Eq. (2.17) on the path of $c_{t+j,i}(z)$.
ii. $p_{t+j} \cdot c_{i,t+j} \equiv \int_0^1 p_{t+j}(z) \cdot c_{i,t+j}(z) dz$ holds when evaluating consumption on the optimal path, and:

$$p_{t+j} \equiv \left[\int_0^1 \left[p_{t+j}(z)\right]^{1-\eta} dz\right]^{\frac{1}{1-\eta}}. \tag{2.19}$$

The second stage of utility-maximizing behavior can be formulated as:

$$\begin{aligned} &\max_{c_{i,t+j}} u(c_{1t}, c_{2t}), \\ &s.t. p_t \cdot c_{1t} + p_{t+1} \cdot c_{2t+1} \leq \delta_t \cdot W_t + \Pi_t, \end{aligned} \tag{2.20}$$

Where: Π_t denotes the nominal profits that are equally delivered to individuals.

iii. Since the lifetime utility function from the consumption stream is assumed to be linear homogenous, elementary calculus leads to the following indirect utility function ID^{KC}:

$$ID^{KC} \equiv \frac{\delta_t \cdot W_t + \Pi_t}{\psi^{KC}(p_t, p_{t+1})} - \delta_t \cdot \alpha, \tag{2.21}$$

Where: $\psi^{KC}(\cdot)$ is a linear homogenous function.

Based on Eq. (2.21), an individual decides whether to work if and only if other individuals commit to work:

$$\frac{W_t}{\psi^{KC}(p_t, p_{t+1})} \geq \alpha, \tag{2.22}$$

Under Assumption 2.1, the equilibrium nominal wage is determined so that Eq. (2.22) might be held as equality. Thus:

$$W_t = \alpha \cdot \psi^{KC}(p_t, p_{t+1}). \tag{2.23}$$

The Decisions of Firms: The Fundamental Equation From the first step of the backward induction in the decision of individuals, the demand function D_{zt} for good z can be derived. That is:

$$\begin{aligned} D_{zt} &= \left[\frac{p_t(z)}{p_t}\right]^{-\eta} \cdot y_t, \\ y_t &\equiv \frac{W_t L_t + \Pi_t}{p_t}, \end{aligned} \tag{2.24}$$

Where: L_t denotes the employment level and y_t is real GDP.

Based on Eq. (2.24), the profits of firm z, $\Pi_t(z)$ can be defined as:

$$\begin{aligned} \Pi_t(z) &\equiv p_t(z) \cdot \left[\frac{p_t(z)}{p_t}\right]^{-\eta} \cdot y_t - W_t \cdot L_t \\ &= \left[p_t(z) \cdot \left[\frac{p_t(z)}{p_t}\right]^{-\eta} - \frac{\alpha \cdot \psi^{KC}(p_t, p_{t+1})}{\gamma}\left[\frac{p_t(z)}{p_t}\right]^{-\eta}\right] \cdot y_t. \end{aligned} \tag{2.25}$$

Maximizing $\Pi_t(z)$ on $p_t(z)$, the following modified fundamental equation in the monetary economy is obtained:

$$p_t \equiv \left[\int_0^1 [p_t(z)]^{1-\eta} dz\right]^{\frac{1}{1-\eta}} = \frac{W_t}{1-\eta^{-1}} = \frac{\alpha \cdot \psi^{KC}(p_t, p_{t+1})}{[1-\eta^{-1}]\gamma}. \tag{2.26}$$

Since ψ^{KC} is a linear homogenous function, the equilibrium inflation rate ρ^{KC} satisfies:

$$\psi^{KC}\left(1, \rho^{KC}\right) = \alpha^{-1}\left[1-\eta^{-1}\right]\gamma. \tag{2.27}$$

Let $f(x) = x$ in Eq. (2.10) and assume that the utility function in the Keynes–Walras model is identical to that in the Keynes–Chamberlin model as outlined in this section. Then, by comparing (2.27) with (2.10), the following important inequality is obtained:

$$\rho^* > \rho^{KC}. \tag{2.28}$$

Thus, the equilibrium inflation rate is lower in the case of monopolistic competition than in the case of perfect competition. As will be discussed in Sect. 2.5, such a property in the dynamic economy will play a key role in discovering the welfare implication of aggregate demand management policy. Furthermore, whenever money is confident in the sense of Definition 2.1, all values of the equilibrium price sequence are uniquely determined and are unrelated to the quantity of money. Thus, as per the Keynes–Walras model, which is extended in SubSect. 2.2.1, money becomes non-neutral.

Market Equilibrium When it is assumed that the government's budget constraint in SubSect. 2.2.1 is intact, the same equilibrium condition exists for the goods market except in respect of the equilibrium inflation rate. Thus, we obtain the modified dynamic Keynesian cross as:

$$y_t = c\left(\rho^{KC}\right) \cdot y_t + \frac{M_t}{p_t}. \tag{2.29}$$

The Welfare Analysis From Eqs. (2.21) and (2.23), the utility level of an individual is:

$$ID^{KC} = \frac{\Pi_t}{\psi^{KC}(p_t, p_{t+1})}. \tag{2.30}$$

Thus, economic welfare improves as much as the real profits evaluated by the price index ψ^{KC}. Hence, the monopolistic competition equilibrium dominates the perfect competition equilibrium in the sense of Pareto.

In addition, Eqs. (2.25) and (2.26) imply $\Pi_t = p_t \eta^{-1} y_t$. Substituting this into Eq. (2.30):

$$ID^{KC} = \frac{\eta^{-1} y_t}{\psi^{KC}\left(1, \rho^{KC}\right)}. \tag{2.31}$$

Accordingly, following from (2.29), expansionary fiscal-monetary policies that increase real GDP must also improve economic welfare. This can be regarded as a welfare-economic foundation of Keynesian discretionary policy. To summarize the result, the following relationship is postulated:

Theorem 2.2
Assume that the lifetime utility function is linear homogenous on the consumption stream and additively separable from the disutility of labor. Further, assume that goods markets are in monopolistic competition. Then, economic welfare is improved by fiscal-monetary policy in the sense established by Pareto.

2.3 The Legitimacy of the Functional Form of the Utility Function

2.3.1 The Utility Function and Price Index Theory

As mentioned above, we assume that the lifetime utility function is linear homogenous on consumption and additively separable from the disutility of the discrete labor supply. Here, additional considerations on the legitimacy of such specifications of the utility function are considered. First, the linear homogeneity of the lifetime utility function from the consumption stream is examined. This problem is closely related to index number theory. The *true* CPI is defined as the ratio of the current value of expenditure function to its previous period value.

First, denote the nominal expenditure e_t and some fixed utility level $\bar{u}$, respectively. An expenditure function e_t can then be written as $e_t \equiv e(\vec{p}_t : \bar{u})$. Then, the *true CPI* during period t is defined as:

$$CPI_t \equiv \frac{e_t}{e_{t-1}} = \frac{e(\vec{p}_t : \bar{u})}{e(\vec{p}_{t-1} : \bar{u})}, \tag{2.32}$$

Because $\bar{u}$ is unknowable, standard index number theory assumes that the expenditure function is multiplicatively separable. That is:

$$e_t \equiv e(\vec{p}_t : \bar{u}) \equiv \hat{e}(\vec{p}_t) \cdot g(\bar{u}). \tag{2.33}$$

Under this assumption, from Eq. (2.31), the *true CPI* becomes independent of the unknowable utility level $\bar{u}$ of each individual and can be written as:

$$CPI_t = \frac{\hat{e}(\vec{p}_t)}{\hat{e}(\vec{p}_{t-1})}. \tag{2.34}$$

It is evident from the discussion in this subsection that whenever the lifetime utility function of the consumption stream is homothetic, the *true CPI* becomes the form indicated by Eq. (2.34). Furthermore, the converse is also true. That is:

Lemma 2.1
If an expenditure function is multiplicatively separable as in Eq. (2.33), *the direct utility function is homothetic.*

Proof
Suppose the expenditure function is Eq. (2.33). Then the corresponding indirect utility function h becomes:

$$h_t \equiv g^{-1}\left(\frac{e_t}{\hat{e}\left(\vec{p}_t\right)}\right). \tag{2.35}$$

Using Roy's identity, the following property of the demand function of each good is obtained:

$$x_i = -\frac{\dfrac{\partial h}{\partial p_i}}{\dfrac{\partial h}{\partial e}} = \frac{e\dfrac{\partial \hat{e}}{\partial p_i}}{\hat{e}} \Rightarrow \frac{x_i}{x_j} = \frac{\dfrac{\partial \hat{e}}{\partial p_i}}{\dfrac{\partial \hat{e}}{\partial p_j}}.$$

Thus, the ratios between any pairs of demand for goods are functions only of the price vector, and hence the propensity of expenditure for good i is:

$$\alpha_i(\vec{p}), \sum_{i=1}^{n} \alpha_i(\vec{p}) = 1. \tag{2.36}$$

Substituting Eq. (2.36) into the direct utility function u and comparing this with the indirect function in Eq. (2.35) produces:

$$u\left(\vec{\alpha}\left(\vec{p}_t\right)\cdot e_t\right) = g^{-1}\left(\frac{e_t}{\hat{e}\left(\vec{p}_t\right)}\right). \tag{2.37}$$

Equation (2.37) reveals that u is homothetic. This completes the proof.

This establishes that the necessary and sufficient condition for *true CPI* to be defined is that the direct utility function be homothetic. Thus, as much as great importance is attached to the more familiar index number theory, the requirements for the lifetime utility function from the consumption stream are not so restrictive. This is a rather natural assumption of macroeconomics, which deals mainly with aggregated variables.

The second problem of the legitimacy of the functional form of utility function is the additive separation of the utility between the consumption stream and disutility of labor. This assumption implies that there is no cross effect between the consumption stream and labor supply. That is, however hard an individual works when young, this does not affect their lifetime utility from consumption. In this sense, the assumption is that consuming goods has rather distant features when compared with enjoying leisure. Although it is difficult to ascertain directly the legitimacy of such a hypothetical property, it must be noted that the CPI does not contain information about wages (the price of leisure) and that the statistics concerning wages belong to another field. This fact suggests that the additively separable assumption is not too restrictive from the viewpoint of macroeconomics.

2.3.2 The Indivisibility of the Labor Supply

The third and final point to note is that it is assumed that there needs to be no adjustment of working hours, and that only employment adjustment is feasible in the model. The reason this assumption is adopted is that full employment is automatically achieved and cannot explain the existence of unemployment, if working-hours adjustments are admissible. The proof of this assertion is based on Otaki (2012). Fukao and Otaki (1993) showed that adjustment by working hours is easier than that by employment level, when there are training costs incurred by new employees. Let h and L denote the working hours per capita and the employment level, respectively. $\bar{L}$ is the full-employment level. Assume that the production function Y is linear on the total working hours, and that the individual's disutility function $G(h)$ is strictly increasing and concave, and satisfies the Inada Condition. Then, the Lagrangean Λ and adjoining Kuhn–Tucker conditions are as follows:

$$\begin{gathered}\Lambda(h,L,\lambda) \equiv hL - G(h)L + \lambda \cdot \left[h - \frac{Y}{\bar{L}}\right], \\ h - G(h) = 0, \\ L - G'(h)L + \lambda \leq 0, \left[h - \frac{Y}{\bar{L}}\right] \cdot [L - G'(h)L + \lambda] = 0, \lambda \cdot \left[h - \frac{Y}{\bar{L}}\right] = 0.\end{gathered} \tag{2.38}$$

If the constraint $h \geq \frac{Y}{\bar{L}}$ does not bind, $\lambda = 0$ holds. Combining these conditions, the equality $G(h) - hG'(h) = 0$ is obtained. Thus, it is clear from Fig. 2.2 that:

$$G(h) - hG'(h) < 0, \forall h.$$

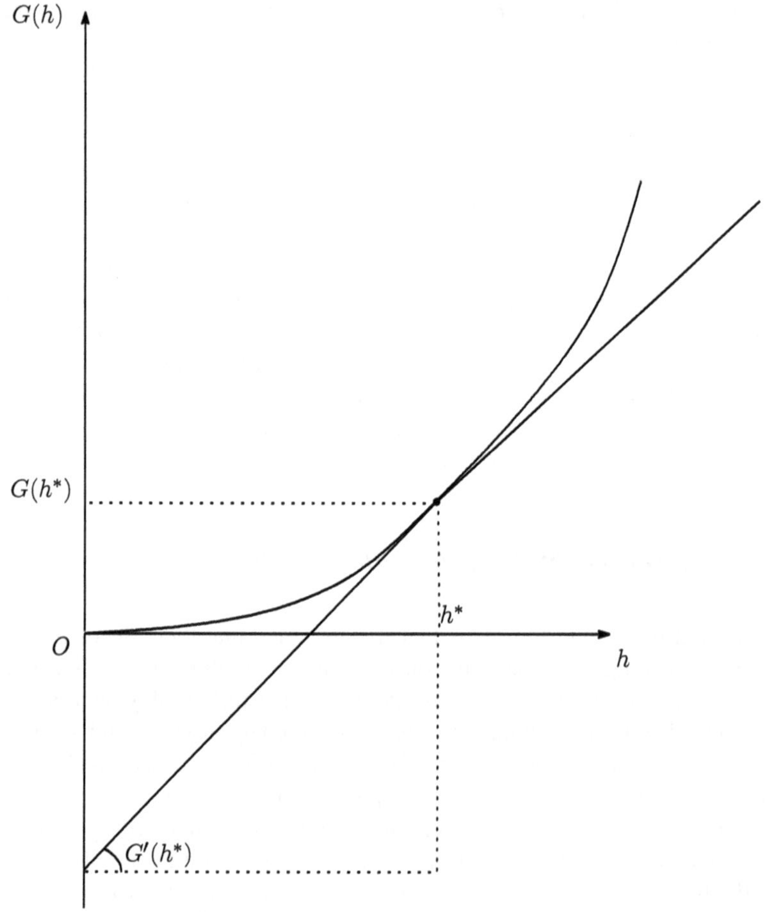

Fig. 2.2 The disutility function of labor

This is a contradiction, and hence $h = \frac{Y}{L}$ holds.

This fact implies that firms strive to reduce working hours per capita and increase employment as much as possible, because additional working hours are associated with higher wages compared with the number of additional individuals employed. Such a property comes entirely from the concavity of function $G(h)$ (the increasing marginal disutility of labor). Accordingly, the assumption of the representative individual, which is a basic presumption of the new Keynesian and real business cycle theorists, is unable to explain the existence of unemployment. To summarize:

Theorem 2.3
Whenever the disutility function of labor $G(h)$ is increasing monotonously and strictly concave, full employment is achieved regardless of the output level Y. That

is, a theory that allows the infinite indivisibility of working hours is unable to explain the existence of unemployment.

Thus, it is necessary to establish an employment theory to introduce the indivisibility of working hours per capita. It is natural to assume that people do not reduce working hours when they are threatened by poverty. Such propensity to work is preserved even in advanced economies for people to maintain minimum standards of civilized life even though working adjoins non-negligible disutility. This lends legitimacy to the concept of the indivisibility of working hours per capita. That is, although an individual feels disutility from working in itself in terms of the utility from their lifetime consumption stream, the marginal disutility is kept at zero within a range $[0,\underline{h})$ as illustrated in Fig. 2.3. This representation of the disutility function F implies that an individual does not reduce their working hours to maintain living standards as long as the working hours offered are permissible. This kinked disutility function is defined as:

$$F\left(h:\bar{h}\right)=\max\left[G\left(\bar{h}\right),G(h)\right], \tag{2.39}$$

Where: F has the corner point at $h=\bar{h}$.

That is:

$$\lim_{h\to+\bar{h}} F'(h)=G'\left(\bar{h}\right),\ \lim_{h\to-\bar{h}} F'(h)=0. \tag{2.40}$$

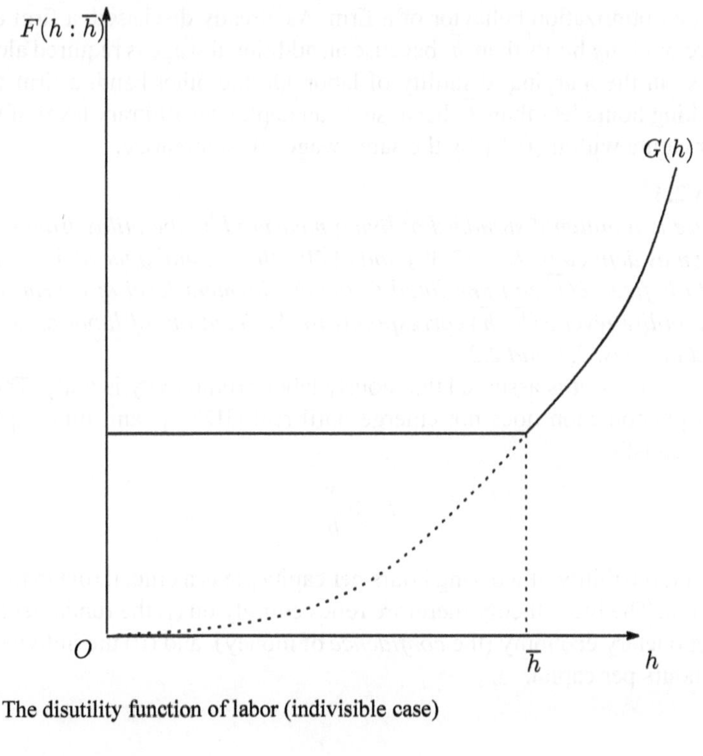

Fig. 2.3 The disutility function of labor (indivisible case)

The Lagrangean Λ^F and Kuhn–Tucker conditions for the profit-maximization problem corresponding to the equations in Eq. (2.38) are:

$$\Lambda^F(h,L,\lambda,\mu) \equiv \left[\overline{h}+v-u\right]L - G\left(\overline{h}+v-u\right)L + \lambda\cdot v + \mu\cdot u \tag{2.41}$$

$$h - G(h) = 0, \tag{2.42}$$

$$L - G'(h)L + \lambda \le 0, v\cdot[L - G'(h)L + \lambda] = 0, \lambda\cdot v = 0, \tag{2.43}$$

$$-L + G'(h)L + \mu \le 0, u\cdot[-L + G'(h)L + \mu] = 0, \mu\cdot u = 0. \tag{2.44}$$

Combining Eqs. (2.42) and (2.43), it can easily be seen that $v = 0$. This is based on the same economic logic used for proving Theorem 2.3. Since $v = 0$, from Eq. (2.40), the value of $G'(h)$ in Eq. (2.44) is equal to zero. Hence, Eq. (2.44) is transformed into:

$$-L + \mu \le 0, u\cdot[-L + \mu] = 0, \mu\cdot u = 0. \tag{2.45}$$

Then, if $u > 0$ and $\mu = 0$ hold, this contradicts the second part of Eq. (2.45). Accordingly, $u = 0$ holds. Thus, the optimal working hours that a firm offers are $\overline{h}(v = u = 0)$. The indivisibility of working hours is endogenously represented through the optimization behavior of a firm. As already discussed, a firm does not offer more working hours than $\overline{h}$ because an additional wage is required along with an increase in the marginal disutility of labor. On the other hand, a firm does not offer working hours less than $\overline{h}$ because it can deploy an arbitrary level of working hours per capita within $[0,\overline{h}]$ by the same wage. To summarize:

Theorem 2.4
When there is a minimal standard of living measured by the utility from consumption stream as defined by Eqs. (2.39) *and* (2.40), *the optimal offer of working hours per capita is fixed at* $\overline{h}$ *and unrelated to the employment level of a firm. Furthermore, the utility level* $F(\overline{h}:\overline{h})$ *corresponds to the disutility of labor,* α, *which has been used in Sects. 2.1 and 2.2.*

In Theorem 2.4, it is assumed that hourly labor productivity is unity. The unemployment phenomenon does not emerge until real GDP, y, and full-employment level, L^f, satisfies:

$$L^f > \frac{y}{\overline{h}}.$$

Thus, the indivisibility of working hours per capita plays a crucial role in theories of employment. The basic theory therefore relies entirely on (i) the fundamental equation in a monetary economy (the *confidence* of money), and (ii) the indivisibility of working hours per capita.

2.4 The Quantity Theory of Money as an Extraneous Belief

Throughout the preceding sections, it has been assumed that money is *confident* in the sense of Definition 2.1. In this section, consideration turns to an extraneous belief in money, in which individuals believe that the value of money decreases proportionately with its quantity. In other words, people believe in the quantity theory of money. This is expressed by Eq. (2.2).

As discussed in Sect. 1.1, owing to the indeterminacy of value intrinsic to the monetary economy, such an extraneous belief possibly becomes self-fulfilling. This problem is dealt with using the Keynes–Walras model analyzed in Sect. 2.2. Since additional money injected by the government via public expenditure can be used to purchase additional goods as long as idle resources exist, it is plausible to assume that the belief is self-fulfilling only when full employment is achieved. Hence, considering the equilibrium condition for the goods market in Eq. (2.15):

$$\overline{y} = c(\rho)\cdot\overline{y} + \frac{M_t}{p_t} = c(\rho)\cdot\overline{y} + \kappa \Rightarrow \kappa = [1 - c(\rho)]\cdot\overline{y}, \tag{2.46}$$

Where: $\overline{y}$ is real GDP, which corresponds to full employment.

When a change in money supply is confined to a once-and-for-all case—that is, the current quantity of money is kept constant hereafter—Eq. (2.2) shows that the equilibrium inflation rate is unity.[4] Thus, the value of κ can be uniquely determined as:

$$\kappa = [1 - c(1)]\cdot\overline{y} \tag{2.47}$$

When labor productivity γ is high enough, the fundamental equation (zero-profit condition as specified in Eq. (2.10)) is modified as the following inequality:

$$\gamma > f^{-1}(\alpha)\cdot\psi(1,1). \tag{2.48}$$

This is because profits earned by a firm should be strictly positive, regardless of the level of effective demand required to achieve full employment under the extraneous belief in Eq. (2.2). Consequently, the following theorem can be constructed:

Theorem 2.5
If labor productivity is high enough to satisfy inequality (2.48), *the extraneous belief* (*in Eq.* (2.2)) *is self-fulfilling and money becomes neutral.*

[4] It can be shown that money is not super neutral in this model if κ is assumed to be unrelated to the inflation rate, although Lucas' (1972) monetarist model preserves this property. Such differences stem from the money-supply rule that the government adopts. This problem is analyzed in more detail in Part 5.

Theorem 2.5 implies that whenever labor productivity γ is high and real unit labor costs are located below unity (real unit revenue from producing goods), every firm is ready to employ new individuals as much as possible, and thus full employment is achieved. As a result, the value of money can decrease proportionately with its quantity. Nonetheless, it must be noted that to uphold Theorem 2.5, people must hold a baseless extraneous belief (Eq. (2.2)) instead of the *confidence* in money as outlined in Definition 2.1. It is hard to imagine such an unrealistic situation in our daily lives. In this sense, the quantity theory of money prominently lacks relevance compared with Keynesian theory.

2.5 Monopolistic Competition in the Dynamic Monetary Economy

This section deals with the counterintuitive result obtained in Sect. 2.2, that resource allocation in monopolistic competition Pareto-dominates that in perfect competition. There are two questions to be asked: Why does lowered inflation enhance economic welfare, and why is the surplus generated by lowered inflation attributed to monopolistic rents?

2.5.1 *Inflation and Economic Welfare*

In general, disinflation improves economic welfare in an endless dynamic monetary economy. Disinflation increases the rate of return of money. That is, as disinflation progresses, any individual is able to receive more goods in exchange for the money that is inherited from the previous generation. For any given real income, y, which is determined by real cash balances, $\frac{M}{p}$, the budget constraint line shifts clockwise around the endowment point $(y,0)$, as illustrated in Fig. 2.4, thus widening the feasible set of consumption behaviors as the shadowed area in Fig. 2.4. As such, it is clear that disinflation improves economic welfare.

It is possible to show that the equilibrium inflation rate under monopolistic competition ρ^{KC} is lower than that under perfect competition ρ^{*} as demonstrated by inequality Eq. (2.28). This is because monopoly pricing heightens current price levels relative to any future price levels that individuals consider when deciding whether to work. Consequently, the monopolistic competition Pareto effect dominates perfect competition via a reduction in the inflation rate. To summarize, the disinflation caused by monopolistic competition is able to enrich every generation without additional structural changes in the economy, because income transfers between

Fig. 2.4 The effect of disinflation

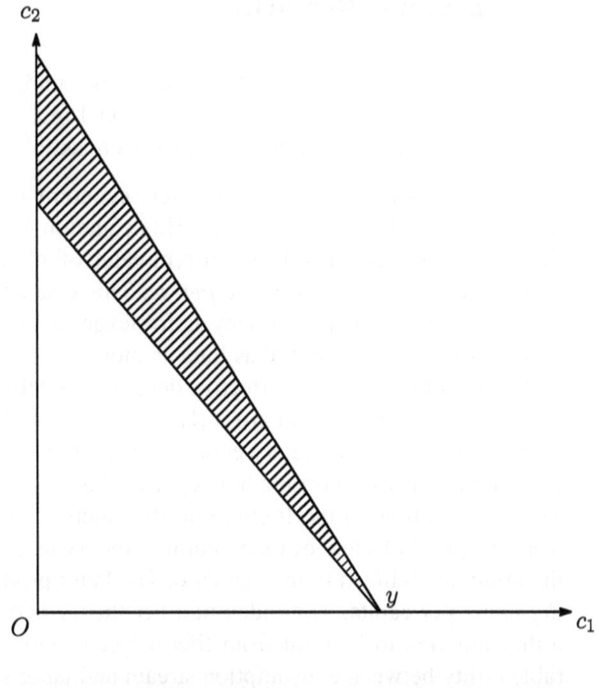

adjacent generations become easier and more sustainable owing to the fact that the economy is viable over the long term.

2.5.2 Why is the Surplus Attributed to Monopoly Rents?

In the previous section, it was demonstrated that monopolistic competition enhances economic welfare by reducing the inflation rate. Meanwhile, benefits from disinflation are attributed entirely to monopoly rents as shown in Eq. (2.31). Here, the discussion analyzes why the benefits are concentrated in monopoly rents.

The vital point is that the nominal reservation wage is lowered by monopolistic competition. Whenever disinflation progresses, *ceteris paribus*, every employee can enjoy a higher standard of living than the minimal level corresponding to the reservation wage, because disinflation widens the lifetime consumption opportunity as discussed above. However, as long as unemployment prevails, individuals who are out of work offer a lower nominal wage to be employed. Such a competitive process continues incessantly until the nominal wage declines sufficiently to offset the economic surplus caused by disinflation. Thus, as long as firms are a monopsony in the labor market, such economic surplus is transferred entirely to monopoly rents. This is the economic interpretation of Eq. (2.31).

2.6 Concluding Remarks

A model of price theory in a monetary economy under Keynesian economics was constructed. This was based on the OLG model in a production economy with an infinite time horizon. The results obtained were as follows:

1. The fundamental equation in a monetary economy has been induced, and depicts the laws of motion of price levels. This equation reveals the nested structure of the value of money. That is, the current value of money is determined by rational expectations on its future value *per se*. This characteristic also implies that, in principle, the quantity of money is irrelevant to the value of money, and thus money becomes non-neutral as long as money is *confident*;
2. A *theory* (not principle) of effective demand is established, which is summarized by the dynamic Keynesian cross (Hicks-Samuelson's 45° line analysis), based on price theory in a monetary economy that comprises the confidence of money and indivisibility of working hours per capita;
3. The specification on the lifetime utility function can be regarded as legitimate from the point of view of index number theory and the existence of a desire for the minimal civilized living standard. The latter produces indivisibility of working hours per capita. The index number theory permits the linear homogenous utility function to be built from lifetime consumption and the additively separable utility between consumption stream and labor supply;
   When monopolistic competition is prevalent in goods markets, an expansionary fiscal-monetary policy improves economic welfare. This theorem comes from the following two properties of the economy: First, since the economy has no end period, the rate of return for money increases by disinflation that originates from monopolistic competition. This brings about economic surplus; and second, such surpluses proportionately increase with effective demand. Accordingly, an expansionary fiscal-monetary policy improves economic welfare.
4. The quantity theory of money is upheld as an extraneous belief in the value of money. This is due entirely to the intrinsic indeterminacy of value in a monetary economy. Once people disbelieve in the intrinsic value of money and understand that its value decreases proportionately with quantity, such belief becomes self-fulfilling under some restrictive conditions.

Mathematical Appendix

1. Homothetic Utility Function and Its Indirect Utility Function In this appendix, it is proven that if a utility function, $u(c_1, c_2)$, is of a linear homogenous form, the corresponding indirect function, h, becomes:

$$h(p_1, p_2, y) = \frac{y}{\psi(p_1, p_2)}, \tag{2.49}$$

Where: ψ is a linear homogenous function.

Proof
Since u is linear homogenous, the optimal consumption plan (c_1^*, c_2^*) satisfies:

$$c_2^* = \varphi\left(\frac{p_2}{p_1}\right)c_1^*. \tag{2.50}$$

By the budget constraint:

$$p_1 c_1^* + p_2\varphi\left(\frac{p_2}{p_1}\right)c_1^* = y \Rightarrow c_1^* = \frac{y}{p_1 + p_2\varphi\left(\frac{p_2}{p_1}\right)}, \quad c_2^* = \frac{\varphi\left(\frac{p_2}{p_1}\right)y}{p_1 + p_2\varphi\left(\frac{p_2}{p_1}\right)}, \tag{2.51}$$

holds. Substituting Eq. (2.51) into $u(c_1^*, c_2^*)$ gives:

$$h(p_1, p_2, y) = \frac{u\left(1, \varphi\left(\frac{p_2}{p_1}\right)\right)}{p_1 + p_2\varphi\left(\frac{p_2}{p_1}\right)} \cdot y. \tag{2.52}$$

Since the inverse of $\dfrac{u\left(1, \varphi\left(\frac{p_2}{p_1}\right)\right)}{p_1 + p_2\varphi\left(\frac{p_2}{p_1}\right)}$ is a linear homogenous function, Eq. (2.52) is equivalent to Eq. (2.49).

2. Continuous CES Utility Function and the Corresponding Price Index In this appendix, the price index is derived:

$p \equiv \left[\int_0^1 \left[p(z)\right]^{1-\eta} dz\right]^{\frac{1}{1-\eta}}$ from the maximization of instantaneous utility $c \equiv \left[\int_0^1 \left[c(z)\right]^{1-\eta^{-1}} dz\right]^{\frac{1}{1-\eta^{-1}}}$

Proof
Given the instantaneous expenditure E, the budget constraint is defined as:

$$E = \int_0^1 p(z)c(z)dz. \tag{2.53}$$

The corresponding Lagrangean L to this maximization problem is:

$$L \equiv \int_0^1 \left[c(z)\right]^{1-\eta^{-1}} dz + \lambda \cdot \left[E - \int_0^1 p(z)c(z)dz\right] = \int_0^1 \left[\left[c(z)\right]^{1-\eta^{-1}} - \lambda\, p(z)c(z)\right]dz + \lambda \cdot E,$$

Where: λ is the Lagrangean multiplier. Since λ does not depend on z, the bracket of the integral can simply be maximized. This gives:

$$c^*(z) = \left[\frac{\lambda\, p(z)}{1-\eta^{-1}}\right]^{-\eta}. \tag{2.54}$$

Substituting Eq. (2.54) into Eq. (2.53) gives:

$$E = \int_0^1 p(z)\left[\frac{\lambda\, p(z)}{1-\eta^{-1}}\right]^{-\eta} dz \quad \Rightarrow \quad \left[\frac{\lambda}{1-\eta^{-1}}\right]^{-\eta} = \frac{E}{\int_0^1 [p(z)]^{1-\eta} dz}. \tag{2.55}$$

Combining Eq. (2.54) with Eq. (2.55) gives:

$$c^*(z) = \frac{[p(z)]^{-\eta} E}{\int_0^1 [p(z)]^{1-\eta} dz} = \left[\frac{p(z)}{\left[\int_0^1 [p(z)]^{1-\eta} dz\right]^{\frac{1}{1-\eta}}}\right]^{-\eta} \cdot \frac{E}{\left[\int_0^1 [p(z)]^{1-\eta^{-1}} dz\right]^{\frac{1}{1-\eta}}} \tag{2.56}$$

$$\equiv \left[\frac{p(z)}{p}\right]^{-\eta} \cdot \frac{E}{p}.$$

Eq. (2.56) is the demand function for good z and the definition of the price index p.

3. Convenient Representation of Budget Constraint Based on the result of the previous appendix, the following convenient formula is constructed:

$$\int_0^1 p(z)c^*(z)dz = pc^*, \qquad c^* \equiv \left[\int_0^1 [c^*(z)]^{1-\eta^{-1}} dz\right]^{\frac{1}{1-\eta^{-1}}}. \tag{2.57}$$

Proof

From Eq. (2.56):

$$[c(z)]^{1-\eta^{-1}} = \left[\frac{[p(z)]^{1-\eta}}{p^{1-\eta}}\right] \cdot \frac{E}{p} \tag{2.58}$$

$$\Rightarrow c^* \equiv \left[\int_0^1 [c(z)]^{1-\eta^{-1}} dz\right]^{\frac{1}{1-\eta^{-1}}} = \left[\frac{\int_0^1 [p(z)]^{1-\eta} dz}{p^{1-\eta}}\right]^{\frac{1}{1-\eta^{-1}}} \cdot \frac{E}{p} = \left[\frac{p^{1-\eta}}{p^{1-\eta}}\right]^{\frac{1}{1-\eta^{-1}}} \cdot \frac{E}{p} = \frac{E}{p}$$

holds. Combining Eqs. (2.53) and (2.58) gives Eq. (2.57).

4. The Kuhn-Tucker Theorem In Sect. 2.3, nonlinear programming permits a boundary solution. The usual Lagrangean method presumes the differentiability and regularity conditions of functions because it uses an implicit function theorem. This property makes it difficult to apply this method to problems that contain a boundary solution where functions are not differentiable. The Kuhn–Tucker theorem is a suitable method to solve such problems because it does not require differentiability. Following Uzawa (1958), this theorem can be described as:

Theorem 2.6 (The Kuhn–Tucker Theorem—sufficiency part: one constraint case)
Consider the following optimization problem:
$\max_x f(x)$, subject to

$$g(x) \geq 0, \tag{2.59}$$

Where: x is n dimensional real vector.

Then, the sufficient condition for x^* to become the solution of (2.59) is that there is λ^* such that:

$$L\left(x,\lambda^*\right) \leq L\left(x^*,\lambda^*\right) \leq L\left(x^*,\lambda\right) \tag{2.60}$$

L is defined as $L(x,\lambda) \equiv f(x) + \lambda \cdot g(x), 0 \leq \lambda$.

Proof
The right side of inequality (2.60) gives:

$$\lambda^* \cdot g\left(x^*\right) \leq \lambda \cdot g\left(x^*\right). \tag{2.61}$$

Since λ can take an arbitrary small non-negative value, inequality (2.61) implies that:

$$\lambda^* \cdot g\left(x^*\right) = 0. \tag{2.62}$$

Applying Eq. (2.62) to the left side of inequality (2.60) gives:

$$f(x) \leq f(x) + \lambda^* \cdot g(x) \leq f\left(x^*\right) \tag{2.63}$$

This inequality completes the proof.

An Application of the Non-Negative Constraint Consider an application of the Kuhn–Tucker theorem. In general, the range of economic values is restricted to a non-negative values. If this constraint is brought into consideration, a typical optimization problem becomes:

$\max_x f(x)$, subject to $0 \leq x$.

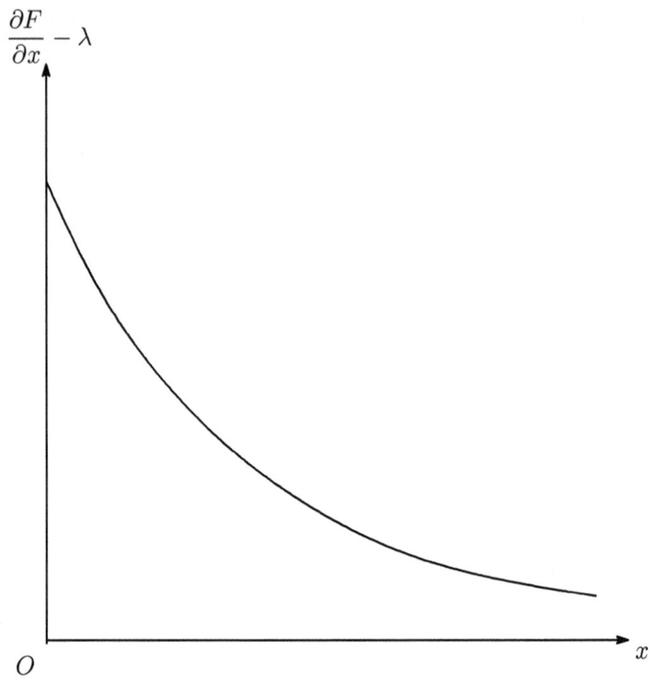

Fig. 2.5 The boundary solution

The corresponding Lagrangean is:

$$L \equiv f(x) + \lambda x \tag{2.64}$$

It must be noted that when the solution is boundary (i.e., $x_i^* = 0, \exists i$),

$$\frac{\partial F}{\partial x_i}|_{x=x^*} - \lambda_i^* \leq 0 \tag{2.65}$$

holds, as Fig. 2.5 illustrates. Otherwise, Eq. (2.65) holds as equality. To summarize:

$$\frac{\partial F}{\partial x_j}|_{x=x^*} - \lambda_j^* \leq 0, \left[\frac{\partial F}{\partial x_j}|_{x=x^*} - \lambda_j^*\right] x_j^* = 0, \forall j. \tag{2.66}$$

Furthermore, from Eq. (2.62):

$$\lambda_j^* x_j^* = 0, \forall j. \tag{2.67}$$

Equations (2.66) and (2.67) are the Kuhn–Tucker conditions corresponding to the non-negative constraints. This formula was used in Sect. 2.3.

References

Blanchard OJ, Kiyotaki N (1987) Monopolistic competition and the effects of aggregate demand. Am Econ Rev 77:647–666

Chamberlin EH (1933) The theory of monopolistic competition: a re-orientation of the theory of value. Harvard University Press, Cambridge

Dewert WE (2009) Cost of living indexes and exact numbers, discussion paper 09–06, department of economics, University of British Columbia, Vancouver. http://www.econ.ubc.ca/diewert/dp0906.pdf. Accessed 25 July 2014

Fukao K, Otaki M (1993) Accumulation of human capital and the business cycle. J Polit Econ 101:72–99

Kahn RF (1931) The relation of home investment to unemployment. Econ J 41:73–198

Keynes JM (1936) The general theory of employment, interest and money. Macmillan, London

Lucas RE Jr (1972) Expectations and the neutrality of money. J Econ Theory 4:103–124

Mankiw NG (1988) Imperfect competition and the Keynesian cross. Econ Lett 26:7–14

Otaki M (2007) The dynamically extended Keynesian cross and the welfare-improving fiscal policy. Econ Lett 96:23–29

Otaki M (2011) A pure theory of aggregate price determination. Theor Econ Lett 1:122–128

Otaki M (2012) The aggregation problem in employment theory: the representative individual model or the individual employees model? Theor Econ Lett 2:530–533

Otaki M, Tamai Y (2011) On the dynamic role of monopolistic competition. Theor Econ Lett 1:114–117

Startz R (1994) Monopolistic competition as a foundation for Keynesian macroeconomic models. Q J Econ 104:737–752

Uzawa H (1958) The Kuhn-Tucker theorem in concave programming. In: Arrow KJ, Hurwicz L, Uzawa H (eds) Studies in linear and non-linear programming. Stanford University Press, Palo Alto, p 32–37

Part II
Applications to Labor Economics and Inflation Theory

Chapter 3
The Existence of an Involuntary Unemployment Equilibrium

3.1 Introduction

Although the preceding chapters have shown that an expansionary fiscal-monetary policy improves economic welfare, unemployment in those models is still voluntary because the equilibrium nominal wage is equalized to the reservation wage. This property raises the question of whether it is possible to represent involuntary unemployment as defined by Keynes (1936) within the theoretical approach taken in this book. This chapter answers the question affirmatively. It is shown that the equilibrium nominal wage can exceed the nominal reservation wage without hampering employment.

Efficient wage bargaining, which originates from McDonald and Solow (1981), plays a crucial role. Efficient wage bargaining is a contract theory that asserts that employer and employees achieve Pareto-efficient allocation via wage-employment bargaining. This theory is of use because it clarifies the fact that nominal wage bargaining, in which the equilibrium nominal wage possibly exceeds that set in the spot market, never prevents efficient resource allocation. However, there are two obstacles to be overcome when attempting to explain the inevitability of involuntary unemployment owing to a shortage in effective demand. That is, McDonald and Solow (1981) assume that not only the nominal wage negotiation but also the employment level are determined by negotiation. In reality, decisions concerning employment levels belong to an employer as a managerial right. Meanwhile, if employees agree with a certain employment level, all existing unemployment is voluntary. Thus, further refinements of the theory are needed to validate the existence of involuntary unemployment.

To separate decisions on nominal wages and employment, a second-stage game is introduced into efficient bargaining theory. In the first-stage game, an employer decides non-cooperatively how many individuals to employ to maximize profits. The next stage is the nominal wage negotiation between the employer and existing employees. The asymmetric Nash bargaining solution is used here as the equilibrium concept.

M. Otaki, *Keynesian Economics and Price Theory*,
Advances in Japanese Business and Economics 7, DOI 10.1007/978-4-431-55345-8_3

Employers should decide employment levels by foreseeing the result of the second stage of this game (assuming the game is in perfect equilibrium). The second stage of the game consists only of sharing the predetermined total surplus (i.e. total sales minus the reservation wage payments), and is optimized for the employer to achieve maximal total surplus in the first stage. Thus, profit maximization becomes equivalent to total surplus maximization. This implies that even though employers are concerned only with their interest in the employment decision, they unconsciously maximize their own and their employees' welfare, or *total* welfare. Accordingly, neither managerial rights nor bargaining processes prevent the efficient allocation of employment levels. Furthermore, the equilibrium nominal wage is at least equal to the nominal reservation wage as long as incumbent employees have some level of bargaining power.

In addition, since the marginal cost that an employer faces is not the equilibrium nominal wage but the nominal reservation wage by virtue of the asymmetric Nash bargaining solution, the equilibrium employment level is equivalent to that of the case dealt with in Chap. 2. That is, the economy achieves its maximal employment level under given effective demand. Consequently, it is possible to prove the existence of an involuntary unemployment equilibrium owing to the shortage of effective demand in the following way. The concept of involuntary unemployment equilibrium thus depends on the following two conditions:

(1) The equilibrium nominal wage is not less than the nominal reservation wage; and
(2) The employment level is never improved by lowering the equilibrium nominal wage via restraining the bargaining power of employees.

This chapter is organized as follows. Section 3.2 discusses the political-economic relevance of full-employment policy. In Sect. 3.3 a general equilibrium efficient wage-bargaining model based on the theory discussed in Chap. 2 is constructed. This model is then used to prove the main theorem advanced in this book, which asserts that an involuntary unemployment equilibrium exists when there is a shortage of effective demand. Section 3.4 contains brief concluding remarks.

3.2 The Political-Economic Meaning of Full-Employment Policy

In the devastating political and economic circumstances of the pre-World War II era, Carr (1939) described how huge amounts of capital investment aimed at creating new employment socially should be deployed, regardless of a country being democratic or totalitarian. That is:

> In nearly every country (and not at least in the United States), large capital investments have been made in recent years, not for the economic purpose of earning profits, but for the social purpose of creating employment.

It is evident that such investment was designed to counter the social instabilities that would eventually trigger World War II. Returning to Carr (1939):

> Employment has become more important than profit, social stability than increased consumption, equitable distribution than maximum production. That is, mass unemployment brings about extreme social strain between the employed and the unemployed because it causes exorbitant income disparity. We could say that war was sought to dissolve such strenuous circumstances by obtaining new economic opportunities via conquering assumed enemies.

Hayashi (1963) also points out the following in the context of Germany being governed by Nazis and thrust into World War II:

> It is evident from the ancient polis to current nation states that the existence of sound middle class citizens is a critical foundation for the stability of a nation. … Inflation destroyed the urban middle income stratum. Savings, the fruits of their lifelong strife, became worthless and their living standards fell to no more than that of the laboring classes. They were proud that they worked as the core of the society that furnished daily life, which differed from the lower income class. It was devastating to realize that they lost such prestige and fell into the poorest class in the society. …. Thus, they naturally came to curse the society which brought about such a disaster, and regard the (Weimar) Republic and the Versailles Treaty as its origins.[1]

This point of view suggests that mass involuntary unemployment under hyperinflation corrupts the basis of a society and distorts its social order. It must be noted that the work of Keynes (1936) was written amid such crisis. Even though the assumption of an exogenously fixed nominal wage is somewhat arbitrary, the social significance that Keynes recognized is far more important than its theoretical flaw. The problem is that his descendants (old and new Keynesians) left the flaw intact.

Pigou (1933) appeared as an antagonist to Keynes and asserted the following:

> But in a period of depression, when all available vacancies are filled, the fact that these men do not desire employment does not cause them to act otherwise than they would do if they did desire it; and, since it is impossible to look directly into people's minds, there are no means of discovering or enumerating them.

His assertion is akin to the neoclassical macroeconomics symbolized by Friedman and Lucas under "laissez-faire" schemes. Since Pigou (1933) considers that no one is able to observe another's intentions, how can his theory relate social strains to the existence of mass unemployment? Unless unemployment was involuntary, the Great Depression would then have been provoked by people's lack of motivation. It is preposterous to propose that the social strains that emerged in this period were due to such a reason.

The aim of full-employment policy is thus to mitigate the social strains caused by involuntary unemployment, and to provide a breathing space within which individuals can go about their daily lives. To qualify this counsel more theoretically, it is necessary to analyze how full employment can be achieved in conjunction with nominal wages that are sufficiently higher than nominal reservation wages to be regarded as the minimum level of income required for living.

[1] Translated by Otaki.

3.3 The Model

3.3.1 *Setting Up the Model*

A Keynes–Chamberlin type model of the kind formulated in SubSect. 2.2.2 was used in this analysis. There exists a continuum of employers who specialize in their own products within the interval $[0,1]$. Each can employ continuum individuals within the interval $[0,1]$. The relationship between them is *reciprocally prescriptive* in the sense that they can produce nothing if they exchange their role with another employer or employees. As discussed in Chap. 11, it may be assumed that there is inseparability between real capital and human capital in an existing firm. That is, specific human capital is accumulated within a firm, which is nurtured by the learning-by-doing effect proposed by Arrow (1962) and is inseparable from real capital. On the other hand, Smith (1776) advocates:

> It is otherwise with common people. They have little time to spare for education. Their parents can scarce afford to maintain even in the infancy. As soon as they are able to work, they must apply to some trade by which they can earn their substance. That trade too is generally so simple and uniform as to give little exercise to the understanding; while, at the same time, their labour is both so constant and so severe, that it leaves them little leisure and less inclination to apply to, or even to think of anything else.

However, at least within developed countries, the current economic environment does not seem as severe, although it cannot be ignored that such tragic situations still exist.

For the purposes of the model, it is assumed that the lifetime utility function U is identical and:

$$U \equiv u(c_1, c_2) - \delta_1 \cdot \alpha, \tag{3.1}$$

Where: $u(\cdot)$ is a linear homogenous and concave function; δ_1 is a definition function that takes value unity when an individual is employed and is zero when unemployed; α denotes the disutility of labor; and c_i is the composite of goods consumed during the i-th stage of life, which is formally defined as:

$$c_i \equiv \left[\int_0^1 \left[c_i(z) \right]^{1-\eta^{-1}} dz \right]^{\frac{1}{1-\eta^{-1}}},$$

Where: $c_i(z)$ is the consumption of good z during the i-th stage of life.

Furthermore, this model assumes that unit labor produces unit goods. By solving the utility maximization problem, the following indirect utility function of the t-th generation's lifetime consumption I_t is obtained:

$$I_t \equiv \frac{\delta_t w_t + \pi_t}{\psi(p_t, p_{t+1})}, \tag{3.2}$$

Where: w_t and π_t are the nominal wage and profits, respectively; and p_i is the price index derived from the utility maximization. That is:

$$p_t \equiv \left[\int_0^1 [p_t(z)]^{1-\eta} dz\right]^{\frac{1}{1-\eta}}$$

Where: $p_t(z)$ is the price of good z.

Using Eqs. (3.1) and (3.2), the nominal reservation wage w_t^R is:

$$w_t^R = \alpha \cdot \psi(p_t, p_{t+1}). \tag{3.3}$$

In addition, the following demand function exists for good z:

$$D_t \equiv \left(\frac{p_t(z)}{p_t}\right)^{-\eta} \cdot y_t, y_t \equiv \frac{w_t L_t + \pi_t}{p_t}, \tag{3.4}$$

Where: L_t is the employment level.

The profit function of an employer is thus defined as:

$$\pi_t(z) \equiv [p_t(z) - w_t(z)] \cdot D_t(z). \tag{3.5}$$

3.3.2 The Nominal Wage Negotiation Process

In this subsection, following Otaki (2009), the negotiation process for the nominal wage is formatted using a two-stage game. In the first stage of the game, an employer decides how many individuals to employ by foreseeing the result of the second stage. The second stage determines the nominal wage in accordance with the asymmetric Nash bargaining solution.

Backward induction is necessary for solving such a game. The threat point of the second-stage bargaining game is assumed to be $\left(0, w_t^R\right)$. This is partly because an employer obtains nothing if the negotiations break down and no individuals participate in the firm, and partly because employees are incentivized only when the nominal wage is not less than the reservation wage. Thus, from Eq. (3.5), the generalized Nash product (*GNP*) corresponding to this game can be formulated as:

$$GNP(w_t(z)) \equiv [\pi_t(z)]^\theta \cdot \left[w_t(z) - w_t^R\right]^{1-\theta} \propto [p_t(z) - w_t(z)]^\theta \cdot \left[w_t(z) - w_t^R\right]^{1-\theta} \tag{3.6}$$

Where: $\theta (0 \leq \theta \leq 1)$ denotes the bargaining power of an employer. Note that the fact that $(p_t(z), D_t(z))$ are predetermined by the first stage of the game to derive Eq. (3.6) is central to this formulation.

Maximizing Eq. (3.6) with respect to $w_t(z)$ gives the following relationship concerning the equilibrium nominal wage:

$$w_t(z) = \theta \cdot w_t^R + [1-\theta] \cdot \left[p_t(z) - w_t^R \right]. \tag{3.7}$$

Equation (3.7) implies that the equilibrium nominal wage becomes the linear combination of the nominal reservation wage w_t^R and the total surplus accrued from unit good production $p_t(z) - w_t^R$. The stronger the bargaining power of an employer (i.e. θ takes a higher value), the cheaper the nominal wage, which approaches the reservation wage. Note also that the equilibrium nominal wage strictly exceeds the nominal reservation wage except for the case $\theta = 1$.

The solution of the first stage of the nominal wage negotiation game is obtained by substituting Eqs. (3.3) and (3.7) into Eq. (3.5):

$$\begin{aligned} &\max_{p_t(z)} \pi_t(z) \equiv \max_{p_t(z)} \left[p_t(z) - w_t(z) \right] \cdot D_t(z) \\ &= \theta \cdot \max_{p_t(z)} \left[p_t(z) - w_t^R(z) \right] \cdot D_t(z) \end{aligned} \tag{3.8}$$

Equation (3.8) reveals that this problem is identical to that dealt with in Chap. 2; that is, the *effective* equilibrium nominal wage that a firm faces is equalized to the nominal reservation wage.

Finally, the maximization problem in Eq. (3.8) must be solved. Taking Eq. (3.4) into account:

$$p_t(z) = \frac{\alpha \cdot \psi(p_t, p_{t+1})}{1-\eta^{-1}} \Rightarrow p_t = \frac{\alpha \cdot \psi(p_t, p_{t+1})}{1-\eta^{-1}}, D_t(z) = y_t. \tag{3.9}$$

This is the same fundamental equation that appears in SubSect. 2.2.2. Thus, the following theorem is supported:

Theorem 3.1
Even though nominal wage negotiation follows a two-step efficient bargaining process, the equilibrium employment level is unchanged from the case in which employees do not have any bargaining power as long as effective demand y_t *is kept constant. That is, the equilibrium nominal wage, which is beyond the nominal reservation wage, is never a hindrance to employment opportunities.*

3.3.3 Market Equilibrium

In the previous subsection, the equilibrium condition for the labor market was formulated. The remaining markets are the goods markets and the money markets, and one of them is not independent according to Walras' law. Henceforth, this discussion focuses on the goods markets. Since the lifetime utility function of consumption is a linear homogenous function, the aggregate consumption function for the young generation C_t is obtained:

$$C_t \equiv c(\rho)\cdot y_t \tag{3.10}$$

Then, the equilibrium condition of the goods markets is:

$$y_t = c(\rho)\cdot y_t + \frac{M_{t-1}}{p_t} + \frac{M_t - M_{t-1}}{p_t} = c(\rho)\cdot y_t + \frac{M_t}{p_t}. \tag{3.11}$$

The second term of Eq. (3.11) is the aggregate demand for goods by the older generation. The third term is real government expenditure financed by *seigniorage*, and ρ is the equilibrium inflation rate that satisfies the fundamental Eq. (3.9).

There are four endogenous variables within the model: (p_t, ρ, y_t, w_t). Adding the condition for confidence in money gives:

$$\frac{dp_{t+1}}{dM_t} = 0, \tag{3.12}$$

There are also four structural equations in the model: Eqs. (3.7), (3.9), (3.11), and (3.12). Thus, the model is closed. Because the structure of the model is the same as that of the Keynes–Chamberlin model used in SubSect. 2.2.2, the equilibrium effective demand is also unchanged from that model. Consequently:

Theorem 3.2
The equilibrium effective demand is unaffected by the interchange in the equilibrium concept of the labor market.

Based on Theorem 3.1 and 3.2, the main theorem can now be stated:

Theorem 3.3
Involuntary unemployment equilibrium exists purely because of the shortage of effective demand. Furthermore, this kind of equilibrium is Pareto inefficient.

Proof
Theorem 3.1 asserts that as long as effective demand is located at the same level as the Keynes–Chamberlin model in SubSect. 2.2.2, the same amount of unemployment emerges even though the equilibrium nominal wage exceeds the nominal reservation wage. Theorem 3.2 proves that the economy faces the same effective demand independent of whether employees have bargaining power in the wage negotiation process. Therefore, an involuntary unemployment equilibrium as defined in the Introduction exists. In addition, it is clear from Theorem 2.2 that this kind of equilibrium is Pareto inefficient.

3.4 Concluding Remarks

In this chapter the existence of the involuntary unemployment equilibrium was proved by extending the efficient wage-bargaining theory of McDonald and Solow (1981). Even though managerial rights concerning employment decisions are separated from the nominal wage negotiation process, efficient bargaining achieves Pareto-efficient allocation in the sense that the process maximizes the total surplus of participants. This implies that the equilibrium nominal wage exceeds the reservation wage, and that the same employment level is achieved as in the case in which employees have no bargaining power. Hence, the involuntary unemployment equilibrium exists owing to the shortage of effective demand.

References

Arrow KJ (1962) The economic implications of learning by doing. Rev Econ Stud 29:155–173
Carr EH (1939) The twenty years crisis, with a new introduction by M. Cox. Palgrave, New York
Hayashi K (1963) Waimaru kyowakoku: Hitler wo tanjo saseta mono (Weimar republic: Hitler's birthplace). Chuo-Koronsha, Tokyo
Keynes JM (1936) The general theory of employment, interest and money. Macmillan, London
McDonald IM, Solow RM (1981) Wage bargaining and employment. Am Econ Rev 71:896–908
Otaki M (2009). A welfare economic foundation for the full-employment policy. Econ Lett 102:1–3
Pigou AC (1933). The theory of unemployment (new impression 1968). Frank Cass, London
Smith A (1776) An inquiry into the nature and causes of the wealth of nations. In: Eonnan E (ed) (1994) The modern liberty. W. Strahan and T. Cadell, New York

Chapter 4
The Phillips Curve and Inflation Theory Reconsidered

4.1 Introduction

Much of the research regarding the Phillips curve presumes artificial and exogenous time lags in price-setting decisions (e.g. Mankiw and Reiss 2002, Gali 2008), together with an assumption of money in the utility function. For example, the Calvo (1983) rule assumes that employers can realign their prices only periodically. It is thus assumed that when the nominal money supply increases, the price level cannot adapt fully to such a shock, because some employers are unable to realign their prices. Hence, business upturns in conjunction with the real cash balance. Therefore, even though price realignments progress as the price level approaches the value that neutralizes the expansionary shock (as long as the adjustment process is stable), it is evident that some inertia emerges in price-level movements once a shock is added to the model.

This implies that money is neutral and that the equilibrium inflation rate becomes zero in the long-run equilibrium of the new Keynesian model, even though, in the short run, inflation can coexist with the business upturn associated with the aforementioned lag structure. However, it is unnatural to assume that the long-run equilibrium rate is zero, and that the long-run Phillips curve is vertical around a zero inflation rate.[1]

The character of Friedman's (1968) vertical long-run Phillips curve does not differ from that of the new Keynesians. A difference is sought as to whether the curve is derived from successive revisions of price expectations (the monetarist case) or from price realignments (the new Keynesian case). Here, a common feature is that the downward-sloping Phillips curve emerges only in a transition process in which adjustments are incomplete. The seminal work of Phillips (1958) nonetheless asserts that there is a significant tradeoff between nominal wages and unemployment even in the long run. In addition, such a long-run tradeoff can also be observed throughout the post-war Japanese economy, although it is based on a rather rough estimation (see Fig. 4.1).

[1] New Keynesians place much importance on exogenous stochastic shocks. This is because they need some substantiation for an economy to always be located out of long-run equilibrium. When such complicated and ornamental lag structures and stochastic shocks are eliminated, however, the basic structure of new Keynesian economics does not progress from the static menu-cost theory.

M. Otaki, *Keynesian Economics and Price Theory*,
Advances in Japanese Business and Economics 7, DOI 10.1007/978-4-431-55345-8_4

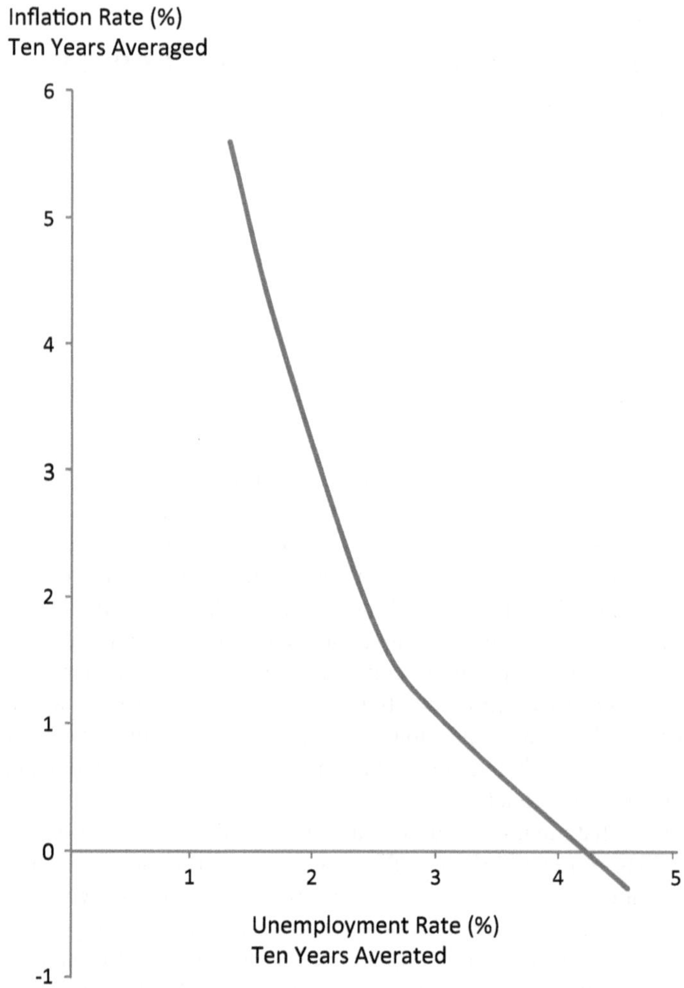

Fig. 4.1 The long-run Phillips curve in Japan

Thus, whether the long-run Phillips curve is vertical is still debatable. However, the curve should be downward sloping in accordance with our fundamental theory exhibited in Chap. 2. This is because money is non-neutral in the fundamental equation even in the long run. Therefore, it is worth constructing a theory that validates the existence of the downward-sloping long-run Phillips curve. A change in labor productivity plays a key role in constructing this theory. As depicted in Table 4.1, the inflation rate correlates positively with the progress of labor productivity. Otaki and Tamai (2012) emphasize this statistical property.

Assume that labor productivity progresses and that this progress is absorbed entirely by an increase in nominal wages. That is, current nominal wages are assumed to increase proportionately with labor productivity. Then, it is clear from the fun-

Table 4.1 The negative correlation between the inflation rate and labor productivity

(% per annum)	1980s	1990s	2000s
Inflation rate by CPI	1.8	1.0	−0.3
The progress of labor productivity	0.7	−0.0	−0.3

Data source: consumer price index, ministry of internal affairs and communications; labor productivity index, Japan productivity center
(The actual labor productivity progresses by 1.06 % on average from 1980 to 2009. We regard this trend as the contribution of physical capital. Subtraction this trend from the actual value, we define the true productivity progress.)

damental equation that the current price level is kept intact. Viewed from another aspect, progress in labor productivity, *ceteris paribus*, reduces production costs, and thus output price should become cheaper relative to any future price. This implies that inflation advances along with any progress in labor productivity. Consequently, a kind of cost push inflation is triggered as long as nominal wages entirely absorb the fruits of this progress, and thus a positive correlation emerges between the inflation rate and labor productivity. Therefore, inflation is a real phenomenon caused by advancement in labor productivity. This contradicts the existing Phillips curve theory in the sense that the opposing theories put much importance on monetary incidents such as nominal money supply.

For this argument, it is assumed that the level of labor productivity is affected more by social incidents than private ones. This is because, as discussed in Chap. 11, some kind of productive coordination is required to achieve process innovation and enhanced labor productivity in firms. The assumed theoretical causality is a variation of Arrow (1962). Potentialities supported by reasonable incomes and stable daily life thus refine abilities beyond generations.

Reflecting on Smith's (1776) argument (Chap. 3), it is realized that his view requires the nurturing of good-natured propensities that facilitate coordination with colleagues, and strong abilities to create innovations that guarantee a stable economic environment, especially those learnt in childhood. Most children are unable to develop these potentialities whenever they face incessant struggle for survival. Involuntary unemployment is a critical factor in hindering the development of such socialized and intellectual personalities. This is because involuntary unemployment immediately implies poverty and/or an unstable family life. Children are disturbed not only by being deprived of educational opportunities but also by instability in their daily lives. Thus, high unemployment within the previous generation is considered to reduce current labor productivity.

As such, the following causality is obtained concerning the long-run Phillips curve:

Higher Unemployment ⇒ Lower Productivity ⇒ Advance in Disinflation.

Thus, a downward-sloping long-run Phillips curve is derived. It must be noted here that such tradeoffs remain even under rational expectation equilibrium with certainty. In this sense, the tradeoff between the unemployment rate and inflation is intrinsic to the market economy.

This chapter is organized as follows. A model is constructed in Sect. 4.2, and from this the stable downward-sloping long-run Phillips curve is derived. Section 4.3 deals with comparative statics and welfare economic analysis. Section 4.4 provides brief concluding remarks.

4.2 The Model

In line with the previous chapter, the Keynes–Chamberlin model is used here, and the nominal wage negotiation process is abbreviated for simplicity. Note that it is not difficult to introduce such a negotiation process into the model outlined in this chapter.

4.2.1 *The Maximization Problem of Economic Agents*

Continuum employers specialize in their own product good within the interval $[0,1]$, and each can employ continuum individuals within the same interval $[0,1]$. The lifetime utility function U is identical and:

$$U \equiv u(c_1, c_2) - \delta_1 \cdot \alpha, \tag{4.1}$$

Where: $u(\cdot)$ is a linear homogenous and concave function; δ_1 is a definition function that takes the value unity when an individual is employed and zero when unemployed; α denotes the disutility of labor; and c_i is the composite of goods consumed during the i -th stage of life, which is formally defined as:

$$c_i \equiv \left[\int_0^1 [c_i(z)]^{1-\eta^{-1}} dz\right]^{\frac{1}{1-\eta^{-1}}},$$

Where: $c_i(z)$ is the consumption of good z during the i -th stage of life.

The indirect utility function of lifetime consumption of an individual who is born at the beginning of period $t, (I_t)$, is:

$$I_t \equiv \frac{\delta_t w_t + \pi_t}{\psi(p_t, p_{t+1})}, \tag{4.2}$$

Where: w_t and π_t are the nominal wage and profits, respectively; and p_i is the price index defined as:

$$p_t \equiv \left[\int_0^1 [p_t(z)]^{1-\eta} dz\right]^{\frac{1}{1-\eta}},$$

Where: $p_t(z)$ is the price of good z.

The nominal reservation wage w_t^R is:

$$w_t^R = \alpha \cdot \psi\left(p_t, p_{t+1}\right). \tag{4.3}$$

In addition, the following aggregate demand function for good z, D_t, and the consumption function during younger ages, C_t, are obtained:

$$D_t \equiv \left(\frac{p_t(z)}{p_t}\right)^{-\eta} \cdot y_t, y_t \equiv \frac{w_t L_t + \pi_t}{p_t}, \tag{4.4}$$

$$C_t \equiv c(\rho_t) y_t, \tag{4.5}$$

Where: L_t is the employment level, and ρ_t is the inflation rate defined by $\frac{p_{t+1}}{p_t}$. The profit function of an employer is defined as:

$$\pi_t(z) \equiv \left[p_t(z) - \frac{w_t^R}{\gamma(U_{t-1})}\right] \cdot D_t(z), \gamma'(U_{t-1}) < 0 \tag{4.6}$$

Where: $\gamma(U_{t-1})$ is the labor productivity function, which is a decreasing function of the unemployment rate of the previous generation U_{t-1}.

As discussed in the Introduction, a high unemployment rate aggravates the conditions of daily life and deprives younger generations of opportunities for higher education and the nurturing of their socialized propensities, which would otherwise have facilitated mutual coordination and communication when they entered jobs, as Dewey (1916) emphasizes. As such, an increase in the unemployment rate *socially* lowers labor productivity. This is the reason why γ is a decreasing function of U_{t-1}. Combining the profit-maximization condition with Eq. (4.3), the fundamental equation that permits varying labor productivity is obtained:

$$p_t = \frac{\alpha \cdot \psi\left(p_t, p_{t+1}\right)}{\left[1-\eta^{-1}\right]\gamma(U_{t-1})}. \tag{4.7}$$

Since $\psi(\cdot)$ is a linear homogenous function, Eq. (4.6) can be transformed into:

$$\psi\left(1, \rho_t\right) = \frac{1-\eta^{-1}}{\alpha} \cdot \gamma\left(U_{t-1}\right), \rho_t \equiv \frac{p_{t+1}}{p_t}. \tag{4.8}$$

Differentiating Eq. (4.8) logarithmically and using Roy's identity:

$$[1-c]\frac{d\rho}{\rho} = \frac{U\gamma'}{\gamma}\frac{dU}{U} \equiv -\nu\frac{dU}{U}, \tag{4.9}$$

Where: ν is the elasticity of labor productivity to the unemployment rate.

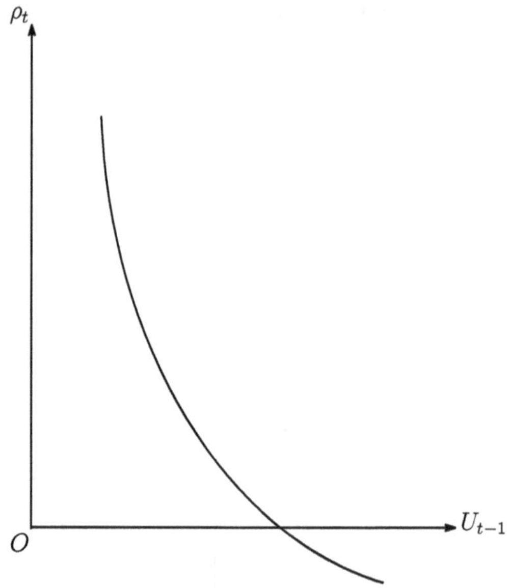

Fig. 4.2 The long-run Phillips curve

Equation (4.9) is the Phillips curve, because disinflation progresses when the unemployment rate during the previous period, U_{t-1}, increases. Thus, the downward-sloping Phillips curve does not assume exogenous price stickiness. This curve is illustrated in Fig. 4.2.[2] This relationship is explained as:

$$\rho = \rho\left(U_{t-1}\right), \rho' < 0. \tag{4.10}$$

4.2.2 *Market Equilibrium*

There are three types of market: the goods market, the money market, and labor markets. Labor markets are in imperfect employment equilibrium when the nominal wage is equal to the nominal reservation wage. That is, $w_t = w_t^R$. Following Walras' law, either the goods market or the money market is not independent, and the equilibrium condition for goods markets:

$$y_t = c\left(\rho_t\right) y_t + \frac{M_{t-1}}{p_t} + g_t, \tag{4.11}$$

Where: M_{t-1} is money carried from the previous period and g_t is real government expenditure.

[2] It must be noted that the real reservation wage in terms of current goods, , increases with the acceleration of the inflation rate, and hence there is a negative correlation between the nominal wage and the unemployment rate.

The first term of the right-hand side in Eq. (4.11) is the aggregate consumption of the younger generation. The second term is that of the older generation, and the third term describes the demand for goods by the government. It is assumed that the government finances its expenditure by issuing new money, and hence the budget constraint for government becomes:

$$g_t = \frac{M_t - M_{t-1}}{p_t}. \tag{4.12}$$

Taking Eq. (4.12) into consideration, Eq. (4.11) can be transformed into:

$$y_t = c(\rho_t) y_t + \frac{M_t}{p_t}. \tag{4.13}$$

Furthermore, we assume that the path of nominal money supply keeps the real cash balance, $\frac{M_t}{p_t}$, constant over time except for the initial value $\frac{M_t}{p_t} = m$. Thus, the equilibrium effective demand is:

$$y_t = c(\rho(U_{t-1})) y_t + m \Rightarrow y_t = \frac{m}{1 - c(\rho(U_{t-1}))}. \tag{4.14}$$

Additionally, since the production function is:

$$y_t = \gamma(U_{t-1})[1 - U_t], \tag{4.15}$$

the equilibrium condition for the aggregate goods market is:

$$U_t = 1 - \frac{m}{\gamma(U_{t-1})[1 - c(\rho(U_{t-1}))]}. \tag{4.16}$$

It is therefore clear that the right-hand side of Eq. (4.16) is an increasing function of U_{t-1} as long as:

$$\eta_s \cdot \eta_\rho > \nu, \tag{4.17}$$

where η_s, η_ρ are the elasticity of savings to the inflation rate, and that of the inflation rate to the unemployment rate, respectively.

The implication of Eq. (4.17) is as follows. An increase in the unemployment rate during the previous period brings about two opposite effects. One effect is that it raises current unemployment through an increase in savings caused by disinflation. This effect appears in the left-hand side of Eq. (4.17). The other effect is that it reduces the current unemployment via stagnation in labor productivity. This corresponds to the right-hand side of Eq. (4.17). It is assumed that the former effect is greater than the latter.

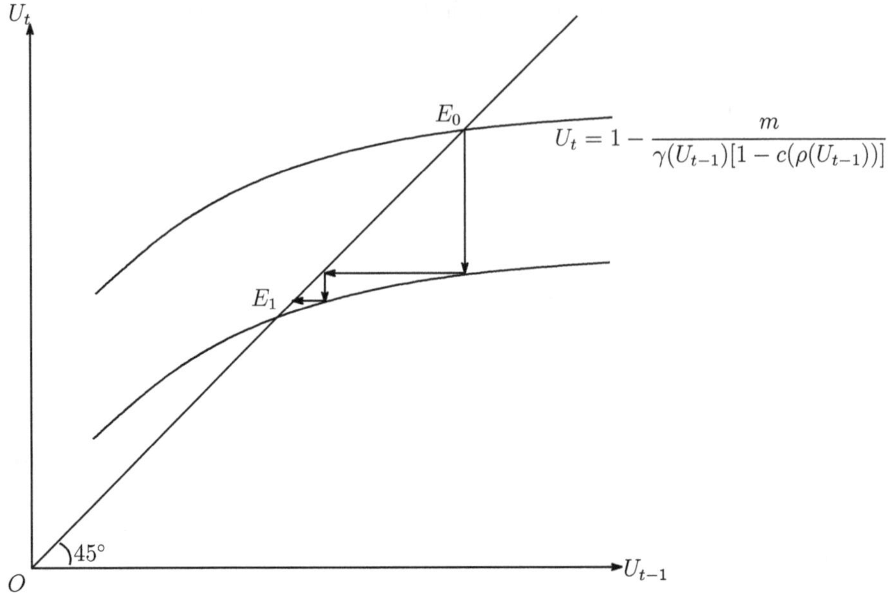

Fig. 4.3 The stability of long-run equilibrium

Equation (4.16) is illustrated by Fig. 4.3. It is evident that local stability around the long-run equilibrium is guaranteed as long as the slope of the curve is less than unity. By differentiating Eq. (4.16):

$$\frac{dU_t}{dU_{t-1}} = \frac{\left[\eta_s \cdot \eta_\rho - \nu\right] m}{\left[\gamma\left(U^*\right)\left[1 - c\left(\rho(U^*)\right)\right]\right]^2 U^*}. \tag{4.18}$$

Hence, if the difference between $\eta_s \cdot \eta_\rho$ and ν is sufficiently small, the dynamic stability of the economy is known.

4.3 Comparative Statics and Welfare Analysis of the Fiscal-Monetary Policy

Consider an expansionary fiscal-monetary policy under imperfect competition. When the real cash balance, m, increases along with real government expenditure, g_t, it is clear that the locus of Eq. (4.16) shifts downwards as illustrated by Fig. 4.3. The long-run equilibrium moves from point E_0 to E_1. Thus, the economy experiences simultaneously a reduction in unemployment and acceleration of inflation. Such consequences are due to the following: first, expansionary policy stimulates effective demand and reduces the unemployment rate; second, labor productivity progresses socially in conjunction with the affluence of the economy. This accelerates inflation because the price of current goods relative to future goods becomes cheaper; and third, the increase in inflation further stimulates aggregate consumption. This favorable cycle continues until the economy reaches a new long-run equilibrium.

Next, the welfare implications of expansionary fiscal-monetary policy are analyzed. Since individuals cannot obtain any surplus from working, the welfare gain is limited to profits that are equally distributed among individuals. Thus, using Eqs. (4.2), (4.3), (4.6), (4.7), and (4.15), social welfare, SW_t, can be written as:

$$SW_t \equiv \frac{\alpha\eta^{-1}\cdot\psi\left(p_t, p_{t+1}\right)}{\left[1-\eta^{-1}\right]\psi\left(p_t, p_{t+1}\right)} L_t = \frac{\alpha\eta^{-1}}{1-\eta^{-1}} L_t. \tag{4.19}$$

Since it is clear from this discussion that the employment level L_t is a monotonously increasing function of time t under expansionary monetary and fiscal policies, the following theorem is obtained:

Theorem 4.1
An expansionary fiscal and monetary policy under imperfect employment equilibrium improves the social welfare of every generation, SW_t, even though the policy raises inflation.

4.4 Concluding Remarks

In this section, the microeconomic foundation for the Phillips curve without exogenous price stickiness was analyzed. The results obtained were as follows:

1. Inflation is essentially a real phenomenon in the sense that improvements in labor productivity accelerate inflation. This is because current goods become cheaper relative to future goods;
2. Improvements in labor productivity are a social concern, because relief from unemployment stabilizes individuals' daily lives and brings positive educational effects for the next generation. Hence, the unemployment rate correlates negatively with labor productivity. Consequently, a negative correlation emerges between the unemployment rate and the inflation rate. This is the interpretation of the downward-sloping long-run Phillips curve; and
3. Finally, an expansionary fiscal-monetary policy improves economic welfare whenever the economy is in imperfect employment equilibrium. This is an extension of Theorem 1.2 in the sense that active aggregate demand management is meaningful even though the policy advances inflation.

References

Arrow KJ (1962) The economic implications of learning by doing. Rev Econ Stud 29:155–173

Calvo GA (1983) Staggered prices in a utility-maximizing framework. J Monetary Econ 12:383–398

Dewey J (1916) Democracy and education: an introduction to the philosophy of education. Free Press, New York

Friedman M (1968) The role of monetary policy. Am Econ Rev 58:1–17

Gali J (2008) Monetary policy, inflation, and the business cycle: an introduction to the new Keynesian framework. Princeton University Press, Princeton

Mankiw NG, Reiss R (2002) Sticky information versus sticky prices: a proposal to replace the new Keynesian Phillips curve. Q J Econ 117:1295–1328

Otaki M, Tamai Y (2012) A microeconomic foundation for the Phillips curve under complete markets without any exogenous price stickiness: a Keynesian view. Theor Econ Lett 2:482–486

Phillips AW (1958) The relation between unemployment and the rate of change of money wage rates in the United Kingdom, 1861–1957. Economica 25:283–299

Smith A (1776) An inquiry into the nature and causes of the wealth of nations. In: Eonnan E (ed) (1994) The modern liberty. W. Strahan and T. Cadell, New York

Part III
Applications to International Economics

Chapter 5
A Basic Model of a Flexible Exchange Rate System Under Perfect Capital Mobility

5.1 Introduction

A small open economy model operating under a flexible exchange rate system is developed in this chapter based on Otaki (2012). A small economy means that it cannot affect real GDP or the inflation rate in foreign economies. Meanwhile, it is assumed that capital mobility is perfect in the sense of Fleming (1962) and Mundell (1963). That is, there are no restrictions on international finance under conditions of certainty. This model provides not only a pivotal point for the following analyses, but also considers the international diffusion problem in the business cycle under a flexible exchange rate system, which was originally raised by Laursen and Metzler (1950). Nevertheless, and unlike preceding research the present analysis is based on a rigorous dynamic microeconomic foundation using an *overlapping generations* (OLG) model. This procedure gives a definite answer to that question. That is, the isolation effect is imperfect and the business cycle diffuses internationally even under a flexible rate system in which the real exchange rate equilibrates the balance of payments.

Such imperfections stem from the fact that an overseas economic upturn will result in an appreciation in the real exchange rate. This appreciation is caused by an increase in foreign demand for domestic goods. The appreciation is advantageous for residents in a domestic economy, and they possibly agree with reducing nominal wages as far as the economy is located at an imperfect employment equilibrium. This is because competition between workers deprives the market of the surplus that emerges from appreciation. Thus, the price of current goods becomes cheaper in relation to future goods. Hence, an appreciation in the real exchange rate accelerates inflation, and this stimulates aggregate domestic consumption via a substitution effect from future goods to current goods. Accordingly, an overseas economic upturn stimulates domestic effective demand. To summarize, the business cycle diffuses internationally even under a flexible exchange rate system in which the real exchange rate is expected to equilibrate the balance of payments.

This chapter is organized as follows. Section 5.2 deals with the relationship between the balance of payments and capital mobility. The discussion shows that, contrary to Fleming (1962) and Mundell (1963), the balance of payments is equili-

M. Otaki, *Keynesian Economics and Price Theory*,
Advances in Japanese Business and Economics 7, DOI 10.1007/978-4-431-55345-8_5

brated even under perfect capital mobility in an OLG model. By using the results of the preceding section, a small open economy model based on an OLG model can be constructed in Sect. 5.3. Section 5.4 considers whether an employment isolation effect exists under a flexible exchange rate system, and Sect. 5.5 gives brief concluding remarks.

5.2 The Equilibrium of the Balance of Payments Under Perfect Capital Mobility

A small open economy model is described here, in which two goods a and b are traded between domestic and foreign economies, using a two-period and infinite time horizon-OLG approach. Each economy specializes in production of a single good: the domestic economy produces Good a, and the foreign economy produces Good b. There are two stores of value in the world economy: domestic and foreign currencies. Each currency is exchangeable only for the corresponding goods. That is, good a is exchangeable only for domestic currency, and good b is exchangeable only for foreign currency. In this discussion, if capital movement is perfect in the sense that there is no restriction for international finance, the equilibrium real exchange rate is determined to equilibrate the balance of payments. Ahead of the analysis, the following assumption for the simplicity of explanation is made:

Assumption 5.1
International commodity trading is settled using foreign currency.

The balance of payments in the home economy B_t is denoted as:

$$B_t \equiv p_t^a\left[E_{1t}^a + E_{2t}^a + E_{gt}^a\right] - p_t^b\pi_t\left[M_{1t}^b + M_{2t}^b + M_{gt}^b\right]$$
$$\Leftrightarrow \frac{B_t}{p_t^a} \equiv \left[\left[E_{1t}^a + E_{2t}^a + E_{gt}^a\right] - e_t\left[M_{1t}^b + M_{gt}^b\right]\right] - e_t M_{2t}^b, \quad (5.1)$$

Where: E_{it}^a is exports towards the i-th generation foreigners during period t ($i = 1$ indicates the younger generation, and $i = 2$ corresponds to the older generation); M_{it}^b is imports of the i-th generation of domestic residents during period t; and E_{gt}^a and M_{gt}^B are the domestic government's exports to the foreign economy and its imports to the home country from the foreign economy, respectively.

The first term in Eq. (5.1) describes the domestic accumulation of foreign currency by the older generation. The second term represents imports by the domestic older generation. Thus, if $B_t > 0$, the domestic older generation passes the foreign currency to descendants. On the contrary, if $B_t < 0$, the older generation leaves a negative inheritance. Since people are assumed to be individualistic, they have no incentive to leave either positive or negative inheritance. Accordingly, the equilibrium condition for the foreign exchange markets under perfect international capital mobility is:

$$\frac{B_t}{p_t^a} \equiv \left[E_{1t}^a + E_{2t}^a + E_{gt}^a\right] - e_t\left[M_{1t}^b + M_{2t}^b + M_{gt}^b\right] = 0. \tag{5.2}$$

This condition is in contrast to the models of Fleming (1962) and Mundell (1963), in which the balance of payments never equilibrates under perfect capital mobility. This difference exists because the present model, by its nature, explicitly contains the due dates of financial transactions, while that of Fleming (1962) and Mundell (1963) does not.

5.3 The Model

5.3.1 Individuals

It is assumed that residents in the two economies have the same lifetime utility function, U, as:

$$U \equiv u(c_{1t}, c_{2t+1}) - \delta_t \alpha, \quad c_{it} \equiv [a_{it}]^{\beta}[b_{it}]^{1-\beta}, \quad 0 < \beta < 1. \tag{5.3}$$

Where: c_{it+j} is the aggregate consumption level during the i-th stage of life at period $t+j$; a_{it+j} and b_{it+j} are the consumption level of goods a and b, respectively; α denotes the disutility of labor; δ_t is a definition function that takes value unity when employed and zero when unemployed; and $u(\cdot)$ is a well-behaved homothetic utility function describing the consumption stream.

Here, an assumption concerning the asset holdings of the domestic younger generation is:

Assumption 5.2
The domestic younger generation saves money in terms of home currency.[1]

By using Assumptions 1 and 2, an elementary calculation leads to the corresponding expenditure function Φ:

$$\Phi \equiv \phi([p_t^a]^{\beta}[\pi_t p_t^b]^{1-\beta}, [p_{t+1}^a]^{\beta}[\pi_{t+1} p_{t+1}^b]^{1-\beta}) f(u), \tag{5.4}$$

Where: u is a utility level.

[1] Although such a restriction on the portfolio selection seems to violate the perfect capital mobility assumption, note that the logic, which leads to the result that the balance of payments is equilibrated under a flexible exchange rate system, is not affected by this restriction.

The following assumption makes the analysis far more facilitative. That is:

Assumption 5.3
The analysis is configured with a stationary state, where the real exchange rate, e, is kept at a constant value, e^*.

Since ϕ is a linear homogenous function, from Assumption 5.3, Eq. (5.4) can be transformed into:

$$\Phi = p_1^a \phi([e_t]^{1-\beta}, \rho^a \cdot [e_{t+1}]^{1-\beta}) f(u) = p_t^a [e^*]^{1-\beta} \phi(1, \rho^a) f(u), \quad (5.5)$$

Where: ρ^a is the equilibrium inflation rate of the domestic good.

From Eqs. (5.3) and (5.5), the nominal reservation wage W^R is:

$$W_t^R = p_t^a [e^*]^{1-\beta} \phi(1, \rho^a) f(\alpha). \quad (5.6)$$

The equilibrium nominal wage is therefore equal to W_t^R as long as the economy has fallen into underemployment equilibrium. This is the market-clearing condition for the labor market.

5.3.2 *Firms*

Since all firms are assumed to be price takers having a linear production function and unit productivity, the zero-profit condition corresponds to the solution of the maximization problem. Thus:

$$p_t^a = W_t^R \quad \Rightarrow \quad 1 = [e^*]^{1-\beta} \phi(1, \rho^a) f(\alpha). \quad (5.7)$$

Equation (5.7) is the fundamental equation of the open economy version. Since ϕ is an increasing function of ρ^a, Eq. (5.7) clearly shows that inflation is accelerated whenever the real exchange rate, e^*, appreciates, as discussed in Sect. 5.1.

5.3.3 *The Government*

In accordance with Otaki (2007, 2009, 2011), the government keeps the real cash level $m_t \equiv \frac{M_t}{p_t^a}$ constant over time once it decides the initial value m_1. Hence the budget constraint of the government becomes:

$$g = [1 - \frac{1}{\rho^a}] m_1, \quad (5.8)$$

Where: g is wasteful real government expenditure.

In addition, the government's propensity to spend on each good is the same as that for individuals. That is, a unit of government expenditure is allocated β to good a, and $1-\beta$ to good b.

5.3.4 Market Equilibrium

The model contains four markets: the domestic goods market; the labor market; the domestic money market; and the foreign exchange market. The equilibrium condition for the domestic money market can be abbreviated in accordance with Walras' law, and the labor market is in interior equilibrium if Eq. (5.7) holds. Also, the foreign exchange market is cleared if $B = 0$ in Eq. (5.2) holds. Again, elementary calculation leads to:

$$E_1^a = \beta \cdot \left[c^b(\rho^b) + \frac{1-c^b(\rho^b)}{\rho^b} + \left[1-\frac{1}{\rho^b}\right]\left[1-c^b(\rho^b)\right] \right] \cdot e^* y^b = \beta \cdot e^* y^b,$$

$$e^* M_1^b = [1-\beta] \cdot \left[c^a(\rho^a) + \frac{1-c^a(\rho^a)}{\rho^a} + \left[1-\frac{1}{\rho^a}\right]\left[1-c^a(\rho^a)\right] \right] \cdot y^a = [1-\beta] \cdot y^a,$$

Where: $c^j\,(j = a, b)$ is the marginal propensity to consume in each economy; and y^j is real GDP in terms of each economy's good.

The first term in these equations corresponds to the younger generation's import demand. The second term covers the older generation. The third term in each equation describes government import demand, which is financed by seigniorage (an inflation tax). Accordingly, the following equation is obtained as the equilibrium condition for the foreign exchange market:

$$\beta \cdot e^* y^b = [1-\beta] \cdot y^a \tag{5.9}$$

Taking Eqs. (5.8) and (5.9) into consideration, the domestic good market is in equilibrium when:

$$y^a = c^a(\rho^a) y^a + \frac{m_1}{\rho^a} + \left[1-\frac{1}{\rho^a}\right] m_1 = c^a(\rho^a) y^a + m_1 \tag{5.10}$$

holds. $c^a(\rho^a)$ is the marginal propensity to consume of the economy.

The first term in Eq. (5.10) is the younger generation's consumption level. The second term is the older generation's consumption level, and the third term corresponds to government expenditure. It should be noted that the real exchange rate e^* does not appear in Eq. (5.10). This is because the real wage in terms of good a, $\frac{W_t^R}{p^a}$, is fixed to unity by Eq. (5.7). Unlike in Laursen and Metzler (1950), the terms of trade effect does not appear directly as a change in real income. It only affects the inflation rate through the fundamental Eq. (5.7) indirectly. To summarize, there are three endogenous variables: (y^a, ρ^a, e^*). These variables are determined by Eqs. (5.7), (5.9), and (5.10). Thus, the model is completely closed.

5.4 The Employment Isolation Effect

This section considers the effect of the foreign economy's business cycle on the domestic economy. The discussion is extended in the Mathematical Appendix. Assume that the world economy expands and y^b increases. This directly stimulates exports and results in the appreciation of the real exchange rate e^*. Since the balance of payments is equilibrated by an appreciation of e^*, the upturn in the foreign economy does not diffuse directly to the domestic economy. However, such an appreciation is in favor of employees because the import price is lowered. Nevertheless, in an imperfect employment equilibrium, where some employees are unemployed, there is room for firms to cut down the nominal wage, and thus the price of the current domestic good p_t^a is also lowered relative to its future price p_{t+1}^a. That is, inflation is accelerated. Hence, if the intertemporal substitution rate is high enough and $\frac{dc^a}{d\rho}$ is positive, real effective demand y^a increases, and the upturn in the foreign economy diffuses to the domestic economy. In this sense, the employment isolation effect is certainly incomplete under a flexible exchange rate system with perfect capital mobility. Thus:

Theorem 5.1
The employment isolation effect is imperfect under a flexible exchange rate system. An upturn in a foreign economy also stimulates a domestic economy by accelerating domestic inflation.

5.5 Fiscal and Monetary Policy

It should be noted that, unlike in the naïve IS/LM analysis, fiscal policy and monetary policy are not independent of the budget constraints imposed by government as Eq. (5.8) indicates. Fiscal expansion always accompanies monetary expansion. To clarify the economic implication, this section considers the aspect of fiscal policy.

Assume that real fiscal expenditure g increases. Then, through the multiplier process, real GDP, y^a increases. However, such an expansionary effect is curtailed compared with a closed economy, in which no international commodity or financial trades exist. This owes much to a depreciation in the real exchange rate. Since imports increase with an upturn in the domestic economy, the real exchange rate depreciates to equilibrate the balance of payments. This depreciation advances disinflation to recover the impacted standard of living, as is clear from Eq. (5.7). Any such disinflation lowers the marginal propensity to consume and reduces the multiplier effect.

In closed economy case, this negative effect does not exist by definition. Thus, the effect of fiscal-monetary policy under an open economy is weaker than that under a closed economy. Although such negative effects are not extreme, it is undeniable that disinflation adjacent to a domestic business upturn reduces the expansionary effect of fiscal-monetary policy under the flexible exchange rate system. Thus:

Theorem 5.2
The effect of fiscal-monetary policy in a small open economy is weaker compared with that in a closed economy. This is because an increase in imports adjacent to a business upturn reduces the marginal propensity to consume by an advance in disinflation through depreciation of the real exchange rate.

5.6 Concluding Remarks

This chapter developed a small open economy model under a perfectly capital mobile, flexible exchange rate system with a rigorous dynamic microeconomic foundation. The results obtained were as follows:

1. First, the balance of payments is equilibrated in this model even though international capital mobility is perfect. This is entirely different from Fleming (1962) and Mundell (1963), in which an economy can borrow money infinitely under a flexible exchange rate. Such differences stem from whether the existence of the due dates of loans is explicitly taken into consideration;
2. Second, the employment isolation effect is incomplete and a business upturn in the foreign economy diffuses into the domestic economy even though real exchange rates equilibrate the balance of payments. This is because any appreciation in the exchange rate resulting from a business upturn in the foreign economy accelerates inflation within the domestic economy. This stimulates domestic consumption, and thus the business cycle diffuses internationally. Although Laursen and Metzler (1950) were unable to provide a definitive view on this question, the success in the present model owes much to its rigorous dynamic microeconomic foundation.
3. Finally, the power of fiscal-monetary policy under a flexible exchange rate system is weaker than that under a closed economy, as Fleming (1962) and Mundell (1963) emphasize. The critical cause of this conclusion is disinflation, which is brought about by the increase in imports deriving from a business upturn.

5.7 Mathematical Appendix

This appendix outlines the mathematical results concerning the theories in Sect. 3, based on the structural Eqs. (5.7), (5.9), and (5.10). Using Roy's identity, $\frac{\phi'}{\phi} = 1 - c^a \equiv s^a$ is obtained. Eq. (5.7) is thus transformed into:

$$[1-\beta]\frac{de}{e} + \rho^a s^a\left(\rho^a\right)\frac{d\rho^a}{\rho^a} = 0. \tag{5.11}$$

Differentiating both sides of Eqs. (5.9) and (5.10) logarithmically and substituting Eq. (5.11):

$$\begin{bmatrix} 1 & \frac{s^a \rho^a}{1-\beta} \\ 1 & -\eta \end{bmatrix} \begin{bmatrix} \frac{dy^a}{y^a} \\ \frac{d\rho^a}{\rho^a} \end{bmatrix} = \begin{bmatrix} \frac{dy^b}{y^b} \\ \frac{dm}{m} \end{bmatrix}, \tag{5.12}$$

Where:

$$\eta \equiv -\frac{\rho^a \left[s^a\right]'}{s^a}$$

.Finally, solving Eq. (5.12) gives:

$$\begin{bmatrix} \frac{dy^a}{y^a} \\ \frac{d\rho^a}{\rho^a} \end{bmatrix} = -\frac{1}{\Delta} \begin{bmatrix} \eta & \frac{s^a \rho^a}{1-\beta} \\ 1 & -1 \end{bmatrix} \begin{bmatrix} \frac{dy^b}{y^b} \\ \frac{dm}{m} \end{bmatrix}, \tag{5.13}$$

Where:

$$\Delta \equiv -\left[\frac{s^a \rho^a}{1-\beta} + \eta\right] < 0.$$

References

Fleming JM (1962) Domestic fiscal policies and floating exchange rates. IMF Staff Pap 9:369–380

Laursen S, Metzler L (1950) Flexible exchange rates and the theory of employment. Rev Econ Stat 32:281–299

Mundell RA (1963) Capital mobility and stabilization policy under fixed and flexible exchange rates. Can J Econ Polit Sci 29:475–485

Otaki M (2007) The dynamically extended Keynesian cross and the welfare-improving fiscal policy. Econ Lett 96:23–29

Otaki M (2009) A welfare economics foundation for the full-employment policy. Econ Lett 102:1–3

Otaki M (2011) A pure theory of aggregate price determination. Theor Econ Lett 1:122–128

Otaki M (2012) A Keynesian model of a small open economy under a flexible exchange rate. Theor Econ Lett 2:278–282

Chapter 6
The Functions of a Key Currency: International Liquidity Provision and Insurance

6.1 Introduction

Although the flexible exchange rate system studied in Chap. 5 equilibrates the current account in the long run, many economies, especially if their nominal exchange rates are pegged to the U.S. dollar, experience persistent imbalance in their current account. Nevertheless, these imbalances are not usually in question except in specific cases such as those found in Latin America. Similarly, although the U.S., the present key-currency country, is also a notable debtor country, no one regarded this fact as a serious international finance problem until the Lehman Shock occurred. How then can such persistent but sustainable (at least seemingly) imbalances in current accounts be understood? Chapter 6 is devoted to the analysis of this problem.

A seminal work exists concerning the selection of a key currency (Matsuyama et al. 1993). This study used an evolutionary game with strategic complement properties. These properties mean that if more economies come to use the same currency, this is more beneficial for the affiliates. Thus, in the long run, a single currency (a key currency) is circulated. Meanwhile, which currency is actually selected depends entirely on contingencies. For example, assume that people in the world disbelieve in the U.S. dollar, and instead become confident in the Mexican peso. Then, the peso may become a key currency. That is, a key currency is a convenient medium that needs no endorsements to sustain confidence in it.

However, this is against historical evidence. During the twentieth century, a change of key-currency country occurred only once; from the U.K. to the U.S. In addition, it must be noted that these countries were and are proud of being the most advanced and affluent economies during their currency's reign. These facts suggest that there is some causality between the economic prosperity of a country and its enthronement or dethronement as a key-currency country. Chapter 2 showed that confidence in a currency plays a crucial role here. The currency of a country that is affected by hyperinflation can hardly become a key currency. This is because once such a currency is hoarded it rapidly devalues and investors lose all their savings. Thus, confidence in a currency, which means the belief that the currency is always convertible to goods at a stable price, is a necessary condition for becoming

M. Otaki, *Keynesian Economics and Price Theory*,
Advances in Japanese Business and Economics 7, DOI 10.1007/978-4-431-55345-8_6

a key currency. In addition, since many economies commonly use the currency, a key-currency country has to possess overwhelming industrial power and enormous gold reserves and/or foreign assets to sustain this confidence. Accordingly, which country becomes a key-currency country is never determined by contingencies, but by the industrial and financial powers it holds.

In turn, affiliated economies also obtain substantive benefits from joining a key-currency system. Since some of these may only have fragile industrial foundations, confidence in the currencies that such economies issue is lower, and hoarding is prone to cause hyperinflation. If, instead, a key currency circulates (or a domestic currency is pegged to a key currency), a difficulty intrinsic to weak currencies is overcome. Thus, a key-currency system is a kind of device that facilitates international liquidity provision.

On the other hand, a key-currency country enjoys its prerogatives. For example, it obtains seigniorage over affiliates in conjunction with its supply of currency. In addition, as observed in the major stock exchange settings such as Wall Street, it can earn huge fees from international financial transaction. As such, a sound key-currency system is reciprocally beneficial for both a key-currency country and its affiliates.

Theoretically, a key currency as described above can be regarded as an international insurance system against sovereign risk within affiliated economies. Since affiliated economies are assumed to be far more fragile in industrial power relative to their key-currency country, they will wish to cover various risks originating from such fragility (e.g. deep stagnation adjacent to hyperinflation) by injecting the key currency into their domestic economy instead of their own currency. That is, affiliated economies are insurers of sovereign risk. In this way, the key-currency country corresponds to an insurance company. Its currency plays an insurance security role although it is far more liquid than that issued by private companies, and is able to circulate as a store of value throughout the world. The insurance due, which substantially means fees and/or taxes incurred in using the key currency, mainly comprises the seigniorage. This implies that a key-currency country can purchase foreign goods simply by printing money, and will profit from international financial intermediation.

Keynes (2013) recorded the actions and sincerity of bankers, politicians, unions, and economists of the U.K. when evacuating the Great Depression. This reference contains the addendum of the Macmillan Committee concerning the devaluation of the pound during the 1930s, written by Keynes. Judging from the proceedings and the letters, the amount of gold hoarded in the U.K. was required to be at a particular critical level to keep the status of key-currency country. Although Keynes admitted that devaluation could become a measure to promote temporal economic recovery, since foreign credits were fixed in terms of sterling not gold, he negated the efficacy of devaluation in his writings. According to Keynes (2013):

> We have already agreed, however, that for a country in the special circumstance of Great Britain in the disadvantage would greatly outweigh the advantages, and we have concurred with our colleagues in rejecting it.

This statement strongly suggests not only how deeply the confidence in a key currency links to its gold reserves, but also how beneficial it is to *keep* the status of a key-currency country.

As is well known, an insurance system relies on the law of large numbers, and thus it is necessary for the maintenance of a key currency that many economies agree to use that currency. Hence, key-currency countries will be limited to those that have not only overwhelming industrial power, but also huge foreign assets to sustain confidence in their currency. Additionally, if the functions of a key currency are as discussed above, persistent imbalances in current accounts, specifically the persistent current account deficits in a key-currency country, are explicable. That is, seigniorage due to the key-currency country makes up for current account deficits. As far as the key-currency country is disciplined by sound fiscal-monetary policy, such deficits never become a serious problem that may result in disbelief in the currency.

This chapter is organized as follows. In Sect. 6.2, a model of a key-currency system is constructed using a two-period overlapping generations (OLG) model with infinite time horizons, based on Otaki (2013). In addition, it is proved that a key-currency system as international insurance also provides international liquidity sufficient to achieve full-employment equilibrium in each affiliated economy. Section 6.3 considers the vulnerability of the key-currency system. In Sect. 6.4, the relationship between the theory extended in this chapter and a theory of an optimum currency area, which is further outlined in Chap. 7, is discussed. Section 6.5 provides brief concluding remarks.

6.2 The Model

6.2.1 *Structure of the Model*

The presentation develops a two-period OLG model with an infinite horizon, and is based on Otaki (2011). Each country produces the same differentiated goods by monopolistic entrepreneur iz, where i generically refers to the characteristics of the country and z refers to those of the good. Each country contains $m\lambda_i$ entrepreneurs who receive all earned profits and $(1-m)\lambda_i$ employees whose incomes come from only nominal wages. In this model the key-currency country K is differentiated from its affiliated countries A only by its huge population λ_k per generation, while the population of each affiliate A is limited by $\lambda_a (n\lambda_a = \lambda_k)$. Since the only production resource is labor, which is supplied by the younger generation, this asymmetric assumption implies that the economy of the key-currency country holds huge potential production power compared with surrounding countries.

In addition, each affiliated country faces a serious though temporary supply shock, or sovereign risk. However, the key-currency country runs no such risk, implying that its production process is far more reliable. For simplicity, when this supply shock is induced, the affiliated country cannot produce any goods. The probability of such a disaster is assumed to be $\varepsilon(0<\varepsilon\ll 1)$. Finally, in the model, all individuals possess an identical lifetime utility function U_i:

$$U_i \equiv U\left(c_{ijt}^1, c_{ijt}^2\right) - \delta_{ij}\alpha, \quad c_{ijt}^h \equiv \left\{\sum_{z=1}^{l}\left[c_{ijt}^h(z)\right]^{1-\eta^{-1}} dz\right\}^{\frac{1}{1-\eta^{-1}}}, \quad \eta > 1, \tag{6.1}$$

Where: U is a well-behaved homothetic function and $c_{ijt}^h(z)$ denotes the consumption of good z by individual j aged h in the i-th country during period t. α is the disutility of labor; l is the number of produced goods; $\delta_{ij}$is a definition function that takes the value of unity when individual j in country i participates in the labor force, and zero when he/she is unemployed. One unit of labor produces one unit of a good.[1]

In this situation, an incentive for insurance emerges between the key-currency country and affiliated countries. In other words, instead of allowing the domestic circulation of the key currency and handing over rents received from issuing their own currencies, affiliated countries import goods in exchange for the key currency. Thus, an almost one-sided capital flow (deficit in the key-currency country, surplus in surrounding countries) emerges. The key-currency system thus becomes sustainable through creating such an incentive.

6.2.2 *Construction of the Model*

Individuals

Since the lifetime consumption utility function is homothetic, the corresponding expenditure function Ψ is represented as:

$$\Psi \equiv \psi(p_t, p_{t+1}) f(u), \quad p_t \equiv \left\{\sum_{z=1}^{l}\left[p_t(z)\right]^{1-\eta} dz\right\}^{\frac{1}{1-\eta}}, \tag{6.2}$$

Where: u is the fixed utility level; and $\psi(\cdot)$ is the increasing linear homogenous function of (p_t, p_{t+1}).

To introduce risk aversion into the utility function, it is assumed that $f''>0$. As long as economies are located at the imperfect employment equilibrium, as Otaki (2007, 2009) shows, the equilibrium nominal wage is kept equal to the nominal reservation wage W_t^R. The latter wage is easily derived from Eq. (6.2) as:

$$W_t^R = \psi(p_t, p_{t+1}) f(\alpha). \tag{6.3}$$

[1] The assumption that the utility functions of all individuals in the world are identical is restrictive. Nonetheless, the main concern here is to show that the imbalance in the current account, namely the international capital movement, is caused without a difference in inflation rates across countries owing to the difference in time preferences. From this perspective, the aforementioned assumption is admissible for simplification purposes.

Firms

From the assumption about the instantaneous utility function, the demand function D_{zt} for good z that is monopolistically produced by a certain firm becomes:

$$D_{zt} \equiv \left[\frac{p_t(z)}{p_t}\right]^{-\eta} y_t,$$

Where; y_t is real GDP in terms of current goods.

From the profit maximization condition and Eq. (6.3), the following fundamental difference equation concerning the evolution of the price level can be postulated:

$$p_t = \frac{\psi(p_t, p_{t+1}) f(\alpha)}{1-\eta^{-1}} = \frac{p_t \psi\left(1, \pi^*\right) f(\alpha)}{1-\eta^{-1}}, \quad \pi^* \equiv \frac{p_{t+1}}{p_t}. \tag{6.4}$$

Equation (6.4) holds for all countries including the key-currency country. Accordingly, the purchasing power of a key currency can be preserved worldwide because the same equilibrium inflation rate π^* is attained in every country, independent of the nominal money supply of the key currency.[2] In other words, the fixed exchange rate system is sustainable even under perfect capital mobility. For simplicity, it is assumed that the nominal exchange rate is fixed at unity and the initial absolute prices in the key currency area are the same.

Governments

The government of the key-currency country adopts the following two segregated monetary and fiscal policies:

1. The key-currency country supplies domestic money through wasteful government expenditure. The expenditure per capita amounts to $\lambda_k G (\equiv \lambda_k \cdot p_{t+j} g)$[3]; and
2. Affiliated countries receive money by exporting the composite goods defined by Eq. (6.1). All imported goods are transferred to younger residents in the key-currency country equally.

To keep the analysis as simple and clear as possible, discussion is confined to the stationary equilibrium. Hence, the monetary authority in the key-currency country keeps the real money supply constant in both the key-currency and affiliated countries. Let these values be denoted as $\lambda_k m^d$ and $n\lambda_a m^f$, respectively. Furthermore, the number of affiliated countries n is assumed to be large enough that the law of large numbers approximately holds.

---

[2] As defined in Chap. 2, it is assumed that people are *confident* with the key currency.

[3] The assumption of wasteful expenditure is adopted for simplicity. Even if the government contributes to economic welfare, the obtained results are unchanged.

6.2.3 Market Equilibrium and International Liquidity Provision

Three kinds of markets exist in this model: goods markets, labor markets, and money markets. The scope of this study is the former two markets, and relies on Walras' Law. Each labor market is in interior equilibrium if the equilibrium nominal wage is equal to the nominal reservation wage W_t^R.[4] Eventually, only the analysis concerning goods markets remains. The equilibrium condition for goods markets is represented by the following two-stage game. At the first stage, the key-currency and affiliated country negotiate for the international implicit insurance. The second stage determines how much the key currency should provide international liquidity to affiliate countries.

The solution for perfect equilibrium begins with solving the solution of the second stage. Since the lifetime utility function of the consumption stream is assumed to be homothetic, the consumption function of a younger individual in each country C_i is:

$$C_i \equiv c\left(\pi^*\right) y_i^d, \quad i = k \text{ or } a, \tag{6.5}$$

Where: y_i^d is the per capita disposable income of country i.

The equilibrium of the aggregate goods market in each affiliated country is conditional on whether the emergent sovereign risk is induced. In other words:

$$y_a = \begin{cases} c\left(\pi^*\right)[y_a - E] + m^f + E, & \text{with probability } 1-\varepsilon, \\ m^f + s, & \text{with probability } \varepsilon, \end{cases} \tag{6.6}$$

Where: y^s is the real GDP per capita; E represents exports to the key-currency country; $y_s - E$ thus denotes its disposal income per capita; and s denotes the implicit insurance payments in an emergency. This specification of the equilibrium of aggregate goods market implies that an affiliated country pays seigniorage for the stock of the key currency, m^f, which amounts to E during every period and that these payments are returned as exports towards itself.

By solving Eq. (6.6) for State 1:

$$y_a - E = \frac{m^f}{1 - c\left(\pi^*\right)} \quad \Leftrightarrow \quad E + \frac{m^f}{1 - c\left(\pi^*\right)} = y_a. \tag{6.7}$$

The sum of the rents received by the key-currency country, E, and each affiliated country's disposal income per capita $\dfrac{m^f}{1 - c(\pi^*)}$ is always equal to each affiliated country's real GDP per capita y_s. Equation (6.6) implies that it is beneficial for

[4] For the properties of the boundary equilibrium, see Chap. 2.

both countries to provide sufficient liquidity m^f to achieve the full-employment equilibrium. Thus, international liquidity guarantees the full-employment equilibrium in every affiliated country. Hence, $y_a = 1$ for all a. This is the solution of the second-stage game.

Next, the first-stage game solution based on the above result can be obtained. The net rent derived from issuing the key currency, B, which is equal to the current account deficit of the key-currency country, is:

$$B\left(m^f, s\right) \equiv [1-\varepsilon]\left[1-\frac{m^f}{1-c(\pi^*)}\right]-\varepsilon\left[m^f+s\right]. \tag{6.8}$$

Where: s denotes the additional aid (or discount) in the case of emergencies in an affiliated country.

Thus, by combining Eq. (6.5), the equilibrium condition for the aggregate goods market in the key-currency country is represented as:

$$\begin{aligned} y_k + B\left(m^f, s\right) &= c\left(\pi^*\right)\left[y_k + B\left(m^f, s\right)\right] + g + \frac{1}{\pi^*} m^d \\ &= c\left(\pi^*\right)\left[y_k + B\left(m^f, s\right)\right] + m^d, \end{aligned} \tag{6.9}$$

Where: y_k is the per capita real GDP in the key-currency country; and the third term of the right-hand side of Eq. (6.9) is the per capita real expenditure of older individuals.

By solving Eq. (6.9) on y_k, the equilibrium GDP of the key-currency country is represented as:

$$y_k^* = \frac{m^d}{1-c\left(\pi^*\right)} - B\left(m^f, s\right). \tag{6.10}$$

Note that the same amount of equilibrium GDP per capita, y_k^*, decreases in line with imports from foreign countries B, while disposable income is fixed as long as the real domestic money supply m^d remains constant. This is because the increment in the savings of younger individuals from real GDP should be entirely crowded out by the increase in imports funded by the net rent from the key-currency system, given that the total purchasing power of the government and older individuals is unchanged.

Since the expected indirect utility is a monotonously increasing function of disposable income, the expected utility of the key-currency country increases with $B(\cdot)$ as long as full employment is maintained by an ample liquidity supply m^d that satisfies $\frac{m^d}{1-c\left(\pi^*\right)} = 1 + B$. Accordingly, the key-currency system attains worldwide full-employment equilibrium, or in other words, the key currency serves as the best international liquidity provision system.[5] From Eq. (6.7), the indirect expected utility of an affiliated country is:[6]

$$\tilde{U}^s \equiv [1-\varepsilon] f^{-1}\left(\frac{m^f}{1-c\left(\pi^*\right)}\right) + \varepsilon f^{-1}\left(m^f + s\right). \tag{6.11}$$

From the law of large numbers, the key currency can become risk-neutral, and thereby the pay-off function is expressed by Eq. (6.8). Consequently, the key-currency system as an optimal contract of insurance system can be described by the following maximization problem:

$$\max_{m^f, s} B\left(m^f, s\right), \quad s.t.\, \tilde{U}^s \geq \bar{U}. \tag{6.12}$$

Using the above result, the Lagrangian L of this problem is written as:

$$L\left(m^f, s, \lambda\right) \equiv [1-\varepsilon]\left[1-\frac{m^f}{1-c\left(\pi^*\right)}\right] - \varepsilon\left[m^f + s\right] + \lambda\left[[1-\varepsilon] f^{-1}\left(\frac{m^f}{1-c\left(\pi^*\right)}\right) + \varepsilon f^{-1}\left(m^f + s\right) - \bar{U}\right], \tag{6.13}$$

Where: λ is the Lagrangian multiplier.

The optimal contract is illustrated by point E_1 in Fig. 6.1. U_1 is the indifference curve of an affiliated country that corresponds to the utility level $\bar{U}$ and I_1 and I_2 are the iso-profit lines of the key-currency country. The line at the bottom left of the Figure (I_2) indicates higher profits. It is clear from Fig. 6.1 that sovereign risk is completely hedged in the solutions for Eq. (6.12), such as points E_1 and E_2, so that each affiliated country receives a fixed income regardless of which of the two states occurs. It is clear from the indifference curves U_1 and U_3 that an affiliated country also becomes better off by being involved in such a system.

6.2.4 *The Persistent Imbalance in the Current Account and the Exchange Rate*

In this subsection, simple comparative statics on the bargaining power of the key-currency country are applied to ascertain why the persistent current account deficit

[5] Note that the full-employment equilibrium is Pareto efficient, even if there is no additional utility gain from the increment in labor. This is because monopolistic profits increase with real GDP. See Chap. 2 for more detail.

[6] It is possible that each argument in $f^{-1}(\cdot)$ should be divided by the price index $\phi(1,\delta^*)$. However, note that the preference ordering is invariant by the multiplicative transformation of each argument.

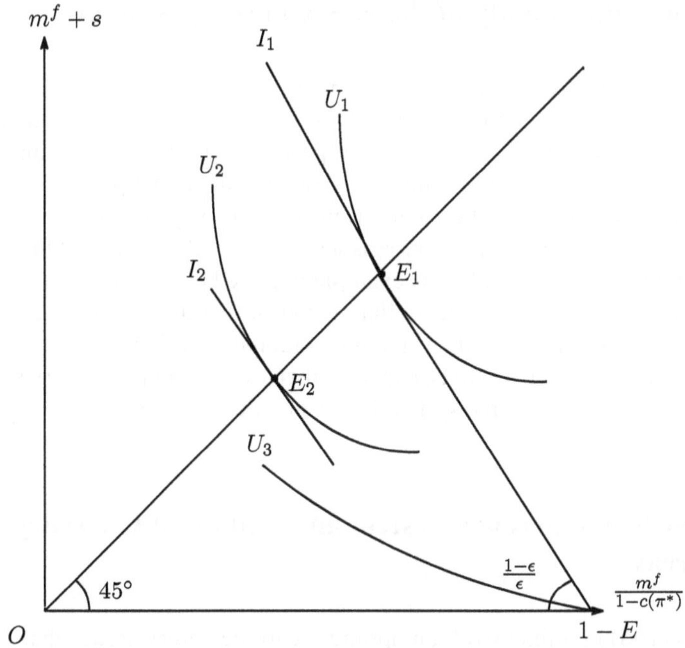

Fig. 6.1 The key-currency system as an implicit insurance

of the key-currency country is sustainable. As discussed with respect to Eq. (6.8), the persistent current account deficit is closely connected with the profits from issuing the key currency in the form of an implicit insurance device. The expected profits from each surrounding country are calculated, with a probability of one, as:

$$B^* \equiv [1-\varepsilon]\left[1-\frac{m^{f*}}{1-c\left(\pi^*\right)}\right]-\varepsilon\left[m^{f*}+s^*\right]. \tag{6.14}$$

The first and second terms in Eq. (6.14) represent the average imports from and average exports to a surrounding country. Thus, Eq. (6.14) expresses the net rent received (insurance due) from issuing the currency. In turn, the net rent is always equal to the current account deficit of the key-currency country. To summarize, the reason why the key-currency country can sustain a persistent current account deficit is based on the rents received from issuing its currency, which is endorsed by its overwhelming industrial and financial power. When the key-currency country's power is strengthened by political decisions, the equilibrium contract moves to point E_2 in Fig. 6.1. This figure clearly shows that the rents received from issuing the currency increase, and that the current account deficit thus becomes prominent.

The problem of the ownership of the worldwide currency rent is very sensitive. For example, at the Bretton Woods conference in, the proposal for a common world currency, *Unitas*, was rejected. Furthermore, Keynes fought strongly to maintain sterling as a key currency (see Moggridge 1992, Chaps. 28 and 29, for more details).

6.3 The Vulnerability of the Key-Currency System

Insurance is ineffective against macroeconomic synchronized shocks, with war the most illustrative example. In World War I, the U.K. was heavily indebted to the U.S. for munitions, fuel, and food for the European, Middle East, and Indian theatres, and herself. In addition to the country's weakened industrial power relative to the U.S., such indebtedness resulted in a serious outflow of gold from the U.K. This is considered to be one of the primary reasons that the U.K. abdicated the right to be a key-currency country. While this example may be beyond the strict scope of the theory advanced in this book, given that it is clear that the unlimited emancipation of capital flow usually strengthens the international cohesion of the business cycle in the key-currency area, it is to be expected that a key-currency country would have much difficulty sustaining the system in the situation of a World War.

6.4 The Key-Currency System and Optimum Currency Areas

Mundell's (1961) seminal work on optimum currency areas argues that factor mobility, including labor force mobility, is indispensable for constructing an optimal currency area. However, it also implies that exogenous shocks are synchronized within the economies that belong to this area. In such a case, the key-currency system is unsuitable because such a risk-sharing system would not work. Furthermore, it is not necessary for an autonomous currency area to be allied to a huge economy such as that of a key-currency country, as will be discussed in Chap. 7. Even if each economy is small, so long as factor mobility is perfect, such economies can unionize a currency area. As such, a currency area may remain a limited body unlike the key-currency system.

6.5 Concluding Remarks

Through describing the key-currency system as a kind of international liquidity provision and insurance system against idiosyncratic sovereign risk, this discussion draws three main conclusions:

1. First, as an international liquidity provision system, the key-currency system works well because there is a common incentive to maximize the expansion of every country's economy. After obtaining the levels of the key currency that are required to attain full-employment equilibrium, affiliated countries divide their fruits in accordance with the implicit insurance contract;
2. Second, risk is completely hedged under the key-currency system. As risk increases, the key-currency country demands higher fees to use its currency,

resulting in a decrease in the disposable incomes of affiliated countries. However, in turn, this indicates that the current account deficit in the key-currency country has become prominent. In this sense, reducing sovereign risk is thus crucial for developing the economy; and

3. Finally, the threat of serious macroeconomic shocks on the key-currency system must be considered. When affiliated countries simultaneously fall into serious slumps and move to convert the key currency into goods (or gold), the key-currency system becomes unsustainable. Instead, a common currency area is recommended in such circumstances.

References

Keynes JM (2013) Activities 1931–1939: world crises and policies in Britain and America. In: Moggridge DE (ed) The collected writings of John Maynard Keynes XXI. Cambridge University Press, Cambridge

Matsuyama K, Kiyotaki N, Matsui A (1993) Toward a theory of international currency. Rev Econ Stud 60:283–307

Moggridge DE (1992) Maynard Keynes: an economist's biography. Routledge, London

Mundell RA (1961) A theory of optimum currency areas. Am Econ Rev 51:509–517

Otaki M (2007) The dynamically extended Keynesian cross and the welfare-improving fiscal policy. Econ Lett 96:23–29

Otaki M (2009) A welfare economic foundation for the full-employment policy. Econ Lett 102:1–3

Otaki M (2011) A pure theory of aggregate price determination. Theor Econ Lett 1:122–128

Otaki M (2013) How a key currency functions as an international liquidity provision and insurance system. Theor Econ Lett 3:43–47

Chapter 7
On the Necessity of Optimum Currency Areas: The Case for Perfect Capital Mobility and Immobile Labor Forces

7.1 Introduction

Income disparity is not limited to developing countries. Advanced economies also face this growing problem. This chapter examines why such an undesirable economic consequence results by constructing a microeconomic foundation for optimum currency area theory based on Otaki (2012) and Mundell's (1961) seminal work. As Mundell (1961) emphasized, the mobility of production resources plays a crucial role when determining which economies should constitute an optimum currency area. Nevertheless, he did not explicitly succeed in clarifying the reason why factor mobility is a key factor for an optimum currency area. This is because the model behind this assertion is not revealed.

This chapter provides a microeconomic foundation for Mundell's theory, and clarifies how factor mobility relates to the constitution of an optimum currency area. Such a relation is considered to be as follows: Assume that there are two indispensable production factors, and one is immobile while the other is mobile between countries without cost. The mobile factor moves towards the country that offers the highest return. However, the government of each country competes to induce the mobile factor to enrich itself, and as a result, income distribution becomes extremely advantageous for owners of the mobile factor. Income disparity also becomes serious through such non-cooperative economic policies. Accordingly, these two countries should be economically unified. Constituting a currency area is part of unification of the two countries.

In this chapter, the case in which both labor forces are immobile and have a nationality, but real capital with no nationality can move internationally at the owners' discretion, is considered. Such a setting is plausible when it is observed that foreign direct investment is generally preferable to certifying working visas. When small twin countries with identical economic structures are in this situation, their central banks compete to invite more real capital to enrich their economy as long as the countries attain full employment. Nonetheless, such competition has the following devastating consequence. If one central bank pursues a high-interest policy to attract more real capital, the other central bank counteroffers with a higher in-

M. Otaki, *Keynesian Economics and Price Theory*,
Advances in Japanese Business and Economics 7, DOI 10.1007/978-4-431-55345-8_7

terest rate. Such a cumulative process does not cease until the surplus from working that is a benefit of the high-interest policy vanishes entirely. Consequently, the non-cooperative behavior of the two central banks brings about a serious income disparity between capital and labor. Furthermore, since capital is assumed to have no nationality, the emerging disparity also results in large welfare losses for these two nations.

The unification of the two central banks is desirable when overcoming such a difficulty. The small twin countries should at least be economically integrated. Then, the same amount of money is supplied to ensure full employment and the interest rates offered to non-national real capital become identical. Accordingly, each country is supplied with an amount of real capital, and thus income disparities and inefficient resource allocations within these economies are entirely resolved. That is, the small twin countries constitute an optimum currency area whenever real capital mobility is complete.

There is prior research on optimum currency areas. Casella (1992) regards a currency area as a device that economizes transaction costs. Basevi et al. (1990) advocate that a kind of network externality results from constituting a currency area. However, these approaches do not have a structural microeconomic foundation in the sense that there is ambiguity concerning the origin of 'transaction costs' and/or 'network externality'. In addition, these studies are far removed from the concern with the relationships between factor mobility and currency area, which originated in Mundell (1961). Unlike preceding research, the theory advanced in this chapter is structural because it succeeds in specifying that the origin of network externality is whether central banks coordinate against the mobile production factor.

Hamada (1981) analyzes not only how past monetary integrations were accomplished, but also how integration can be maintained using the IS/LM model in an open economy. Although his analyses differ from the above two studies and contain abundant policy implications, the welfare evaluation of monetary integration is not feasible, because his models are not based on the optimization of economic agents.

The remainder of this paper is structured as follows: in Sect. 7.2, a small twin country model is constructed based on Otaki (2009, 2012); in Sect. 7.3, non-cooperative and cooperative monetary policies are compared, and the inevitability of optimum currency areas is proven. In Sect. 7.4, brief concluding remarks are provided.

7.2 The Model

7.2.1 Structure of the Model

This analysis is based on a two-period overlapping generations model in a production economy with money. The world consists of twin countries A and B, whose economic structures are identical, and the rest of the world. Each country has residents who cannot move elsewhere and who live in two periods with the density

[0, 1]. Each resident specializes in producing one differentiated good with the help of real capital when young. Real capital, whose owners have no nationality, exists with the density $[0,1]\times[0,2]$. Hence, each resident can potentially deploy real capital with the density $[0,1]$. Capital income is also earned when the owner is young, and then capital itself is passed to a descendant. Once an owner determines the location of capital, he or she lives in that country even after retirement. The minimum rate of return from the rest of the world $(\tilde{r})$ is guaranteed to all capital owners. Furthermore, for simplicity, a unit of real capital combined with a resident's business skills produces a unit of goods.

The income distribution between residents and capital owners is determined by negotiation. The negotiation process, developed by Otaki (2009), is assumed to be the following two-stage game. First, a resident determines how much capital to deploy to maximize income from business skills. Second, given the volume of capital deployed and goods produced, residents and owners mutually determine income distribution in accordance with the asymmetric Nash bargaining solution. In addition, there is a central bank in each country that pursues the social welfare of its residents. The policy variables for each central bank are the nominal money supply and the real interest rate (i.e. the rate of return on capital). It is assumed that central banks manipulate real interest rates by intervening in the negotiation process between residents and non-nationality capital owners. That is, a central bank can control the bargaining power of residents through moral suasion.

7.2.2 Construction of the Model

Individual Utility and Consumption Functions

Assume that all individuals (including capital owners) have the same concave and linear homogenous lifetime function:

$$U \equiv u(c_1, c_2), c_i \equiv [\int_0^1 [c_i(z)]^{1-\eta^{-1}} dz]^{\frac{1}{1-\eta^{-1}}}$$

Where: $c_i(z)$ is the consumption of good z during the i -th stage of life who is born at period t.

From this, the following corresponding indirect utility function, IU, is derived:

$$IU \equiv \frac{Y_t}{\varphi(p_t, p_{t+1})} = \frac{y_t}{\varphi(1, \rho)}, y_t \equiv \frac{Y_t}{p_t}, \rho \equiv \frac{p_{t+1}}{p_t}, \tag{7.1}$$

Where: Y_t is the nominal income and p_t is the price index defined by:

$$p_t \equiv [\int_0^1 [p_t(z)]^{1-\eta} dz]^{\frac{1}{1-\eta}}.$$

Furthermore, the consumption function of the younger generation, C, is:

$$C \equiv c(\rho)y_t. \tag{7.2}$$

Finally, the demand function for good z is:

$$D(z) \equiv \left[\frac{p(z)}{p}\right]^{-\eta} y^d, \tag{7.3}$$

Where: y^d is aggregate demand.

The Production Process in the Two-Stage Game

To develop the aforementioned production process, the following two-stage game is considered:

I. Each resident maximizes his income from business skills by deploying non-nationality capitals; and
II. The resident and capital owners negotiate their income distribution in accordance with the asymmetric Nash bargaining solution, the threaten point of which is $[0, r^*]$.

This problem can be solved by backward induction. In the second-stage game, the corresponding generalized Nash product $G(z,i)$ is:

$$GP(z,i) \equiv [p(z) - r^i]^{\theta - \varepsilon_i}[r^i - r^*]^{1-\theta+\varepsilon_i}, \tag{7.4}$$

Where: θ is the genuine bargaining power of a resident and $\theta - \varepsilon^i$ is the modified (actual) power of a country i's resident; that is, ε^i denotes the power of moral suasion of i country's central bank; and r^i is the domestic rate of return for a unit capital.

The shape of the product is derived from two properties of the model. First, the objective function is linear on the nominal income as indicated by Eq. (7.1). Second, the production (or demand) volume is already determined by the first stage of the game. Maximizing Eq. (7.4) with respect to r^i, the equilibrium domestic rate of return r^{i*} is obtained:

$$r^{i*} = [1 - \theta + \varepsilon^i]p(z) + [\theta - \varepsilon^i]\tilde{r}. \tag{7.5}$$

Taking Eq. (7.5) into consideration, the maximization problem of the first stage can be expressed as:

$$\pi^i(z) \equiv \max_{p(z)}[p(z) - r^{i*}]D(z) = [\theta - \varepsilon^i]\max_{p(z)}[p(z) - \tilde{r}]D(z). \tag{7.6}$$

The solution to Eq. (7.6) is:

$$p^*(z) = \frac{\tilde{r}}{1 - \eta^{-1}}, \forall z. \tag{7.7}$$

Hence, the price level p is constant over time and the equilibrium inflation rate is $\rho^* = 1$.

Substituting Eqs. (7.3) and (7.7) into Eq. (7.6):

$$\frac{\pi^i(z)}{p^*} = [\theta - \varepsilon^i]\eta^{-1} y^{di}, \tag{7.8}$$

Where: y^{di} denotes the real GDP of country i.

From Eq. (7.1), it is clear that Eq. (7.8) corresponds to the social welfare of residents in country i.

The Market Equilibrium

In both countries, new money is supplied through wasteful government expenditure; thus, taking Eq. (7.2) into consideration, the equilibrium condition for the domestic aggregate goods market becomes:

$$y^{di} = c(1) y^{di} + m^i \Rightarrow y^{di} = \frac{m^i}{1 - c(1)}, \tag{7.9}$$

Where: m^i denotes the real money supply within country i.

The second term of (7.9) corresponds to the sum of the aggregate expenditure of the older generation and the government expenditure. Finally, with perfect mobility, the real capital market achieves equilibrium when:

$$k^i = \begin{cases} 2, & if\ \varepsilon^i > \varepsilon^j \\ 1, & if\ \varepsilon^i = \varepsilon^j \\ 0, & if\ \varepsilon^i < \varepsilon^j \end{cases} \tag{7.10}$$

Where: k^i is the amount of capital that has been invested in country i.

The model contains five types of endogenous variable $(r^{i*}, p^*, \pi^i, y^{di}, k^i)$, two types of exogenous variable (ε^i, m^i), and five structural Eqs. (7.5), (7.7), (7.8), (7.9), and (7.10). Thus, the model is closed.

7.2.3 *The Non-cooperative Game Between Central Banks and the Disparity in Income Distribution*

As a result of the international mobility of real capital and the representation of social welfare (7.8), each central bank is eager to attract more capital and enrich its country. Such competition is described by the following two-stage game. In the first stage, central banks determine $(\varepsilon^A, \varepsilon^B)$. Next, they decide how much money they supply (i.e. (m^A, m^B)).

To solve the equilibrium of this game, the second stage is examined first. Since the outcomes of the first stage are summarized by Eq. (7.10), taking social welfare (7.8) and the equilibrium condition for each aggregated goods market (7.9) into consideration, the best response of each central bank is to maintain full-employment equilibrium, which is prescribed by the amount of real capital that is associated with its country. Hence, the following dominant strategy in this game corresponds to the result of the first-stage game. That is:

$$m^i = \begin{cases} 2, & \textit{if } \varepsilon^i > \varepsilon^j \\ 1, & \textit{if } \varepsilon^i = \varepsilon^j . \\ 0, & \textit{if } \varepsilon^i < \varepsilon^j \end{cases} \tag{7.11}$$

Since full employment is assured in the second stage, central banks strive to invite as much real capital as possible. The following theorem holds concerning the uniqueness of the Nash equilibrium:

Theorem 7.1
The unique Nash equilibrium is characterized by:

$$\left(m^{i*}, \varepsilon^{i*}, \frac{\pi^{i*}}{p^*} \right) = (1, \theta, 0). \tag{7.12}$$

Proof
Sufficiency
If Eq. (7.12) is satisfied, there is no active incentive to diverge the strategies because no additional gain is obtained by lesser $(m^{i*}, \varepsilon^{i*})$. Hence, Eq. (7.12) is a Nash equilibrium.

Necessity
Suppose that $\frac{\pi^{i*}}{p^*}$ is strictly positive in some Nash equilibrium. Then:

$$\frac{\pi^{i*}}{p^*} \geq \frac{\pi^{j*}}{p^*} \Leftrightarrow \varepsilon^{i*} \geq \varepsilon^{j*}.$$

By selecting a ε^{j**} slightly larger than ε^{i*}, country j improves its social welfare as much as:

$$[\theta - \varepsilon^{j**}]\eta^{-1} > 0.$$

Thus, there is an incentive to diverge from the equilibrium. This is a contradiction.

The economic implication of Theorem 7.1 is quite serious. As long as two central banks extend the non-cooperative game to attract more capital, income disparities deepen against their intentions. Owing to this competition, residents' earnings from business skills are utterly absorbed by capital income. Since, as seen in Eq. (7.8), the social welfare of residents is proportional to their income, deepening income disparity also results in a less efficient economy. Such a phenomenon is prominent in East Asia, for example. In this area, foreign direct investment flows mainly from Japan and China to other countries. Although their capital accumulation sufficiently advances, and a limited number of capitalists surprisingly become rich, the labor income of most residents, including those in Japan and China, stagnates. Income disparity is one of the most urgent problems in East Asia.

7.3 The Optimum Currency Area as the Unification of Central Banks

In the previous section it was shown that the non-cooperative actions of central banks can have quite harmful effects on both countries. To offset this, the unification of central banks is advocated. According to Mundell (1961), a currency area is defined as follows:

> A single currency implies a single central bank (with note-issuing power) and therefore a potentially elastic supply of interregional means of payment.

This definition of a currency area is adopted.

When central banks are unified and a currency area is formed, the twin countries A and B can be treated as a single country, and monetary coordination becomes possible. Because of the symmetry of the countries, the optimal coordination policy is also symmetrical. Hence the two-step game extended in subsection 7.2.3 requires equal allocations of real capital. Thus, $m^A = m^B = 1$ and $\varepsilon^A = \varepsilon^B = 0$. It is evident that the social welfare of each country in Eq. (7.8) becomes $\theta\eta^{-1}$. This is the maximal value that each country attains. In this sense, the twin countries together constitute an optimum currency area.

7.4 The Difficulty of Constituting a Currency Area in Reality

In the previous section, optimism in relation to the incentive for coordination between the two countries was expressed. However, as Hamada (1981, Chap. 3) argues, historical evidence suggests that political unification generally advances before monetary integration. This implies that monetary integration is more difficult than political unification, because the return from issuing money is exorbitant as such.

In reality, there is no movement towards political unification even in European Union countries. As will be discussed in Chap. 8, the Eurozone is far from an optimum currency area, and might be regarded as countries that have adopted a fixed exchange rate system in which the nominal exchange rate is at unity and non-adjustable. As a result, imbalances in the current accounts between Euro countries provoke serious political-economic problems. Nevertheless, it should be noted that such imbalances always exist within a country, and in a sense are regarded as compensation for maintaining the unification of a country. Thus, although the Euro might aim at the economic unification of European countries, unless creditor countries become more patient, such unification will not easily be accomplished, nor will true monetary integration be achieved.

7.5 Concluding Remarks

In this chapter the theory of the optimum currency area was considered from the perspective of resource allocation and income distribution. The results were as follows:

1. The discussion concentrated on the case of twin countries under perfect capital mobility and immobile labor forces. This assumption seems natural if the significance of nation states is acknowledged;
2. When each central bank pursues its national interests—that is, the social welfare of its immobile labor force (i.e. the residents)—dire economic consequences emerge. Each central bank is led to adopt an artificial high-interest policy because more capital induced by a rate slightly higher than those of its rival central bank brings about higher incomes for the business skills possessed by the residents of that nation. However, such competitive and escalating interest-raising is devastating and cumulative, and does not end until all the residents' income is absorbed by real capital without nationality. Thus, serious income disparities and large decreases in social welfare occur. It is clear that such a nation is not in an optimum currency area;
3. When the two central banks are unified and monetary coordination becomes possible, the present discussion shows that such catastrophic competition becomes avoidable. Real capital is then allocated equally by abolishing the competitive and artificial high-interest policy, and just enough external money is supplied to ensure full-employment equilibrium in each country. Thus, social welfare achieves its maximum. In other words, the twin countries under perfect capital mobility constitute an optimum currency area. It is also noteworthy that this approach is based on a rigorous dynamic microeconomic foundation. In this sense, it succeeds in updating and extending the theory of Mundell (1961);
4. Finally, there are some limitations to this analysis. The first lies in the difficulty of central bank unification. Bureaucrats who operate the unified central bank may be of different nationalities. Differences due to culture, ethnicity, tradition, and so on are not as easy to overcome as the theory assumes. It takes more time than expected to ensure fair policy coordination. The second limitation concerns the glut of foreign direct investment. In reality, the volume and mobility of real capital is large and wide ranging. Thus, it is feared that the world as a whole may become a unique optimum currency area. Nevertheless, it is certain that such a tremendous and enlarged organization would never work well. It may therefore be more practical to place a levy on international capital movement, like the Tobin tax.

References

Besevi G, Delvono F, Delnicolo V (1990) International monetary cooperation and economic influence. J Int Econ 28:1–23
Casella A (1992) Participation in monetary union. Am Econ Rev 82:847–863
Hamada K (1981) Kosusai kinyu no seijikeizaigaku (The political economy of international finance). Sobunsha, Tokyo
Mundell RA (1961) A theory of optimum currency area. Am Econ Rev 51:657–665
Otaki M (2009) A welfare economics foundation for the full-employment policy. Econ Lett 102:1–3
Otaki M (2012) A microeconomic foundation for optimum currency area. Theor Econ Let 2:395–399

Chapter 8
Universal Discipline or Individual Discipline: On the Viability of the Eurozone as a Nonadjustable Local Fixed Exchange Rate Regime

8.1 Introduction

The Eurozone is an ambitious attempt to transcend the concept of the nation state and unite most parts of Europe. This seems to be based on the theory of an optimal currency area developed by Mundell (1961) whose microeconomic foundation was provided in Chap. 7. However, in reality the Eurozone is far from being an optimal currency area in the sense that Mundell (1961) envisioned. The European Central Bank (ECB) is not the only organization that determines monetary policies within the Eurozone; each country retains its central bank intact. Furthermore, each central bank has discretion concerning the fine-tuning of domestic aggregate demand management policy to a substantive extent.

This implies that affiliated countries are possibly in conflict on the value of imbalances in the current account, as the recent Euro Crisis reveals. In this respect, there are massive and persistent current account imbalances even within a country. Nevertheless, as long as the governance of the country is well organized, such imbalances are regarded as an implicit income redistribution policy from the wealthy to the non-wealthy regions. Even though this is not based on the voluntary intention of residents in wealthy regions, they tacitly permit such income transfers because the unification of the nation is far more beneficial for them. Unfortunately, the difficulty in such a tacit income redistribution policy is that it is a critical economic deficiency that prevents the Euro from becoming a properly functioning united currency. In other words, as Otaki (2012) points out, the current situation is that the Euro is not a united currency but rather a regionally fixed exchange rate system in which the nominal exchange rate is unity and nonadjustable. In this fixed exchange rate regime, which does not permit the realignment of nominal exchange rates, the imbalance in current accounts becomes a grievous problem, unless economic welfare and/or political-economic growth exceeds the incurred costs, as noted above.

Single exchange rates inevitably mean that countries whose potential equilibrium exchange rates are located at a more realistic level than such a rate become creditor countries. On the other hand, those whose potential equilibrium exchange rate is located at a more devalued level become debtor countries. As such, when

M. Otaki, *Keynesian Economics and Price Theory*,
Advances in Japanese Business and Economics 7, DOI 10.1007/978-4-431-55345-8_8

attempting to avoid unnecessary conflicts and equilibrate the current accounts of the affiliate countries, universal rules (e.g. fiscal deficits should not exceed 3 % of GDP) are ineffective. Specifically, it must be emphasized that differences in the marginal propensity to import are important in this situation. Countries in which this value is high, for example owing to the immaturity of domestic industry, are apt to become debtor countries under universal regulations.

To summarize, countries that belong to the Eurozone face a policy tradeoff. If they keep the unified exchange rate and equilibrate current accounts, it becomes necessary to adopt individual disciplines in accordance with the macroeconomic characteristics of each affiliated country, even though adjacent political costs are estimated to be quite high. On the other hand, if universal disciplines remain intact, imbalances in current accounts are unavoidable to some extent.

Specific austere policy choices are required in countries that record persistent current account deficits. This chapter considers an austerity policy that orders the levying of additional tax in a serious debtor country to compensate for its deficits, and analyzes the resultant effects. Although it seems cruel to force such burdens on a debtor country, it must be noted that austere policies promote confidence in that country. This facilitates the liquidity provision of Euros and promotes the growth of the country at least in the long run. In other words, besides the maturity of the domestic industry, the tax-levying ability of a government buttresses the sustainability of the Euro.

This chapter is organized as follows. In Sect. 8.2, a model of a small open economy, which is an affiliate of an unadjustable flexible exchange rate system based on a two-period overlapping generations model, is constructed. The analysis looks at how the immaturity of a domestic economy affects the stability of such a system, and clarifies the necessity for the imposition of austere policies (individual discipline). Meanwhile, it is shown that such a policy heightens the welfare of the economy at least in the long run. Section 8.3 offers brief concluding remarks.

8.2 The Model

8.2.1 Structure of the Model

A small open economy ω, which is an affiliate of a currency alignment area, is considered. The nominal exchange rate is fixed to unity within the alignment, and is not adjustable. The economic aim of the currency alignment can be variously determined. For example, a large currency area supported by rich economic powers might enjoy international seigniorage by constituting a new key currency as analyzed in Chap. 6. However, the economic aim of the currency alignment is not made explicit at this point; attention is confined to the sustainability of such an alignment.

The assumptions relating to this model are: that there are continuum residents uniformly distributed within interval $[0,1]$ in country ω; consumption goods are also differentiated within interval $[0,1]$, but country ω can only produce the consumption goods that are located between $[0,\alpha_{\omega}]$. That is, along with an increase in α_{ω}, country ω becomes mature and able to produce a greater variety of consumption goods, and each good is produced monopolistically by a single firm.

8.2.2 The Maximization Problems of Economic Agents

Individuals

All residents within the currency alignment have the same utility function:

$$U \equiv u\left(c_{1t}, c_{2t+1}\right) - \delta_t \cdot \beta, \quad c_{it+k} \equiv \left[\int_0^1 \left[c_{it+k}(z)\right]^{1-\eta^{-1}} dz\right]^{\frac{1}{1-\eta^{-1}}}, \quad \eta > 1, \tag{8.1}$$

Where: $u(\cdot)$ is a strictly concave and linear homogenous function; $c_{it+k}(z)$ is the demand for good z of an individual who is the i-th stage of life during period $t+k$; β denotes the disutility of labor; and δ_t is a definition function, which takes the value of unity when a young person works, and zero when they are unemployed.

From the maximization of utility, the demand function for good z, $c_{it+k}(z)$ is:

$$c_{it+k}(z) = \left[\frac{p_t(z)}{p_t}\right]^{-\eta} \cdot y_{it+k}, \quad y_{it+k} \equiv \frac{Y_{it+k}}{p_t}, \quad p_t \equiv \left[\int_0^1 \left[p_t(z)\right]^{1-\eta} dz\right]^{\frac{1}{1-\eta}}, \tag{8.2}$$

Where: Y_{it+k} is the total expenditure of individuals in the i-th stage of life during period $t+k$.

Aggregating Eq. (8.2) on z, the following intertemporal budget constraint is obtained:

$$Y_t = \int_0^1 p_t(z) c_{1t}(z) dz + \int_0^1 p_{t+1}(z) c_{2t+1}(z) dz = p_t c_{1t} + p_{t+1} c_{2t+1}, \tag{8.3}$$

Where: Y_t is the total income of the younger generation.

Maximizing Eq. (8.1) under the constraint of Eq. (8.3), the aggregate consumption function of the younger generation c_{1t} is obtained:

$$c_{1t} = c\left(\frac{p_{t+1}}{p_t}\right) \cdot y_t. \tag{8.4}$$

The corresponding indirect lifetime utility function of consumption, h_t, becomes:

$$h_t = \frac{Y_t}{\Psi(p_t, p_{t+1})} \tag{8.5}$$

Where: Ψ is a linear homogenous function.

Since the nominal reservation wage, W_t^R, satisfies $h_t = \beta$:

$$W_t^R = \beta \cdot \Psi(p_t, p_{t+1}). \tag{8.6}$$

Firms

The aim of firm z is to maximize profits. For simplicity, labor productivity is set to unity. Furthermore, it is again assumed that economy ω is located at imperfect employment equilibrium, because there are always some unemployed individuals within the economy. Hence, as long as an individual worker does not have bargaining power, the equilibrium wage becomes equal to the nominal reservation wage W_t^R.

Thus, the objective function of firm z, $\Pi_t(z)$, becomes:

$$\max_{p_t(z)} \Pi_t(z) = \max_{p_t(z)} \left[p_t(z) - W_t^R \right] c_t(z),\ c_t(z) \equiv c_{1t}(z) + c_{2t}(z). \tag{8.7}$$

Taking Eq. (8.6) into consideration, the solution of Eq. (8.7) is:

$$p_t(z) = p_t = \frac{\beta \cdot \Psi(p_t, p_{t+1})}{1 - \eta^{-1}}. \tag{8.8}$$

This is the fundamental equation that implies the non-neutrality of money as discussed in Chap. 2. Since Ψ is a linear homogenous function, Eq. (8.8) can be transformed into:

$$\Psi\left(1, \rho^*\right) = \beta^{-1}\left[1 - \eta^{-1}\right],\quad \rho^* \equiv \frac{p_{t+j+1}^*}{p_{t+j}^*}. \tag{8.9}$$

Thus, the equilibrium inflation rate, ρ^*, is invariant across economies. Accordingly, a necessary condition for maintaining the fixed exchange rate system is satisfied.

The Government

As discussed in Sect. 8.1, the equilibrium of the surplus account of each affiliate is crucial in sustaining a politically immature currency union. Imbalances in the surplus account provoke serious conflict between creditor and debtor economies, as is shown in the current Euro Crisis. To avoid such distress, some fiscal-monetary disciplines, which are represented as the rules of a policy game, are necessitated beforehand.

Fiscal and monetary disciplines are genetically not universal, but economy-specific when sustaining the unified nominal exchange rate. This is partly because structural parameters such as the propensity to import and a government's tax-levying ability differ across affiliated economies, and partly because the universally fixed nominal exchange rate cannot reflect the characteristics of each economy woven in the traditional fixed exchange rate regime. This implies that existing universal disciplines in the Eurozone are likely to become ineffective. Economy-specific disciplines, which can be called *austere policies*, are unavoidable when there is a necessity to equilibrate current accounts. However, the order of the policy game is quite important for the effectiveness of these policies and for success in stabilizing currency alignments.

Macroeconomic policies are disciplined by two goals: (i) equilibrate the current account, and (ii) achieve high employment level. The rational and effective order of these requires that goal (i) should be met prior to goal (ii). If goal (ii) is advanced, a hold-up problem is provoked. That is, if unrestricted stimulation is permitted in fiscal and monetary policy, a debtor economy resolves the problem of current account by bankruptcy. If bankruptcies are prevalent, it is certain that the currency alignment will collapse. Hence, to hinder such irresponsible behavior, equilibrating each current account should be a priority.

The policy measures available to governments are as follows. One is that the government levies a lump-sum tax from its residents, T, and uses this to compensate the current account. The other is that the government issues money, M_t, to achieve a high employment level. For the purposes of the model developed in this chapter, it is assumed that real government expenditure, g, is wasteful and financed by seigniorage emerging from inflation while the real cash balance, m, is kept constant over time. Thus:

$$\frac{M_t}{p_t} - \frac{M_{t-1}}{p_t} = g \Rightarrow \left[1 - \frac{1}{\rho^*}\right] m = g \tag{8.10}$$

holds.[1]

8.2.3 Market Equilibrium

There are three kinds of market: the aggregate goods market, the domestic money market, and labor markets. In addition, one political constraint exists under the austere policies framework. That is, the current account should be equilibrated by fiscal and monetary policy. Labor markets are in interior (imperfect employment) equilibrium when the equilibrium nominal wage is equal to the nominal reservation wage, W_t^R, as already discussed in the previous section. The domestic money market is cleared whenever the aggregate goods market is cleared under austere policies by the nature of the overlapping generations model. Hence, attention can be confined

[1] The *confidence in money*, which is defined in Chap. 2, is upheld.

to the equilibrium condition for the aggregate goods market and the constraint imposed by austere policies. These two structural equations are represented as follows:

$$y = c(\rho^*)[y - T_\omega] + m + \left[T_\omega - [1 - \alpha_\omega]\left[c(\rho^*)[y - T_\omega] + m_\omega\right]\right], \tag{8.11}$$

$$B_\omega \equiv T_\omega - [1 - \alpha_\omega]\left[c(\rho^*)[y - T_\omega] + m_\omega\right] = 0. \tag{8.12}$$

Where: y is real GDP.

Equation (8.11) is the equilibrium condition for the aggregate goods market. The first term is the aggregate consumption by the younger generation. The second term denotes the sum of the government and the older generation expenditure. The third term corresponds to the surplus in the current account.[2] Equation (8.12) is the policy constraint imposed by any austere policies. That is, fiscal and monetary policy should be maneuvered lest the current account, B, is in imbalance. Thus:

Definition 8.1
Austere policies are defined by the pair of (T_ω, m_ω) *that satisfy Eq. (8.12).*

Using Eqs. (8.9), (8.11), and (8.12), for a given government's tax-levying ability, T_ω, the endogenous variables $(\rho^*, y_\omega, m_\omega)$ are determined. As such, the model is completely closed.

8.2.4 *Comparative Statics and Welfare Implications of Austere Policies*

This section considers how equilibrium real GDP, y_ω, and economic welfare are affected by the tax-levying ability of the government, T_ω, and the variety of consumption goods, α_ω, which represent an economy's industrial maturity. Then, solving Eq. (8.11):

$$y_\omega = T_\omega + \frac{\alpha_\omega}{1 - c(\rho^*)\alpha_\omega} \cdot m_\omega. \tag{8.13}$$

Equation (8.13) implies that an economy must increase its real cash balance, m_ω, to increase its disposable income, $y_\omega - T_\omega$. This is because the value of the balanced-budget multiplier is unity and the only way to increase the disposable income is to stimulate the economy without a tax burden (i.e. printing new money).

Next, solving Eq. (8.12) on T_ω gives:

$$T_\omega = \frac{1 - \alpha_\omega}{1 - c(\rho^*)\alpha_\omega} \cdot m_\omega. \tag{8.14}$$

[2] For simplicity, we abbreviate exports of private sector in Eqs. (8.11) and (8.12).

Equation (8.14) implies that the permissible real cash balance under austere policies, m_{ω}, is proportional to the government's tax-levying ability, T_{ω}. It is apparent from Eq. (8.14) that imports:

$$[1-\alpha_{\omega}]\left[c(\rho^{*})[y_{\omega}-T_{\omega}]+m_{\omega}\right]$$

are an increasing function of m_{ω}, and thus, along with an increase in real cash balances, imports will also increase. Hence, to permit an adequate money supply in the domestic economy, more stringent fiscal discipline is required. This is the economic meaning of Eq. (8.14).

Combining Eqs. (8.13) and (8.14):

$$y_{\omega}-T_{\omega}=\frac{\alpha_{\omega}}{1-\alpha_{\omega}}\cdot T_{\omega}. \tag{8.15}$$

Thus, disposable income, $y_{\omega}-T_{\omega}$, is an increasing function of α_{ω} and T_{ω}. That is, an economy that produces a variety of goods and does not heavily depend on imports achieves higher disposable income for a given government tax-levying ability T_{ω}. In addition, if a government has a high tax-levying ability, this also enriches its residents under an austere policies regime. Although this might seem paradoxical, it should be remembered that a high tax-levying ability implies that the government is able to provide ample liquidity and can stimulate the economy sufficiently to achieve policy ends.

To summarize: where (i) there is autonomy in the sense that the propensity to import from an economy, $1-\alpha_{\omega}$, is low, and (ii) there exists a high tax-levying ability on the part of a particular government, these two factors will play a key role in relation to prosperity under the austerity policies necessary for maintaining a currency alignment. This is because both economic factors mitigate the constraint of balancing the current account.

Next, the argument moves to consider economic welfare analysis. Since it is assumed that the equilibrium nominal wage is equal to the nominal reservation wage (the assumption of imperfect employment equilibrium), no additional surplus emerges from additional employment. Accordingly, from the indirect lifetime utility function (Eq. 8.5), the lifetime utility, h_{ω}^{*}, is:

$$h_{\omega}^{*}=\frac{\int_{0}^{\alpha_{\omega}}\Pi_{t}^{*}(z)\,dz-p_{t}^{*}T_{\omega}}{\Psi(p_{t}^{*},p_{t+1}^{*})}. \tag{8.16}$$

Substituting Eqs. (8.8) and (8.15) into Eq. (8.16), since Ψ is a linear homogenous function, the following relationship is obtained:

$$h_{\omega}^{*}=\frac{\alpha_{\omega}\eta^{-1}y_{\omega}^{*}-T_{\omega}}{\Psi(1,\rho^{*})}=\frac{\dfrac{\alpha_{\omega}\eta^{-1}}{1-\alpha_{\omega}}T_{\omega}-T_{\omega}}{\Psi(1,\rho^{*})}. \tag{8.17}$$

Equation (8.17) implies that if an economy is sufficiently mature, a high value of α_ω produces well-differentiated goods (a high value of η^{-1}), and:

$$\alpha_\omega \geq \frac{1}{1+\eta^{-1}} \tag{8.18}$$

holds.

Austere policies, as outlined in Definition 8.1, improve an economy's welfare level. To summarize:

Theorem 8.1
*If Inequality (*8.18*) is satisfied for all ω that belong to the currency alignment, an expansionary policy under the austere regime in Definition 8.1 improves economic welfare in every economy, and the alignment becomes sustainable.*

8.2.5 The Hold-Up Problem

In this section, the hold-up problem is dealt with. This occurs in a reversal of the order of policy priorities. It is assumed that equilibrium in the current account is possible prior to achieving a high employment level. This implies that every affiliate economy pledges its money supply subject to its tax-levying ability, so that the current account equilibrates. If this policy priority is reversed and the government puts high employment first after levying tax, the hold-up problem might be experienced, since the incentive to equilibrate its surplus account is lost. As a policy game, this hold-up problem can be formatted as the following two-stage game. First, the government of an economy decides its real cash balance, m_ω, so that full employment is attained for a given T_ω. Second, the government makes payments overseas. The payoff of the second stage should then be:

$$\max\left[0, T_\omega - [1-\alpha_\omega]\left[c\left(\rho^*\right)[y_\omega - T_\omega] + m_\omega\right]\right]. \tag{8.19}$$

under limited liability, where the second term represents the surplus of the current account.

Equation (8.19) implies that there is no substantial constraint concerning the current account. Furthermore, if the hold-up problem occurs, it is clear from Eq. (8.19) that:

$$T_\omega < [1-\alpha_\omega]\left[c\left(\rho^*\right)[y_\omega - T_\omega] + m_\omega\right] \tag{8.20}$$

holds. Therefore, at the first stage of the game, the government provides enough liquidity to achieve full employment. This is because the indirect lifetime utility function (8.16) is an increasing function of real GDP, y_ω, for any predetermined tax payments, T_ω. Thus, the equilibrium of the aggregate goods market (8.11) under the optimal real cash balance, m_ω^*, becomes:

$$y_\omega^f = T_\omega + \frac{\alpha_\omega}{1-\alpha_\omega c\left(\rho^*\right)} \cdot m_\omega^*, \tag{8.21}$$

Where: y_ω^f is the full-employment real GDP.

Combining Inequality (Eq. 8.20) with Eq. (8.21), the necessary and/or sufficient condition for an economy falling into default is:

$$\left[1+\frac{\alpha_\omega}{1-\alpha_\omega}\right]T_\omega < y_\omega^f. \tag{8.22}$$

Equation (8.22) implies that three crucial economic factors exist that provoke the hold-up problem (i.e. economic default). The first factor is the immaturity of a domestic economy. If an economy has a lower ability to produce goods and α_ω takes a lower value, the propensity to import becomes high. This means that the economy is apt to experience current account deficits.

The second factor is the tax-levying ability of the government, T_ω. When a government cannot collect sufficient tax, there is little room for importing goods, as long as it is concerned with equilibrium in the current account. However, imports are an increasing function of real GDP and high levels of liquidity are necessary for the achievement of full employment. Thus, it is not unusual that such an economy will experience imbalances in its current account.

The final factor is the scale of an economy, which is summarized by the term full-employment GDP, y_ω^f. In conjunction with an economy becoming large, *ceteris paribus*, a high real cash balance that can sustain the full-employment equilibrium is necessary. This implies that a large economy asks for many benefits compared with its incurred tax burden. This also induces a crisis in the current account. To avoid such a disaster, the levied tax for joining the currency alignment, T_ω, should be increased in proportion to the scale of an economy.

8.3 Concluding Remarks

This chapter analyzed how a nonadjustable regional fixed exchange rate system such as the Eurozone could be made sustainable. The results obtained were as follows:

1. First, the maturity and/or variety of domestic industrial structures plays a crucial role. This is because a higher propensity to import hinders the equilibrating of the current account, which is indispensable in sustaining currency alignments. In addition, a government's tax-levying ability in relation to collecting the implicit fee for joining the alignment is also important. This eases the problem of

providing an economy with sufficient liquidity through mitigating the constraint of the current account, and thus maintains high employment levels;

2. Second, more austere policies, which put priority on the equilibrium in the current account in relation to high employment, are desirable. Such policies prevent the hold-up problem, which is a kind of moral hazard owing to limited liability, and possibly causes a devastating consequence for the alignment of a currency as a whole. Meanwhile, against naïve intuition, along with empowering the levying ability, austere policies improve economic welfare. As discussed earlier, fiscal abundance connects directly to ample domestic liquidity under a sustainable currency alignment;
3. Finally, the level of collected tax needed to maintain a currency alignment should be proportional to the potential scale of an economy, which is summarized by full-employment GDP unless austere policies are enacted. The reason is that costs large enough to sustain a currency alignment are sunk costs if there is no direct regulation for equilibrating the current account to avoid the hold-up problem.

References

Mundell RA (1961) A theory of optimum currency area. Am Econ Rev 51:657–665

Otaki M (2012) The stability of a regionally fixed exchange rate system: can euro be sustained by austere fiscal discipline? J Bus Econ 3:243–248

Chapter 9
Industrial Hollowing Under a Flexible Exchange Rate System

9.1 Introduction

This chapter analyzes the macroeconomic consequences of foreign direct investment (FDI). The barter theory of international economics is known as the Hecksher-Ohlin-Samuleson (HOS) model. It predicts that although the liberalization of production resources changes the income distribution within a country, it never affects economic welfare in the sense of Pareto because production resources never become idle, and are always fully employed. However, as FDI progressed during the 2000s in Japan, unemployment rates soared from around 3 to 5 %. In reality, Japan imports profits and unemployment mainly from East Asian economies in exchange for its FDI. Thus, full employment cannot be achieved in a monetary economy in the way that the HOS model asserts for a barter economy.

This phenomenon that FDI induces unemployment is characterized as industrial hollowing. Based on Otaki (2012), this chapter explores why such a phenomenon occurs, and considers its implications for welfare economics. Industrial hollowing is the consequence of the following. First, the reduction of domestic worker incomes curtails aggregate consumption and induces a business downturn. Second, wage payments towards foreign workers almost never occur as aggregate demand to the domestic economy. This makes the resulting stagnation more serious. Furthermore, it should be noted that the upturn in the foreign economy does not improve this situation. Even though the demand for tradable goods increases in the foreign economy, the remittance of profits appreciates the domestic currency under a flexible exchange rate system. If the savings of the domestic economy are insensitive to the real exchange rate, this increase in remittances is absorbed wholly by appreciation, and thus the business upturn in the foreign economy does not diffuse to the domestic economy.

To sum up, industrial hollowing is a kind of collective irrationality (i.e. a fallacy of composition). The cause of such irrationality relates to the prospect of changes in the real exchange rate. Although the real exchange rate is an exogenously given variable for each foreign invested firm, it is an exogenous variable in the economy as a whole. Even when FDI is profitable at particular real exchange rates, if all

M. Otaki, *Keynesian Economics and Price Theory*,
Advances in Japanese Business and Economics 7, DOI 10.1007/978-4-431-55345-8_9

firms remit their profits simultaneously, the rate appreciates enough to cancel out the benefits of FDI. Since most firms do not perceive that their economic behavior appreciates the real exchange rate by itself, FDI advances until the gain from such investment vanishes entirely. Accordingly, the only economic consequence of FDI is these harmful effects, which are defined as industrial hollowing. As such, against the intuition that the extension of investment opportunities never aggravates economic welfare, FDI aggravates a nation's wellbeing via the reduction of effective demand in a monetary economy.

The remaining sections of this chapter are organized as follows. A small open economy model with FDI is constructed and discussed in Sect. 9.2. Furthermore, the comments consider the welfare economics implications of industrial hollowing. Section 9.3 gives brief concluding remarks.

9.2 The Model

Much research has been accumulated in the field of FDI. For example, Caves (1971) defines FDI as the transfer of nexus of managerial resources to overseas. Hood and Young (1979) and Caves (1982) argue that a multinational firm is a device to economize on the transaction costs incurred by such transfer. However, previous research remains oriented towards analyzing the behavior of individual multinational firms. It does not provide a wide enough scope for considering how a surge of FDI affects the efficiency of a national economy as a whole.

Applying the HOS model, MacDougal (1960) and Kemp (1964) prove that if a country is large enough to manipulate world interest rates by adjusting its capital exports, it can heighten its economic welfare. Nevertheless, such theories are an application of the optimal tariff theory in a barter economy. A different theory is required for analyzing the economic implication of FDI under a flexible exchange rate system in a monetary economy.

9.2.1 *Structure of the Model*

In this chapter, a two-period overlapping generations model with infinite time horizon is derived. The world economy comprises the home and the foreign economy. The home economy is small in the sense that it cannot affect the economic situation in the foreign economy.

There are two kinds of goods in the home economy: tradable goods and non-tradable goods. Firms that belong to the tradable goods sector can choose the location of their factory, whereas those in the non-tradable goods sector cannot. In each sector, goods are differentiated within the interval $[0,1]$. All firms have the same production technology, within which marginal/average labor productivity is unity. Every resident in the home economy has the same preferences on lifetime consumption and labor supply. People provide unit labor at their discretion when young. The government of the home country has the same consumption propensity to tradable and non-tradable goods as its residents. The expenditure is financed by the seigniorage (i.e. printing new money). For simplicity, it is assumed that government consumption does not affect the economic welfare of residents.

9.2.2 Optimization Problems of Economic Agents

Individuals

All individuals have the same utility function as follows:

$$u(c_1, c_2, \delta_1) \equiv [c_1]^c [c_2]^{1-c} - \delta_1 \cdot \alpha, \tag{9.1}$$

$$c_i \equiv \left[c_i^T\right]^{\frac{1}{2}} \left[c_i^{NT}\right]^{\frac{1}{2}}, \tag{9.2}$$

$$c_i^k \equiv \left[\int_0^1 \left[c_i^k(z)\right]^{1-\eta^{-1}} dz\right]^{\frac{1}{1-\eta^{-1}}}, \quad k = T, NT, \tag{9.3}$$

$$0 < c < 1, \ 1 < \eta.$$

Where: c_i denotes the aggregate consumption level during the i-th stage of life.

This comprises the geometric mean of tradable and non-tradable goods as indicated by Eq. (9.2). The geometric mean implies that the potential scale of each sector is equal, that $c_i^k(z)$ is the consumption of good z, which belongs to sector k (T expresses the tradable sector, and NT corresponds to the non-tradable sector) during the i-th stage of life, that α denotes the disutility of labor, and that δ_1 is a definition function, which takes the value of unity if a resident works when young, and becomes zero when that person is unemployed.

The optimization problem is solved by the following three steps:

1. Given the expenditure y_i^k, maximize c_i^k on $c_i^k(z)$;
2. Since c_{ki} becomes a function of y_{ki} under symmetric equilibrium, maximize Eq. (9.2) on y_i^k for a given total expenditure of the i-th stage of life, y_i; and
3. Since c_i becomes a function of y_i, maximize (9.1) with respect to y_i, subject to the lifetime budget constraint.

From the first step of the maximization:

$$c_i^k(z) = \left[\frac{p^k(z)}{p^k}\right]^{-\eta} \cdot y_i^k, \tag{9.4}$$

$$p^k \equiv \left[\int_0^1 \left[p^k(z)\right]^{1-\eta} dz\right]^{\frac{1}{1-\eta}}, \tag{9.5}$$

$$y_i^k \equiv \frac{Y_i^k}{p_i^k}, \tag{9.6}$$

Where: Y_{ki} is the nominal expenditure to $k(k = T, NT)$ goods during the i-th stage of life.

Since the equilibrium prices are the same within a sector, Eq. (9.4) is reduced to:

$$c_i^k(z) = y_i^k. \tag{9.7}$$

Accordingly, the budget constraint of the second-step optimization is:

$$y_i = e \cdot y_i^T + y_i^{NT}, \tag{9.8}$$

Where: e denotes the relative price of the tradable goods to the non-tradable goods, which corresponds to the real exchange rate in the model; and y_i is the real expenditure in terms of non-tradable goods during the i-th stage of life.

Thus, the solution of the second step of the optimization becomes:

$$\frac{1}{2} y_i = e \cdot y_i^T = y_i^{NT} \tag{9.9}$$

Finally, using the results obtained above, the third step of the optimization becomes:

$$e^{-\frac{1}{2}} \max_{y_i} [y_1]^c \cdot [y_2]^{1-c}, \text{ s.t. } y_1 + \rho \cdot y_2 = y, \tag{9.10}$$

Where: ρ denotes the inflation rate of the non-tradable goods; and y is income in terms of non-tradable goods earned when young.

Equation (9.10) immediately leads to a Keynes-type consumption function for the younger generation. That is:

$$y_1 = c \cdot y. \tag{9.11}$$

Substituting Eq. (9.11) into Eq. (9.10), the indirect lifetime utility function IU concerning consumption is obtained as:

$$IU(e, \rho, y) = A \cdot e^{-\frac{1}{2}} \cdot \rho^{-[1-c]} \cdot y, \quad A \equiv c^c \cdot [1-c]^{1-c}. \tag{9.12}$$

From Eqs. (9.1) and (9.12) the nominal reservation wage, W_t^R, is:

$$W_t^R = A^{-1} p_t^{NT} \cdot e^{\frac{1}{2}} \cdot \rho^{[1-c]} \cdot \alpha. \tag{9.13}$$

Whenever the home economy is in imperfect employment equilibrium, Eq. (9.13) corresponds to the domestic labor market equilibrium condition.

Firms

A firm that belongs to the non-tradable sector maximizes the following profit function, Π_t^{NT} on $p_t^{NT}(z)$:

$$\Pi_t^{NT} \equiv \left[p_t^{NT}(z) \cdot \left[\frac{p_t^{NT}(z)}{p_t^{NT}} \right]^{-\eta} - W_t^R \cdot \left[\frac{p_t^{NT}(z)}{p_t^{NT}} \right]^{-\eta} \right] \cdot \frac{y^h}{2}, \tag{9.14}$$

Where: y^h is the real GNP of the home economy in terms of non-tradable goods.

The solution is:

$$p_t^{NT} = p_t^{NT}(z) = \frac{W_t^R}{1-\eta^{-1}} = \frac{A^{-1} p_t^{NT} \cdot e^{\frac{1}{2}} \cdot \rho^{[1-c]} \cdot \alpha}{1-\eta^{-1}}. \tag{9.15}$$

This is the fundamental equation in the present model.

A firm that belongs to the tradable sector can choose its location. If it is located in the home economy, the profit function Π_t^T becomes:

$$\Pi_t^T \equiv \left[p_t^T(z) \cdot \left[\frac{p_t^T(z)}{p_t^T} \right]^{-\eta} - W_t^R \cdot \left[\frac{p_t^T(z)}{p_t^T} \right]^{-\eta} \right] \cdot \frac{e^{-1} y^h + y^f}{2}, \tag{9.16}$$

Where: y^f is the real GNP of the foreign economy.[1]

The solution is:

$$p_{Tt} = p_{Tt}(z) = \frac{W_t^R}{1-\eta^{-1}} = \frac{A^{-1} p_{NTt} \cdot e^{\frac{1}{2}} \cdot \rho^{[1-c]} \cdot \alpha}{1-\eta^{-1}}. \tag{9.17}$$

[1] We assume that the foreign economy does not initially produce the tradable goods. Even after firms of the home economy constructs factories in the foreign economy, the real exchange rate within that economy is kept at unity because any firm faces the same nominal reservation wage.

Combining Eqs. (9.15) and (9.17), the equilibrium real exchange rate, e^*, and inflation rate, ρ^*, when the tradable goods sector stays within the home economy, are:

$$e^* = 1,\ \rho^* = \sqrt[1-c]{\alpha^{-1} A\left[1-\eta^{-1}\right]} \tag{9.18}$$

Denoting the nominal exchange rate (the relative price of the foreign currency to the domestic currency) during period t as E_t, if the nominal reservation wage within the foreign economy, $E_t \cdot \widetilde{W_t^R}$, is lower than that within the home economy, all firms that belong to the tradable goods sector move overseas. That is, if $E_t \cdot \widetilde{W_t^R} < W_t^R \Leftrightarrow E_t \cdot \widetilde{p_t^{NT}} < p_t^{NT}$ the price of the non-tradable goods of the foreign country, $E_t \widetilde{p_t^{NT}}$, is lower than that of the domestic economy, p_t^{NT}, and industrial hollowing occurs. In this case, the equilibrium real exchange rate, e^*, becomes:

$$e^* = \frac{E_t \cdot \widetilde{W_t^R}}{W_t^R} < 1 \tag{9.19}$$

Equation (9.19) is the necessary and sufficient condition for industrial hollowing. Henceforth, it is assumed that this condition is satisfied. In such a case, the equilibrium inflation rate is determined by the fundamental Eq. (9.15), and is expressed as:[2]

$$\rho^h = \sqrt[1-c]{\alpha^{-1} A\left[1-\eta^{-1}\right] e^{-\frac{1}{2}}}. \tag{9.20}$$

9.2.3 Market Equilibrium

Before discussing the following analysis, it must be noted that the following two approximations are used to avoid the complexity intrinsic to the nonlinearity of the model. It is assumed that the equilibrium real exchange rate is located in the vicinity of 1, and the following formulae hold. That is:

$$y^T \equiv \frac{e^{-1} y^h + y^f}{2} = \frac{y^h + e y^f}{2} + [1-e]\frac{e^{-1} y^h + y^f}{2} \approx \frac{y^h + e y^f}{2}, \tag{9.21}$$

[2] The equilibrium path of the nominal exchange rate, E_t, is determined by the fundamental equations within the home and the foreign economy; that is, by the fundamental equation within the foreign economy, where the prices of tradable and non-tradable goods are equal, $\alpha A^{-1}\left[1-\eta^{-1}\right]^{-1}\left[\rho^f\right]^{1-c} = 1$. Here, ρ^f is the inflation rate within the foreign economy. This equation is essentially the same as Eq. (9.18). The fundamental equation of the home economy is Eq. (9.20). Then $\left[\frac{\rho^f}{\rho^h}\right]^{1-c} \cdot e^{\frac{1}{2}} = 1$ Since the relative prices between the tradable and non-tradable goods are kept constant over time, it is clear that $\frac{\rho^f}{\rho^h} = \frac{E_t}{E_{t+1}}$ holds. Thus, the path of the nominal exchange rate is determined as $\left[\frac{E_t}{E_{t+1}}\right]^{1-c} \cdot e^{\frac{1}{2}} = 1$.

$$\frac{E_t \cdot \widetilde{W_t^R}}{p_t^{NT}} = \frac{p_t^T}{p_t^{NT}} \cdot \frac{E_t \cdot \widetilde{W_t^R}}{p_t^T} = \frac{E_t \cdot \widetilde{W_t^R}}{p_t^T} + \left[e^* - 1\right] \cdot \frac{E_t \cdot \widetilde{W_t^R}}{p_t^T} \approx \frac{E_t \cdot \widetilde{W_t^R}}{p_t^T}. \quad (9.22)$$

Equation (9.21) implies that the total world expenditure towards tradable goods, $\frac{e^{-1}y^h + y^f}{2}$, which is nonlinear on endogenous variables (y^h, e), is exchangeable for the expenditure towards the non-tradable goods, $\frac{y^h + ey^f}{2}$, around the vicinity of $e^* = 1$. On the other hand, Eq. (9.22) implies that the wage reduction gain per worker, $\left[e^* - 1\right] \cdot \frac{E_t \cdot \widetilde{W_t^R}}{p_t^T}$, is negligible around $e^* = 1$.

The Equilibrium of the Foreign Exchange Market

There are four kinds of market in this model: the labor market, the foreign exchange market, the home currency market, and the aggregate goods market. By the nature of the model, one of the latter three kinds of market is not independent, as will be shown later. Here the concentration is on the foreign exchange market and the aggregate goods market.

As discussed in Chap. 5, the real exchange rate is determined to equilibrate the balance of payments in a two-period overlapping generations model without bequest motive. By using Eqs. (9.21) and (9.22), the total imports of the home economy are:

$$\frac{1}{2e}\left[y^h - \frac{E_t \cdot \widetilde{W_t^R}}{p_t^{NT}} \cdot y^T\right] = \frac{1}{2e}\left[y^h - \left[1 - \eta^{-1}\right]\frac{y^h + e \cdot y^f}{2}\right], \quad (9.23)$$

or the deficit of the trade balance. Inside the brackets is the disposable income of the home country, which subtracts overseas wage payments from the real GNP. A surplus in the income account corresponds to the remittance of profits of the tradable goods sector, which is located overseas. This amounts to:

$$\frac{\eta^{-1}}{2} y^f. \quad (9.24)$$

Using Eqs. (9.23) and (9.24), the equilibrium condition for the foreign exchange market in stationary state is:[3]

$$\frac{1}{2e}\left[y^h - \left[1 - \eta^{-1}\right]\frac{y^h + e \cdot y^f}{2}\right] = \frac{\eta^{-1}}{2} y^f \Rightarrow y^h = e \cdot y^f \quad (9.25)$$

[3] Since the carried-over money of the older generation depends on the income of the previous period, there is an adjustment process towards stationary state. To clarify the discussion, we abbreviate the process.

The Equilibrium of the Aggregated Goods Market

Since $y^h \equiv e \cdot y^T + y^{NT}$ by definition, the aggregated goods market is cleared when:

$$y^h = c \cdot \left[y^h - \frac{E_t \cdot \widetilde{W_t^R}}{p_t^{NT}} \cdot y^T \right] + m + \left[\frac{\eta^{-1}}{2} y^f - \frac{1}{2e} \left[y^h - \frac{E_t \cdot \widetilde{W_t^R}}{p_t^{NT}} \cdot y^T \right] \right], \quad (9.26)$$

Where: the first term of Eq. (9.26) is the aggregate consumption of the younger generation, and the second term is the sum of government expenditure and the total expenditure of the older generation. This is equal to the real cash balance $m \equiv \frac{M_t}{p_t^{NT}}$, where M_t is the nominal money supply during period t.[4] The third term is the surplus of the balance of payments, which is zero as a result of the equilibrium condition of the foreign exchange market.

Substituting Eqs. (9.21) and (9.25) into Eq. (9.26):

$$y^h = \frac{m}{1 - c\eta^{-1}}. \quad (9.27)$$

In the present model there are three endogenous variables (ρ, e, y^h). The corresponding structural equations are Eqs. (9.20), (9.25), and (9.27), and thus the model is completely closed.[5]

Since $\eta > 1$, we obtain the following theorem:

Theorem 9.1

The fiscal multiplier under industrial hollowing is less than that under the closed economy $\frac{1}{1-c}$. *Thus, industrial hollowing lessens the effectiveness of fiscal and monetary policy, and is harmful if the real cash balance is kept constant.*[6]

---

[4] The government of the home economy is assumed to keep the real cash balance constant over time. Then, the budget constraint of the government implies: $g_t = \frac{M_t - M_{t-1}}{p_t^{NT}} = m - \frac{M_{t-1}}{p_t^{NT}}$.
Where: g_t is the real government expenditure in terms of the non-tradable goods.

Since the total real cash balance that the older generation carried over is $\frac{M_{t-1}}{p_t^{NT}}$, the sum of the government and the older generation's expenditure is: $g_t + \frac{M_{t-1}}{p_t^{NT}} = m$.

[5] Equation (9.26) is transformed taking Eq. (9.25) into consideration:

$$y^h - c \cdot \left[y^h - \frac{E_t \cdot \widetilde{W_t^R}}{p_t^{NT}} \cdot y^T \right] = m.$$

This implies that whenever the foreign exchange market and the aggregated goods market are cleared, the home currency market is also in equilibrium.

[6] Note that, as shown in Chap. 2, social welfare is an increasing function of real profits that are proportionate to real GNP.

The reason why industrial hollowing lowers the value of the fiscal multiplier is found in the leakage of wage payments overseas, which appears within the first brackets of Eq. (9.26). That is, even though the home economy experiences a business upturn, wage payments to residents who are engaged in the tradable goods sector in the foreign economy reduce the disposable income of the home country. Thus, a part of the expanded domestic effective demand leaks overseas. However, since the income distribution ratio between labor income and profits is $1-\eta^{-1}$ to η^{-1}, the larger η^{-1} is, the more advantageous a position a firm will enjoy. Hence, in conjunction with an increase in η^{-1}, the leakage overseas becomes small and the fiscal multiplier takes a higher value.

Next, consider the relationship between FDI and the real exchange rate. Combining Eqs. (9.25) and (9.27) gives the following theorem concerning the macroeconomic consequence of FDI under a flexible exchange rate system:

Theorem 9.2
Assume that the foreign economy is enjoying a boom and real GDP y^f *increases. However, this does not affect the business in the home economy at all, and only appreciates the real exchange rate.*

This theorem is validated by the fact that the real GNP of the home economy does not depend on y^f (see Eq. (9.27)). In addition, from Eq. (9.25), the equilibrium real exchange rate, e, appreciates just enough to offset the upturn of the foreign economy. Such an economic phenomenon belongs to a kind of *fallacy of composition.* Every firm, which produces its own tradable good, seeks cheap labor from overseas as a result of the differences in non-tradable goods prices (industrial hollowing). However, such cost-saving behavior is canceled by an appreciation of the real exchange rate owing to an increase in the remittance of profits, even though the business of the foreign economy upturns (Theorem 9.2). Only an increase in wage payments overseas remains, and this brings a depressive effect into the home economy (Theorem 9.1). It is rational behavior for an individual firm to be located in the lower nominal wage economy. Nevertheless, if such behaviors occur simultaneously in an economy as a whole, they conversely lower economic welfare because of wage payments overseas. This is the economic consequence of industrial hollowing.

9.3 Concluding Remarks

In this chapter, a small open economy model incorporating the opportunity of FDI was constructed. The results obtained were as follows:

1. First, industrial hollowing is an economic phenomenon, which is provoked by the nominal wage differential brought about by the existence of non-tradable goods. Since the assumption that labor is an immobile production resources applies, the nominal wage arbitrage across economies is imperfect. Thus, firms in a high nominal wage economy move their factories overseas. This lowers domestic employment opportunities and causes serious unemployment problems;

2. Second, industrial hollowing is a kind of fallacy of composition. Although individual rationality asks firms to invest in low-wage economies, this is accompanied by a massive reduction of domestic effective demand since wage payments flow out overseas, which is an exogenous factor for an individual firm. In addition, earnings from foreign economies cannot offset this depressive effect. This is because the massive remittance of profits appreciates the real exchange rate; and
3. Finally, since a leakage of effective demand (i.e. wage payments to foreign economies) emerges in conjunction with industrial hollowing, the value of the fiscal multiplier is lowered. This curtails the positive effect of aggregate management policy. In reality, many advanced economies face fiscal hardships. As such, industrial hollowing also relates to the maintenance of fiscal discipline.

References

Caves RE (1971) International corporations: the industrial economics of foreign investment. Economica 38:1–27

Caves RE (1982) Multinational enterprise and economic analysis. Cambridge University Press, Cambridge

Hood N, Young S (1979) The economics of multinational enterprise. Longman, London

Kemp MC (1964) The pure theory of international trade. Prentice-Hall, Upper Saddle River

MacDougal GDA (1960) The benefits and costs of private investment from abroad: a theoretical approach. Econ Rec 36:13–35

Otaki M (2012) A macroeconomic consequence of foreign direct investment: the welfare economics of industrial hollowing. Theor Econ Lett 2:412–417

Chapter 10
On the Function of Gold Standard in Idealism and Reality

10.1 Introduction

The gold standard was believed to be an ideal cohesive international financial system until the early 1930s. The adjustment process in this system is known as the specie flow theory and is outlined below. This theory works at least in the long run, and isolates affiliated countries, thus protecting them from the international diffusion of the business cycle.

Specie flow is a theory that combines the quantity theory of money with the purchasing power parity theory of money. That is, domestic price levels are assumed to increase proportionately with the quantity of fiduciary currency. In other words, the total purchasing power of gold is kept constant. Simultaneously, by arbitrage, the ratio of a country's domestic price level to a foreign country's price level is equal to the nominal exchange rate, which is fixed by the parities of both fiduciary currencies. Consequently, if the home country is a small country in the sense that it cannot affect the economic activities of the foreign country, from purchasing power parity theory, its domestic price level is fixed by the foreign country's price level. By interpreting the quantity theory of money conversely, this implies that the permissible amounts of gold or fiducial currency are also endogenously fixed. Hume (1752b) was the pioneer of the specie flow theory. He asserted:

> Suppose four-fifths of all the money in GREAT BRITAIN to be annihilated, and the nation reduces to the same condition, with regard to specie, as in the reign of the HARRYS and EDWARDS, what would be the consequence? Must not the price of all labour and commodities sink in proportion, and everything be sold as cheap as they were in those ages? What nation could then dispute with us in any foreign market, or pretend to navigate or to sell manufactures at the same price, which to us would afford sufficient profit? In how little time, therefore, must bring back the money which we had lost, and raise us to the level of all the neighboring nations? Where, after we have arrived, we immediately lose the advantage of the cheapness of labour and commodities; and the farther flowing in of money is stopped by our fullness and repletion.

Thus, once the hoarding of gold exceeds such amounts, the domestic price level becomes relatively high compared with that of the foreign country, and thus the home country temporarily experiences deficits in its balance of payments. This implies

M. Otaki, *Keynesian Economics and Price Theory*,
Advances in Japanese Business and Economics 7, DOI 10.1007/978-4-431-55345-8_10

that a part of its gold stockpiles flows overseas, and thus the excess gold or fiducial currency is entirely dissolved.

In the opposite case, when business within the foreign country expands and its goods become expensive, the home country experiences surpluses in its balance of payments and corresponding amounts of gold inflow. Nevertheless, domestic prices also become expensive by such inflows. Consequently, the foreign business upturn is entirely absorbed by inflation in the home country, and there is no substantial change in outputs. This is the employment-isolation mechanism assumed in specie flow theory. Such an idealistic function was advanced by advocates of the gold standard during the 1920s.

However, around the time of the Great Depression in the 1930s, the inherent cruelty of the gold standard was revealed. The synchronization of business cycles under the gold standard all over the world became prominent. Every advanced country fell into a serious slump that originated from the United States. By the middle of the 1930s, most advanced countries had abandoned the gold standard and moved to a flexible exchange rate regime. This chapter analyzes why the actual workings of the gold standard were so different to its hypothetical prospect.

There are two points of departure between the ideal and actual. First, goods produced by various countries are differentiated, and the perfect competition that the specie flow theory presumes is never upheld. In such a case, the income effect within reciprocal demand functions cannot be ignored. Thus, the purchasing power parity is violated. Second, and more important, is whether individuals are *confident* about the value of gold. Specie flow theory assumes that the value of gold decreases proportionately with its quantity. This implies that people *disbelieve* in the intrinsic value of gold, which is defined by the exchange ratio to goods (i.e. the inverse of the price level), and the value varies with the existing quantity within the country.

However, under the regime of the gold standard, people were confident in the value of gold. That is, people were *confident* that gold could be converted to goods at the same rate at that time, in the future, and independently of the existing quantity. Keynes (1924) was quite anxious about the collapse of *confidence* in gold owing to its imbalanced distribution. According to Keynes:

> I hold that gold flows to America because America offers in return for it a greater value in commodities than the gold is worth to the rest of the world. As none know better than Sir Henry Strakosch, gold is freely offered for sale in London every week; America is open to buy unlimited quantities of it at an almost fixed price in terms of goods; … It is not true, therefore, that she 'has secured a free option to acquire goods, services, and securities in exchange for the gold whenever it happens to suit her', if it means 'getting as much as goods for the gold as she originally gave for it'.

Mundell (1997) argues that people are more confident about gold than the U.S. dollar, which is the present key currency. He is also anxious about the inflation caused by the disbelief in the worldwide glut of dollars. Hence, he recommends that gold should play a more important role as a foreign reserve to discipline monetary policy, especially in the United States. This fact suggests that there is an internal inconsistency in the specie flow theory. That is, the specie flow theory assumes that although the value of gold is *disbelieved* within the domestic economy, there is *confidence* internationally and this serves as a reliable store of value. It is natural to assume that people's *confidence* about or *disbelief* in the value of gold should not depend on where gold is transacted.

Although Hume (1752a) admits that money stimulates economic activities at least in the short run, he asserts:

> And no other satisfactory reason can be given, why all prices have not risen to a much more commodities exorbitant height, except that which is derived from a change of customs and manners. Besides that more commodities are produced by additional industry, the same commodities come more to market, after men depart from their ancient simplicity of manners. And though this increase has not been equal to that of money, it has, however been considerable, and has preserved the proportion between coin and commodities nearer the ancient standard.

That is, Hume was skeptical about the role of money in the real economy in the long run. However, the stable proportion between money and commodities indicates that people are confident about money (gold), and this suggests that money is non-neutral even in the long run.

To summarize, in reality, the gold standard rests on two economic conditions: (i) the dominance of the income effect relative to the substitution effect caused by a change in the real exchange rate, and (ii) absolute confidence in the value of gold. The second condition makes the real exchange rate stable, because the relative prices of goods remain in narrow ranges and each nominal exchange rate is fixed by parities. Thus, adjustment by price levels is relatively difficult when the balance of payments is in disequilibrium. Conditions (i) and (ii) imply that the imbalance in the balance of payments is adjusted mainly by the flow of gold under some stable price level, once a country experiences a change of business environment. This also implies that, in reality, serious international diffusion of business cycles is unavoidable under the gold standard, because an imbalance in the balance of payments immediately links to a change in the supply of gold within a country. Thus, in contrast to the idealism, the gold standard system is actually a critical transmitter of the international business cycle. This assertion is endorsed by world economic history between the 1920s and 1930s.

This chapter is organized as follows. In Sect. 10.2, a "specie flow" model is developed, and the isolation effect from foreign business cycles ascertained. Section 10.3 deals with the model of the gold standard in reality, based on Otaki (2007, 2012). In addition, the discussion shows that deepening confidence in gold overseas, which brings about deflation, diffuses to the home country, and mitigates the depressive effects of the outflow of gold. In other words, in contrast to historical conjecture, the imported deflation adjoining the outflow of gold contributes to eliminating the depressive effect of monetary contraction, because it heightens the purchasing power of gold. Section 10.4 contains brief concluding remarks.

10.2 The Gold Standard in Idealism: Disbelief in Gold

10.2.1 A Model of the Specie Flow Theory and the Isolation Effect

As suggested in the Introduction, specie flow theory can be regarded as a combination of the quantity theory of money and the purchasing power parity theory of nominal exchange rates. These characteristics are captured in a two-period overlapping generations model of a production economy with an infinite time horizon.

It is assumed that only one good exists in the world and that the home country is too small to be able to affect economic conditions in the rest of the world. Perfect competition prevails in the goods market. That is, the home country behaves as a price taker in the integrated goods market. Again, it is assumed that the utility function of each individual U is identical to and additively separable between the lifetime consumption stream and the labor supply. That is:

$$U \equiv u\left(c_{1t}, c_{2t+1}\right) - \delta_t \cdot \alpha, \tag{10.1}$$

Where: $C_{it+i\text{-}1}$ is the consumption level of an individual who is born at the beginning of period t and located at the i-th stage of life; α denotes the disutility of labor; and δ_t is a definition function, which takes the value unity when the individual is employed and zero when he is unemployed. We also assume that $u(\cdot)$ is a well-behaved concave and linear homogenous function. Finally, let us assume that labor productivity is unity.

The lifetime budget constraint is then:

$$p_t c_{1t} + p_{t+1} c_{2t+1} \leq w_t + \pi_t, \tag{10.2}$$

Where: (p_t, p_{t+1}) is the price vector of the good; and w_t and π_t denote the nominal wage and the nominal profits, respectively.

An elementary calculus leads us to the following indirect utility function $h(\cdot)$ concerning lifetime consumption:

$$h\left(p_t, p_{t+1}, w_t\right) \equiv \frac{w_t + \pi_t}{\psi\left(p_t, p_{t+1}\right)}, \tag{10.3}$$

Where: $\psi(\cdot)$ is a linear homogenous function.

Based on Eq. (10.3), the nominal reservation wage can be calculated by the following procedure. The nominal reservation wage is the wage at which an individual is indifferent to whether to work, and thus:

$$h - \frac{\pi_t}{\psi\left(p_t, p_{t+1}\right)} = \alpha \Leftrightarrow w_t = \alpha \cdot \psi\left(p_t, p_{t+1}\right) \Leftrightarrow w_t = \alpha \cdot p_t \cdot \psi\left(1, \frac{p_{t+1}}{p_t}\right) \tag{10.4}$$

holds.

As long as private firms are sustainable, they must be able to earn non-negative profits. Accordingly, the following inequality (the fundamental equation) must hold:

$$\pi_t \equiv [p_t - w_t] L_t \geq 0 \Leftrightarrow 1 - \alpha \cdot \psi \left(1, \frac{p_{t+1}}{p_t}\right) \geq 0 \tag{10.5}$$

Where: L_t is the employment level.

Since prices are unchanged in equilibrium where the specie flow ceases, the inflation rate becomes unity, and thus the non-negative profit condition (5) is transformed into:

$$1 - \alpha \cdot \psi \ (1,1) \geq 0 \tag{10.6}$$

Whenever α is sufficiently small, Inequality (10.6) is satisfied. It must be noted that as long as Eq. (10.6) is upheld as a strict inequality, all firms have an incentive to expand their production as much as possible, and hence the economy attains full-employment equilibrium. This is the final comment describing the economic decisions of individuals and firms, and the equilibrium conditions of the labor market. The discussion now turns to the equilibrium conditions of the goods market. Ahead of this analysis, the following assumption of the value of gold or fiducial money is made. That is:

Assumption 10.1
People disbelieve in the intrinsic value of money in the sense that the value decreases proportionately with its quantity.

That is:

$$M_t = \kappa \cdot p_t \tag{10.7}$$

holds where M_t is the stock of fiducial money during period t, and κ is some positive constant, which is determined endogenously.

Since the utility function, $u(\cdot)$, is a linear homogenous function, the aggregate consumption function of younger individuals, C_t, becomes:

$$C_t \equiv c\left(\frac{p_{t+1}}{p_t}\right) \cdot y_t = c(1) \cdot y_t, \tag{10.8}$$

Where: y_t is the real GDP in terms of the current goods.

Then, we obtain the following equilibrium condition for the goods market:

$$y^f = c(1) \cdot y^f + \frac{M_{t-1}}{p_t} + \left[\frac{M_t}{p_t} - \frac{M_{t-1}}{p_t}\right], \tag{10.9}$$

Where: y^f is GDP in full employment.

The second term of the right-hand side of Eq. (10.9), $\frac{M_{t-1}}{p_t}$, denotes the aggregate consumption demand of older individuals. The third term $\frac{M_t}{p_t} - \frac{M_{t-1}}{p_t}$

corresponds to the surplus in the balance of payments. Rearranging the terms and substituting Eq. (10.7) into Eq. (10.9) results in:

$$y^f = \frac{\kappa}{1-c(1)}. \tag{10.10}$$

If κ is determined to satisfy Eq. (10.10), the macroeconomic equilibrium is the rational expectation equilibrium (REE) under the expectation (10.7).[1] Thus, it is clear that the imbalance in the balance of payment never affects the domestic economy and unemployment prevails as long as α is sufficiently small. That is, we obtain the following theorem:

Theorem 10.1
A disturbance in business overseas never diffuses to the home country under the idealistic gold standard.

10.2.2 Specie Flow

In conjunction with this theorem, it is possible to consider how the imbalance in the balance of payments is adjusted: the mechanism of specie flow. First, by measuring the unit of good properly, the nominal exchange rate is set at unity. Second, since purchasing power parity is assumed to be upheld, the following equation is obtained:

$$p^* = p_t. \tag{10.11}$$

When business upturns overseas and p^* rises (for example, owing to finding new gold ore), *ceteris paribus*, goods are exported from the home country because the home goods are cheaper relative to overseas goods. Thus, gold or fiduciary money is imported to the home country. As such, the domestic price rises because people are in disbelief about the value of money as expressed in Eq. (10.7).

The total imported amounts of gold are calculated by differentiating Eqs. (10.7) and (10.11). That is:

$$\frac{dp^*}{p^*} = \frac{dp}{p} = \frac{dM_t}{M_t}. \tag{10.12}$$

Thus, the total increase rate of money $\frac{dM_t}{M_t}$ is equal to the temporary inflation rate overseas $\frac{dp^*}{p^*}$ around the vicinity of the equilibrium.

[1] The procedure for determining REE is essentially the same as that of Lucas (1972).

10.3 The Gold Standard in Reality: Confidence in Gold

10.3.1 *Confidence in the Intrinsic Value of Gold*

Whenever the intrinsic value of gold is *disbelieved*, and Eq. (10.7) holds, the gold standard functions as a cohesive international financial settlement system. Nonetheless, there is an internal inconsistency within the specie flow theory. That is, although there is disbelief in gold domestically, the theory also assumes that all affiliate countries are *confident* in that intrinsic value internationally. In other words, people in every affiliate country that experiences surpluses in its balance of payments are ready to receive gold, despite the fact that the inflows of gold never benefit that country's economy and only serve to cause inflation. Thus, it is natural to assume that the price of gold should be either held in confidence or disbelieved, independently of where it is exchanged.

Hence, it is hereafter assumed that every individual is confident in the intrinsic value of gold independent of where it is exchanged. That is, instead of Assumption 10.1, it is presumed that:

Assumption 10.2
Every individual is confident in the intrinsic value of gold and rationally expects that gold is exchanged for goods independently of its quantity.

That is:

$$\frac{dp_t}{dM_t} = 0 \tag{10.13}$$

holds.

10.3.2 *The Gold Standard in Reality: Business Cycles Diffuse Internationally*

As briefly mentioned in the Introduction, it is natural to regard goods that are traded internationally as being differentiated. This implies that the income effect to tradable goods cannot be neglected, and the model advanced here should be reformatted to take this into account. Assume that there are two kinds of goods; *a* and *b*. The home country specializes in the production of good *a*, and the rest of the world produces good *b*. The consumption bundle in the utility function (1) C_{it+i-1} becomes:

$$c_{it+i-1} \equiv \left[a_{it+i-1}\right]^{\beta} \cdot \left[b_{it+i-1}\right]^{1-\beta}, 0 < \beta < 1, \tag{10.14}$$

Where: a_{it+i-1} and b_{it+i-1} are the consumption levels of goods *a* and *b*, respectively, by those who are born in period *t* during the *i*-th stage of their lives.

Since $u(\cdot)$ is linear and homogenous, the following indirect utility function h^1 is obtained:

$$h^1 \equiv \frac{w_t + \pi_t}{\psi\left(\left[p_t^a\right]^{\beta}\left[p_t^b\right]^{1-\beta}, \left[p_{t+1}^a\right]^{\beta}\left[p_t^b\right]^{1-\beta}\right)}, \tag{10.15}$$

Where: $\left(p_{t+j}^{a}, p_{t+j}^{b}\right)$ are the prices of goods a and b, respectively, during period $t+j$. In addition, the value of the nominal exchange rate approaches unity without loss of generality. Because it is assumed that people have confidence in the intrinsic value of gold and Eq. (10.13) holds, the equilibrium price level is constant over time except for the case in which the price level of goods produced overseas, p_t^b, changes. Thus, by the linear homogeneity of $\psi(\cdot)$, Eq. (10.15) can be transformed into:

$$h^1 \equiv \frac{w_t + \pi_t}{p_t^a \psi\left([e]^{1-\beta}, \left[\frac{p_{t+1}^a}{p_t^a}\right]^{\beta} [e]^{1-\beta}\right)} = \frac{w_t + \pi_t}{p_t^a [e]^{1-\beta} \psi(1,1)} \tag{10.16}$$

Where: $e\left(\equiv \frac{p_t^b}{p_t^a}\right)$ is the real exchange rate.

From Eqs (10.1 and 10.16), the nominal reservation wage can be calculated as:

$$w_t = \alpha p_t^a [e]^{1-\beta} \psi(1,1). \tag{10.17}$$

Henceforth, the following assumption is made:

Assumption 10.3
The economy of the home country is always located at an interior equilibrium. That is, there are some individuals who are unemployed in equilibrium.

As will be clarified later, if the stockpile fiducial money is small enough, such an equilibrium point surely exists. From Assumption 10.3, the nominal reservation wage corresponds to the nominal equilibrium wage. Furthermore, the zero-profit condition of firms also requires that:

$$\pi_t \equiv p_t^a \left[1 - \alpha e^{1-\beta} \psi(1,1)\right] = 0 \Leftrightarrow e^* = \frac{1}{\sqrt[1-\beta]{\alpha \cdot \psi(1,1)}} \tag{10.18}$$

Thus, the equilibrium real exchange rate, e^*, takes a constant value independent of the balance of payments, and so does the domestic equilibrium price level p^{a*}.

Since the utility function $u(\cdot)$ is assumed to be linear and homogenous, the aggregate consumption function of younger individuals, C_t, is:

$$C_t \equiv c(1) \cdot y_t.$$

Then, similar to Eq. (10.9), the equilibrium condition of the good a market is:

$$y_t = c(1) \cdot y_t + \frac{M_t}{p^{a*}}. \tag{10.19}$$

Besides the equilibrium condition of the goods market, we must consider the specie flow in conjunction with the imbalance in the balance of payments. Fiduciary money, which is supplied by those who reside overseas, is equivalent to the total imports of good α. This amounts to $\beta e y^b$, where y^b is the real GDP of the rest of the world. The demand is the total imports of good b of the home country. This amounts

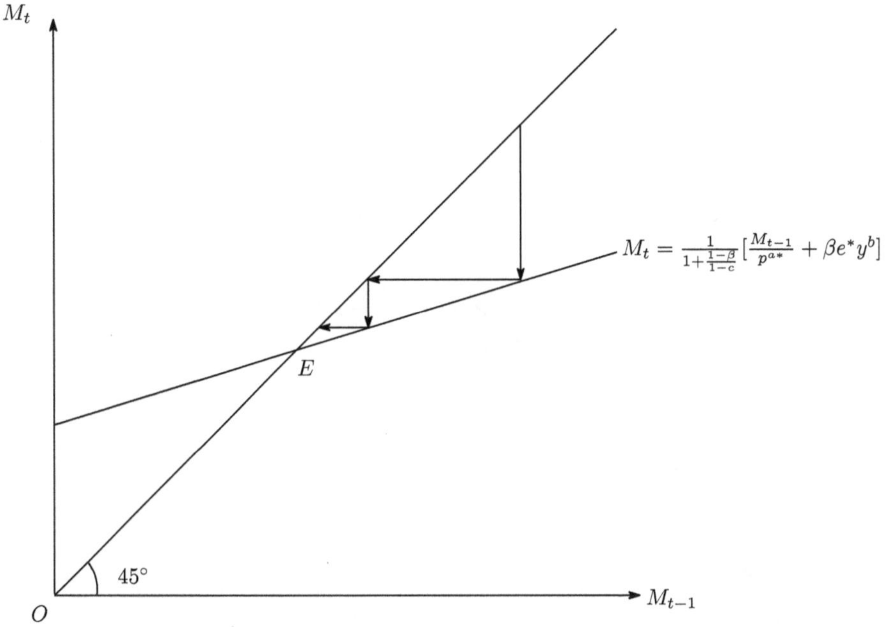

Fig. 10.1 The adjustment process

to $[1-\beta]y_t$. The difference between the two values is the total amount of inflows of the fiduciary money, and thus:

$$\frac{M_t - M_{t-1}}{p_t^{a*}} = \beta e^* y^b - [1-\beta] y_t. \tag{10.20}$$

Equations (10.19 and 10.20) describe the dynamics of this model under REE. Solving Eq. (10.19) on y_t:

$$y_t = \frac{1}{1-c(1)} \cdot \frac{M_t}{p^{a*}}, \tag{10.21}$$

Substituting Eq. (10.21) into (10.20), the following dynamics of the stock of the fiduciary money are observed:

$$\frac{M_t}{p^{a*}} = \frac{1}{1+\frac{1-\beta}{1-c}} \cdot \left[\frac{M_{t-1}}{p^{a*}} + \beta e^* y^b \right]. \tag{10.22}$$

Figure 10.1 illustrates the adjustment process. It is clear that the long-run equilibrium (Point *E*), where the flow of the fiducial money equilibrates, is unique and stable. If the initial stock exceeds the long-run equilibrium, imports are boosted since the business in the home country upturns. However, the circulated fiduciary money gradually decreases because the country experiences deficits on its balance of payments. Thus, the temporary boost to the economy converges to the long-run equi-

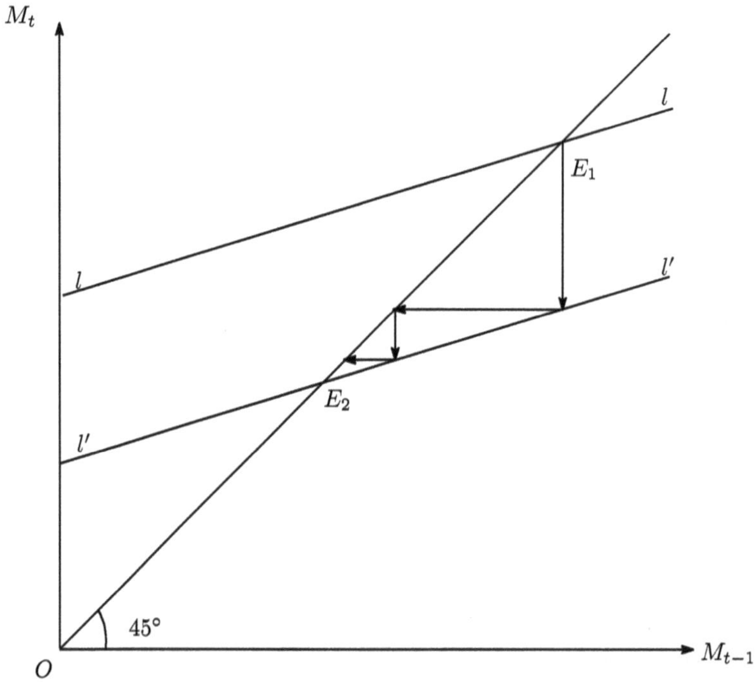

Fig. 10.2 The diffusion of business cycle

librium. In turn, Fig. 10.2 illustrates how the business cycle diffuses internationally. Whenever the world economy stagnates and the value of y^b decreases, the line that represents Eq. (10.22) shifts downward from *ll* to *l'l'*. In this case, the long-run equilibrium moves from E_1 to E_2. Since exports from the home country are curtailed, there is a deficit in the balance of payments and circulated money decreases. This triggers a financial contraction, and thus the home country cannot be immune from the business downturn. Thus, we have the following theorem:

Theorem 10.2
As long as people are confident in the intrinsic value of gold , the isolation effect becomes imperfect and business cycles diffuse among countries.

10.3.3 Perturbations in the Level of Confidence in the Intrinsic Value of Gold

In reality, business downturns under the gold standard often deepen confidence in the value of gold. This might be due to a psychological propensity for people to rely heavily on gold for precautionary savings for their unforeseeable future. This section analyzes how the deepened confidence in gold worldwide affects the home country's economy.

On differentiating Eq. (10.18):

$$-\frac{dp^{a*}}{p^{a*}} = -\frac{dp^{b*}}{p^{b*}}. \tag{10.23}$$

This implies that deepened confidence overseas entirely diffuses into the home country. In other words, temporary deflation overseas is transmitted to the home country under the gold standard. Since this increases the real value of the existing fiduciary money, $\frac{M_{t-1}}{p^{a*}}$, the transmitted deflation also mitigates the contractionary pressure caused by stagnation overseas. More formally:

Theorem 10.3

As the sequences of the equilibrium in real GDP with and without deflation are $\left\{\bar{y}^*_{t+j}\right\}_{j=0}^{+\infty}$ *and* $\left\{y^*_{t+j}\right\}_{j=0}^{+\infty}$, *respectively, then:*

$$y^*_{t+j} < \bar{y}^*_{t+j}, \forall j \tag{10.24}$$

holds.

Proof

Assume that the initial nominal stock of fiducial money, M_{t-1}, is the same in both cases. Then, by the difference of Eq. (10.22), the real cash balance $\frac{M_{t+j}}{p^{a*}}$ with deflation is larger than that without deflation for all j. Since it is apparent from Eq. (10.21) that real GDP increases proportionately with the real cash balance, Eq. (10.24) holds.

Thus, the deflation in conjunction with severe recession overseas discussed in subsection 10.3.2 mitigates damage from the recession. This is because the imported deflation raises the real cash balance, and thus contributes to moderating the financial contraction owing to outflows of gold.

10.4 Concluding Remarks

The function of the gold standard was analyzed in this chapter and the discussion shows that people are confident in the intrinsic value of gold. The results obtained were as follows:

1. First, the gold standard in idealism, which is called the specie flow theory and originated from Hume (1752b), can be regarded as the combination of the quantity theory of money and purchasing power parity concerning the nominal exchange rate. There is no economic factor other than commodity prices that

would transmit the business cycle between countries. As a result, full-employment equilibrium is always achieved and changes in the overseas economic environment never affect the domestic economy. That is, the employment-isolation effect is perfect under the idealistic gold standard, although this runs counter to the historical evidence;

2. Second, although the specie flow theory presumes disbelief in the intrinsic value of gold, people are confident in that value in the sense that they rationally expect that a unit of gold will always be convertible to commodities at some fixed ratio. Based on such a reality, the discussion revealed that a downturn of business overseas reduces exports from the home country, and hence gold as fiduciary money flows out. This triggers a financial contraction and makes the domestic economy slump. As such, the gold standard in reality is a transmitter of international business cycle diffusion;
3. Finally, the coexistence of deflation with stagnation overseas mitigates any depressive effect from these outcomes. This is because deflation raises the existing real cash balance and partly moderates the financial contraction owing to deficits in the balance of payments.

References

Hume D (1752a) Of money. In: Political discourses, 2nd edn. Oxford University, Oxford, p 41–59. http://books.google.co.uk/books?id=m0gVAAAAQAAJ&hl=ja&source=gbs_navlinks_s. Accessed 21 July 2014

Hume D (1752b) Of the balance of trade. In: Political discourses, 2nd edn. OxfordãUniversity, Oxford, p 79–114. http://books.google.co.uk/books?id=m0gVAAAAQAAJ&hl=ja&source=gbs_navlinks_s. Accessed 21 July 2014

Keynes JM (1924) The prospects of gold. In: The collected writings of John Maynard Keynes XIX: activities 1922–1929: the return to gold and industrial policy. Cambridge University Press, Cambridge, p 177–182

Lucas RE Jr (1972) Expectations and the neutrality of money. J Econ Theory 4:103–124

Mundell RA (1997) The international system in the 21st century: could gold make a comeback? Lecture delivered at St. Vincent College, Letrobe, Pennsylvania, 12 March 1997. http://www.columbia.edu/~ram15/LBE.htm. Accessed 27 July 2014ã

Otaki M (2007) The dynamically extended Keynesian cross and the welfare-improving fiscal policy. Econ Lett 96:23–29

Otaki M (2012) A Keynesian model of a small open economy under a flexible exchange rate. Theor Econ Lett 2:278–282

Part IV
Applications to Economic Growth Theory

Chapter 11
Dexterity as a Source of Economic Growth

11.1 Introduction

Investment function theory relies heavily on the existence of adjustment functions. Uzawa (1969) emphasizes the point that the quality of installed real capital within a firm utterly differs from new capital sold in the market. Real capital is assumed to become productive only via an *adjustment* process. He defines the ability of adjustment as a management skill (the Penrose effect). However, the components of adjustment costs are quite ambiguous in Uzawa's model (Uzawa 1969). Why do automatic changes in the quality of real capital necessarily incur adjustment costs? It would seem natural that the dexterity of employees contributes to increasing the capacity of real capital. The intangible human capital that employees accumulate therefore plays a crucial role in the growth of a firm. In other words, it is quite important for the growth of a firm to internalize a positive externality from skilled labor to capital via the formal/informal education of employees.

Once this is recognized, it is plausible to regard labor as a quasi-fixed production factor instead of as real capital. The growth of a firm is equivalent to that of employees' skills, thus investment function theory should be replaced with a theory of human-capital accumulation. Such a reconstruction of investment theory facilitates the economic interpretation of the adjustment cost function. The additional costs necessary for a firm's growth are the costs of the education that is needed to enhance and/or furnish the human capital held by employees. In this reconstruction, human-capital q theory is established and corresponds to Tobin's (1969) q theory concerning real-capital accumulation.

This discussion also considers the case where such internalization does not work well. In this case, an employer neglects the existence of the important intangible asset (i.e. labor dexterity), and regards the firm as being entirely constructed of marketable and substitutable production resources, as the elementary neoclassical theory of production assumes. In such a situation, the employer recognizes that the firm's production opportunities face diminishing returns to scale because the important production factor (the *dexterity*) is lacking from the firm's perspective.

M. Otaki, *Keynesian Economics and Price Theory*,
Advances in Japanese Business and Economics 7, DOI 10.1007/978-4-431-55345-8_11

The surplus gained from such dexterity is regarded as an autonomous technological progress (a kind of goodwill) whose return should be attributed to the employer.

Given that the recognized production function shows diminishing returns to scale and the optimal size of a firm is known, it is easy to show that the equilibrium growth rate of such a firm is zero in the long run. That is, how efficiently internalized the accumulation of intangible assets is will determine whether a firm can continue to grow.

The contents of this chapter are as follows. In Sect. 11.2, a dynamic theory of human-capital accumulation is constructed (human-capital q theory); Sect. 11.3 considers the importance of the internalization of employee dexterity for promoting the growth of a firm; and Sect. 11.4 gives brief concluding remarks.

11.2 The Model

There are two types of employees at the start of an economy. Among these, L_0 are skilled workers who can contribute to improve the productivity of physical capital by their skills. L_0^U are unskilled workers whose occupation is simple work, which does not affect the productivity of physical capital. To avoid the unemployment problem, it is assumed that the real reservation wage ω is high enough, and that imperfect employment has been prevailed.[1] It is also assumed that there is a single perishable good that can not only be consumed but also be used for the formal and/or informal education of employees.

In this chapter the problem of how the correct evaluation of employees' dexterity contributes to economic well-being is considered. An elementary calculus of variation is deployed for solving such a problem. The lifetime utility function of each skilled employee U_t is:

$$U_t \equiv \int_t^{\infty} c_\tau e^{-\rho[\tau - t]} d\tau, \tag{11.1}$$

Where: c_τ denotes the consumption level at time τ; and ρ is the time preference rate.

Using Otaki and Yaginuma (2012) and Otaki (2013), the production function is specified as follows:

$$Y_\tau = F\left(\Psi(L_\tau, k_\tau), L_\tau + L_\tau^U\right), \tag{11.2}$$

Where: $\Psi(\cdot)$ is a linear homogenous function that represents the effective capital input; Y_τ and k_τ denote the volume of output and the deployed real capital used for it, respectively. In addition, it is assumed that $F(\cdot)$ is also a linear homogenous function.

[1] The properties of monetary economic growth under imperfect employment equilibrium are dealt with in Chap. 13.

The economic meaning of Eq. (11.2) is as follows. As well as the increment in output owing to real capital $\frac{\partial F}{\partial \Psi}\frac{\partial \Psi}{\partial k}$, an improvement in the efficiency of a skilled labor force brings about two positive effects. One is direct, in the sense that employees can deal with the procedures involved in their jobs more efficiently $\frac{\partial F}{\partial L}$. The other is indirect, as real capital works more productively because of the dexterity of a skilled labor force $\frac{\partial F}{\partial \Psi}\frac{\partial \Psi}{\partial L}$. The internalization of the second effect is regarded as meaning that the appropriate enhancement of employees' dexterity is the raison d'être of a firm. Elementary economics deploys the linear homogenous production function, and so excludes an externality such as $\frac{\partial F}{\partial \Psi}\frac{\partial \Psi}{\partial L}$ from labor to capital, and thus a firm can ultimately be decomposed into these two production resources. As Coase (1937) suggests, such a firm without this externality can only be constructed by assembling production resources. Hence, this cannot explain how an organization is differentiated from the market. What it is that differentiates a firm from the market is therefore quite ambiguous in the Coase–Tobin–Uzawa theory. To advance discussion of this point, it is necessary to emphasize that the substance of a firm is determined by the inseparability of labor and capital originating from employee dexterity; namely, the externality from labor to capital.

Thus, net cash flow per employee, NCF_τ, which in the model presented in this discussion is always equal to the difference between current consumption c_τ and the disutility of labor, can be written as:

$$NCF_\tau \equiv \frac{1}{L_0}\left[F(\Psi(L_\tau, k_\tau), L_\tau + L_\tau^U) - k_\tau - \omega\left[L_\tau + L_\tau^U\right] - \Phi(g_\tau)L_\tau\right], \quad g_\tau \equiv \frac{\dot{L}_\tau}{L_\tau}, \tag{11.3}$$

Where: g_τ denotes the growth rate of the efficiency of labor; and $\Phi(\cdot)$ is the educational cost function of heightening dexterity. This corresponds to the adjustment cost function (the Penrose function) in the Tobin–Uzawa theory.

Taking the linear homogeneity of F and Ψ into consideration, from the short-run maximization decision for NCF_τ, the Euler theorem transforms Eq. (11.3) into:

$$NCF_\tau = \left[\frac{\partial F}{\partial \Psi}\frac{\partial \Psi}{\partial L} - \Phi(g_\tau)\right]\frac{L_\tau}{L_0}. \tag{11.4}$$

From Eqs. (11.1) and (11.4), the objective function of a representative firm becomes:

$$U_t^* \equiv \max_{g_\tau}\int_t^\infty \left[\frac{\partial F}{\partial \Psi}\frac{\partial \Psi}{\partial L} - \Phi(g_\tau)\right]L_\tau e^{-\rho[\tau - t]}d\tau. \tag{11.5}$$

It is well known that under such a linear homogenous environment the only optimum path of $\{g_\tau\}$ involves a growth rate g^* that is constant over time (see Mathematical Appendix 3 based on Arrow and Kurz (1970)). Thus, Eq. (11.5) can be rewritten as:

$$U_t^* \equiv \max_g \int_t^{\infty} \left[\frac{\partial F}{\partial \Psi} \frac{\partial \Psi}{\partial L} - \Phi(g) \right] L_t e^{-[\rho - g][\tau - t]} d\tau . = \max_g \frac{\frac{\partial F}{\partial \Psi} \frac{\partial \Psi}{\partial L} - \Phi(g)}{\rho - g} L_t . \tag{11.6}$$

By differentiating Eq. (11.6) with respect to g, the optimal skill accumulation rate g^* is:

$$\Phi'(g^*) = \frac{\frac{\partial F}{\partial \Psi} \frac{\partial \Psi}{\partial L} - \Phi(g^*)}{\rho - g^*} \equiv q. \tag{11.7}$$

In accordance with that of Uzawa (1969) in the case of real-capital accumulation, the right-hand side of Eq. (11.7) denotes human capital q, which corresponds to the shadow price of an employee measured by the efficiency unit, and thus this equation implicitly defines the q theory of human capital investment. Hence, it is also clear that the following theorem derived from Eqs. (11.5) and (11.7) holds:

Theorem 11.1
The equilibrium lifetime utility of a skilled worker U_t^* *is represented by:*

$$U_t^* = qL_t . \tag{11.8}$$

Equation (11.8) shows that the lifetime utility per employee is equal to their human capital q. In addition, the equilibrium growth rate of employee skills g^* is defined by Eq. (11.7).

11.3 Dexterity as the Engine for the Growth of a Firm

In the previous section it was assumed that a firm can fully internalize the dexterity of employees. However, such a mechanism works only when the employer can properly evaluate each employee's performance. This implies that employees are not anonymous within the firm. This lack of anonymity characterizes the difference between the internal and external transactions of the firm (market transactions). It must be noted that transactions under anonymity imply the standarization of transacted goods and services as long as the market works soundly. As such, jobs that require few skills are transacted by the market.

When employers do not concern themselves with the dexterity of employees and deal with them anonymously, as the standard neoclassical-type firm theory postulates, such internalization is not possible. As the production function (Eq. 11.2) reveals, such an employer fails to count the externality emerging from the dexterity of employees $\frac{\partial F}{\partial \Psi}\frac{\partial \Psi}{\partial L}$ in this situation. The growth in productivity due to increasing dexterity is seen as an autonomous progress that is independent of employees' skills. The first-order conditions for the maximization problem in such firms are:

$$\frac{\partial}{\partial k}F(\Psi(L_0,k^*),L^*)=1,\quad \frac{\partial}{\partial L}F(\Psi(L_0,k^*),L^*)=\omega, \tag{11.9}$$

Where: L^* is the sum of skilled and unskilled workers; and * means the optimal value.

From Euler's theorem and Eq. (11.9):

$$F(\Psi(L_0,k^*),L^*)=\frac{\partial F}{\partial k}k^*+\frac{\partial F}{\partial \Psi}\frac{\partial \Psi}{\partial L}L_0+\frac{\partial F}{\partial L}L^*>k^*+wL^*, \tag{11.10}$$

Equation (11.10) implies that an employer who does not evaluate the contribution of dexterity to the production process recognizes that the production function is diminishing returns to scale, and misinterprets the value of the dexterity to be the rent that is intrinsically attached to the firm itself.[2] The optimal firm size is determined by Eq. (11.9). This implies that the growth rate of such a firm becomes zero. This leads to the following theorem:

Theorem 11.2

If an employer is not concerned with the development of employee dexterity, then they rationally interpret the production function to be one of diminishing returns to scale. Hence, there is no opportunity for the growth of such a firm. In this sense, whether a firm can continue to grow crucially depends on how efficiently dexterity is internalized. In other words, the correct evaluation of dexterity is the engine for the growth of a firm.

---

[2] It is a necessary and sufficient condition for a diminishing return-to-scale production function G that there is a non-negative and strictly increasing function Φ such as: $\Phi(\lambda)\equiv\lambda y-G(\lambda K,\lambda L)$, where: λ is a non-negative number and y is the output, and function Φ represents the seriousness of diminishing returns to scale. Differentiating both sides of the above equation with respect to λ and applying Euler's theorem:

$$\Phi'=y-rK^*-wL^*.$$

Thus, if the right-hand side of the above equation is positive, such a production function gives diminishing returns to scale.

11.4 Concluding Remarks

This chapter has considered the role of employee dexterity in the growth of a firm. Dexterity is represented by a positive externality from skilled labor force to real capital within a firm. The results obtained are as follows:

1. First, when an employer succeeds in internalizing such an externality, the production function is perceived as giving constant returns to scale, and thus there is infinite opportunity for the growth of the firm. In relation to this human-capital investment, this chapter developed the concept of human capital q, replacing Tobin's q (Tobin 1969), which placed too much importance on a kind of vintage effect concerning real capital (Uzawa 1969);
2. Second, the reason why the adjustment cost function (Penrose function) exists has been clarified. Here, Uzawa's interpretation is quite ambiguous as it did not expose the mechanism by which real capital is made productive. The present discussion suggests that a convex adjustment function properly expresses the non-negligible informal and/or formal educational costs for nurturing the various skills of employees;
3. Finally, it is proven here that the production function becomes one of decreasing returns to scale, and overlooks the opportunity of the growth of a firm whenever an employer fails to internalize dexterity. Such inefficiency comes from the fact that the employer confuses the surplus derived from dexterity with the goodwill of the firm. Although it is an intangible asset, dexterity is the embedded engine for the growth of a firm.

Mathematical Appendix: A Heuristic Explanation of the Calculus of Variation

1. The Euler Equation

A typical problem of the calculus of variation is:

$$\max_{\{\dot{x}_t\}} \int_0^T f(x_t, \dot{x}_t, t)dt, \quad x_0 = \underline{x}, x_T = \overline{x}.$$

To solve this problem, consider the following perturbation:

$$J(\varepsilon) \equiv \int_0^T f(x_t^* + \varepsilon\eta_t, \dot{x}_t^* + \varepsilon\dot{\eta}_t, t)dt, \quad \eta_0 = \eta_T = 0.$$

Where: $(x_t^*, \dot{x}_t^*)$ indicates the optimal path.
Expanding $J(\varepsilon)$ around the optimal path:

$$J(\varepsilon) = J(0) + \varepsilon \int_0^T \left[\frac{\partial f}{\partial x} \cdot \eta_t + \frac{\partial f}{\partial \dot{x}} \cdot \dot{\eta}_t \right] dt + o(\varepsilon). \tag{11.11}$$

Integrating part of the second term of the right-hand side of (Eq. 11.11) gives:

$$J(\varepsilon) = J(0) + \varepsilon \int_0^T \left[\frac{\partial f}{\partial x} - \frac{d}{dt}\left[\frac{\partial f}{\partial \dot{x}}\right]\right] \cdot \eta_t dt + o(\varepsilon). \tag{11.12}$$

Here it must be noted that $J(\varepsilon) \leq J(0)$ holds by definition.

Since $|\varepsilon|$ is a non-zero arbitrary small number, which can take both a positive and negative value, and $\eta_t \neq 0$ in general, Eq. (11.12) implies:

$$\frac{\partial f}{\partial x} - \frac{d}{dt}\left[\frac{\partial f}{\partial \dot{x}}\right] = 0. \tag{11.13}$$

The optimal path must satisfy this partial differential equation. This is the Euler equation.

2. Calculus of Variation with a Constraint

The dynamic optimization problem with a constraint is considered next. That is:

$$\max_{\{u_t\}} \int_0^T f(x_t, u_t, t)dt, \text{ subject to } \dot{x}_t \leq g(x_t, u_t, t). \tag{11.14}$$

Now, $x_0 = \underline{x}$, $x_T = \overline{x}$. In this problem, x_t and u_t are called state variable and control variable, respectively. To solve this problem, we must make the following Euler–Lagrangean, L:

$$L(x_t, u_t, \lambda_t, t) \equiv f(x_t, u_t, t) + \lambda_t[g(x_t, u_t, t) - \dot{x}_t]. \tag{11.15}$$

This problem can be decomposed into two parts. First, by the Kuhn–Tucker theory introduced in Chap. 2, the optimal value, u_t^*, satisfies:

$$\frac{\partial f}{\partial u} + \lambda_t \frac{\partial g}{\partial u} = 0 \tag{11.16}$$

together with:

$$\lambda_t^*[g(x_t^*, u_t^*, t) - \dot{x}_t^*] = 0 \tag{11.17}$$

is the necessary condition for optimality because $f(\cdot)$ should be maximized on u_t under the constraint in Eq. (11.14) for a given $(x_t^*, \dot{x}_t^*)$.

The second part comprises the optimality of the path of x_t. Since (u_t^*, λ_t^*) is determined by Eqs. (11.16) and (11.17), the value of the Euler–Lagrangean (Eq. 11.15) is the same as $f(x_t^*, u_t^*, t)$. Hence the Euler Eq. (11.13) can be applied to the Euler–Lagrangean (Eq. 11.15). Thus:

$$\frac{\partial f}{\partial x_t} + \lambda_t^* \frac{\partial g}{\partial x_t} + \dot{\lambda}_t^* = 0. \tag{11.18}$$

It must be noted that instead of $\dot{x}_t^*$, the Lagrangean multiplier, λ_t^*, plays a key role in Eq. (11.18). If the redundancy of the constraint is excluded and $\lambda_t^* \neq 0$, it is convenient to summarize the obtained results by the Hamiltonian, H. That is:

$$H \equiv f(x_t, u_t, t) + \lambda_t \cdot g(x_t, u_t, t). \tag{11.19}$$

Then Eqs. (11.16), (11.17), and (11.18) are expressed by:

$$\frac{\partial H}{\partial u} = 0, \quad \frac{\partial H}{\partial \lambda} = \dot{x}, \quad -\frac{\partial H}{\partial x} = \dot{\lambda}. \tag{11.20}$$

This is a useful formula. Equation (11.10) is a two-dimensional differential equation concerning (x_t, λ_t), and thus contains two indeterminate constants. These constants are determined by an initial and a terminal condition.

3. A Useful Terminal Condition (A Transversality Condition)
In an optimization problem with infinite time horizons, it is generally difficult to impose a plausible terminal condition. However, there is a *useful* terminal condition:

Theorem 11.3
Suppose a Hamiltonian satisfies:

$$H(x_t, u_t, \lambda_t^*, t) \leq H(x_t^*, u_t^*, \lambda_t^*, t) + \frac{\partial H}{\partial x} \cdot [x_t - x_t^*], \tag{11.21}$$

Where: $\frac{\partial H}{\partial x}$ *is evaluated along the optimal path. Then:*

$$\lim_{t \to \infty} \lambda_t^* x_t^* = 0 \tag{11.22}$$

*becomes a sufficient condition for the optimality of Eq. (*11.14*).*

Proof
Substituting Eqs. (11.20) into (11.21) gives:

$$H(x_t, u_t, \lambda_t^*, t) \leq H(x_t^*, u_t^*, \lambda_t^*, t) - \dot{\lambda}_t^* \cdot [x_t - x_t^*]$$

By the definition of the Hamiltonian:

$$f(x_t, u_t, t) \leq f(x_t^*, u_t^*, t) - \dot{\lambda}_t^* \cdot [x_t - x_t^*] - \lambda_t^* \cdot [\dot{x}_t - \dot{x}_t^*] \tag{11.23}$$

Integrating both sides of Eq. (11.23):

$$\int_0^T f(x_t, u_t, t) dt \leq \int_0^T f(x_t^*, u_t^*, t)\, dt - \lambda_T^* \cdot [x_T - x_T^*]. \tag{11.24}$$

Taking the limit $T \to \infty$, it is easy to verify that if Eq. (11.22) holds:

$$\int_0^{+\infty} f(x_t, u_t, t)dt \le \int_0^{+\infty} f(x_t^*, u_t^*, t)\, dt$$

4. The Economic Meaning of the Lagrangean Multiplier

The Lagrangean multiplier λ_t^* has an important economic meaning. To clarify this property, multiply $\exp\left[\int_0^t \frac{\partial g}{\partial x} ds\right]$ on both sides of Eq. (11.18) and rearrange the terms. Then:

$$\left[\dot{\lambda}_t^* + \frac{\partial g}{\partial x}\lambda_t^*\right] \cdot \exp\left[\int_0^t \frac{\partial g}{\partial x} ds\right] = -\frac{\partial f}{\partial x} \cdot \exp\left[\int_0^t \frac{\partial g}{\partial x} ds\right]. \tag{11.25}$$

Integrating Eq. (11.25):

$$\lambda_0^* - \lim_{t\to\infty} \lambda_t^* \exp\left[\int_0^t \frac{\partial g}{\partial x} ds\right] = \int_0^\infty \frac{\partial f}{\partial x} \cdot \exp\left[\int_0^t \frac{\partial g}{\partial x} ds\right] dt \tag{11.26}$$

If a transversality condition admits $\lim_{t\to\infty} \lambda_t^* \exp\left[\int_0^t \frac{\partial g}{\partial x} ds\right] = 0$, Eq. (11.26) becomes:

$$\lambda_0^* = \int_0^\infty \frac{\partial f}{\partial x} \cdot \exp\left[\int_0^t \frac{\partial g}{\partial x} ds\right] dt \tag{11.27}$$

In general:

$$\lambda_t^* = \int_t^\infty \frac{\partial f}{\partial x} \cdot \exp\left[\int_t^\tau \frac{\partial g}{\partial x} ds\right] d\tau \tag{11.28}$$

holds. Thus, λ_t^* is the discounted value of increment of the gain obtained from a unit increase of the initial state variable. In other words, this is the imputed price of the state variable. If $f(x_t, u_t, t) \equiv h(x_t, u_t)e^{-\rho t}$, Eq. (11.18) can be transformed into:

$$\lambda_t^* = e^{-\rho t} \int_t^\infty \frac{\partial h}{\partial x} \cdot \exp\left[-\int_t^\tau \left[\rho - \frac{\partial g}{\partial x}\right] ds\right] d\tau \tag{11.29}$$

and thus the economic meaning of Eq. (11.28) becomes clearer.

5. Uzawa's (1969) Investment Function

Uzawa (1969) considers the following maximization problem:

$\max_{[g_t]} \int_0^\infty [r - \varphi(g_t)] K_t e^{-\rho t} dt$, subject to

$$\dot{K}_t = g_t K_t \tag{11.30}$$

Where: $\varphi(g)K$ is the investment adjustment cost function (the Penrose function). The corresponding Hamiltonian is:

$$H \equiv [r - \varphi(g_t)]K_t e^{-\rho t} + \lambda_t g_t K_t. \tag{11.31}$$

Uzawa assumed that an optimal path is steady growth, and hence g^* is constant over time. Such an assumption satisfies the Arrow–Kurz sufficient condition, which is exhibited in Mathematical Appendix 3. Assume that the growth rate is constant. Then, the value of Eq. (11.30), which represents the current market value of a firm, becomes:

$$\frac{r - \varphi(g^*)}{\rho - g^*} K_0, \tag{11.32}$$

where g^* satisfies:

$$\varphi'(g^*) = \lambda_t^* e^{\rho t} = const. \Rightarrow \dot{\lambda}_t^* = -\rho \lambda_t^* \tag{11.33}$$

From Eqs. (11.31) and (11.33):

$$\dot{\lambda}_t^* = -[r - \varphi(g^*)]e^{-\rho t} + \lambda_t g^* \Rightarrow \lambda_t^* = \frac{r - \varphi(g^*)}{\rho - g^*} e^{-\rho t} \tag{11.34}$$

$$\varphi'(g^*) = \lambda_t^* e^{\rho t} = \frac{r - \varphi(g^*)}{\rho - g^*}. \tag{11.35}$$

$\lambda_t^* e^{\rho t}$ is Tobin's marginal q, which means the imputed price of capital as was shown in the previous appendix.

To this must be added a convenient property for empirical analyses of the capital investment function. That is, Tobin's average q (the ratio of the market value of a firm to its replacement cost), which is an observable variable, is equal to the marginal q, which uniquely determines the capital investment ratio, but is unobservable. This is clear from Eqs. (11.32) and (11.35). Let the Hamiltonian expand to a Taylor series around the optimal plan:

$$H\left(K_t, g_t, \lambda_t^*, t\right) \le H\left(K_t, g_t^*, \lambda_t^*, t\right) = H\left(K_t^*, g_t^*, \lambda_t^*, t\right) + \frac{\partial H}{\partial K_t}\Big|_{\substack{K_t = K_t^* \\ g_t^* = g^*}} \cdot \left[K_t - K_t^*\right]. \tag{11.36}$$

Thus, condition (11.21) is satisfied. From Eq. (11.34), the corresponding transversality condition is:

$$\lim_{t\to\infty} \lambda_t^* K_t^* = \lim_{t\to\infty} e^{-\rho t} \cdot \frac{r - \varphi(g^*)}{\rho - g^*} K_t = \lim_{t\to\infty} \frac{r - \varphi(g^*)}{\rho - g^*} K_0 e^{-[\rho - g^*]t} = 0. \tag{11.37}$$

Economically, this condition implies that the far future market value of a firm converges to zero because individuals discount future consumption at the rate ρ. It is evident that this condition is satisfied as long as the analysis retains economic meaning.

References

Arrow KJ, Kruz M (1970) Public investment, the rate of return, and optimal fiscal policy. The Johns Hopkins University Press, Baltimore

Coase RH (1937) The nature of the firm. Economica 4:386–405

Otaki M (2013) Evaluation of dexterity and a theory the growth of a firm. Mod Econ 4:226–229

Otaki M, Yaginuma H (2012) Kigyo seicho to jinteki shihon no chikuseki: keieiken to kigyo seicho no conflict [The growth of a firm and accumulation of human capital: the conflict between the managerial right and the growth of a Firm]. DBJ Discussion Paper Series No. 1208, Research Institute of Capital Formation, Development Bank of Japan. http://www.dbj.jp/ricf/research/discussion.html. Accessed 22 July 2014

Tobin J (1969) A general equilibrium approach to monetary theory. J Money Credit Bank 1:15–29

Uzawa H (1969) Time preference and the penrose effect in a two-class model of economic growth. J Polit Econ 77:628–652

Chapter 12
Monetary Economic Growth Theory Under Perfect Competition: Can Monetary Expansion Really Enhance Economic Growth?

12.1 Introduction

How the market structure of goods markets affects economic growth in a monetary economy is almost unknown. Although Dixit and Pindyck (1994) built models of investment function under uncertainty and pointed out that this function depends on the level of effective demand, it was not their concern to analyze how such investment relates to economic growth as a whole. As noted in Chap. 13, Otaki (2013) developed a general equilibrium growth model under monopolistic competition, and also found that there exists no endogenous economic force for sustainable growth in a monetary economy without a government's incessant stimulating policies.

On the other hand, in his seminal work, Uzawa (1969) analyzed the properties of the investment function under perfect competition in the context of a general equilibrium model. Although this theory entirely excludes the existence of money, he found that the optimal investment ratio to capital is free of the level of effective demand. The equilibrium growth ratio is dependent on the profit rate, which is endogenously determined only by relative prices. Such a prominent property of the investment function implies that unlike the monopolistic competition case analyzed in Chap. 13, capital investment enables an economy to sustain its growth. This is because employers can invest without referring to the condition of effective demand,[1] and these resources are rewarded by whole-earned quasi-rents within the firm. To summarize, the driving force of growth in a barter economy is perfect competition.

The main theoretical issue addressed in this chapter is, based on Otaki and Tamura (2013), to check the validity of Uzawa's (1969) assertions that capital investment calls forth future investment expansion under perfect competition, and that economic

[1] It is quite ambiguous why more capital enhances more investment in physical capital q theory. This theory attributes such a property to the existence of *managerial resources*. However, it seems difficult to reveal the substance of *managerial resources*, as discussed in the previous chapter. The previous chapter, instead, introduced the concept of *dexterity* in labor forces, which provides physical capital with positive externalities such as process innovations. A firm is regarded as an ingenious device for the internalization of such externalities, and thus, since there is no limit to sale under perfect competition, a firm attains sustainable growth along with the accumulation of *dexterity*.

M. Otaki, *Keynesian Economics and Price Theory*,
Advances in Japanese Business and Economics 7, DOI 10.1007/978-4-431-55345-8_12

growth is sustainable even in a monetary economy. The result is as follows: since the effective demand principle works because of the indeterminacy of the equilibrium price sequence (see Chap. 2), an economy is not necessarily able to attain a level of Net Domestic Product (NDP) that guarantees full resource utilization even though goods markets are competitive. However, since human capital investment becomes an autonomously expanding expenditure independent of effective demand, its suspending power on economic growth becomes fortified compared with that seen in the case of monopolistic competition (Otaki 2013). This is refined in Chap. 13. Consequently, government deficits, which are necessary for achieving a high employment level, grow only at a constant rate (i.e. at the real NDP growth rate).

In addition, as the growth model developed in this book includes the monetary factor, it is possible to analyze how money affects economic growth through the inflation rate. Here, *asset crowding out* is a key concept. As long as real NDP per capita is unchanged by economic growth in the stationary state, an increase in the real cash balance per capita implies that the capital investment is curtailed because of the limitations on the aggregate supply of funds.[2] This phenomenon is defined as asset crowding out. This induces a lower inflation rate (a higher rate of return for money) because inflation must be tranquilized to equilibrate the money market. Thus, when capital investment is an increasing function of the inflation rate, a monetary expansion conversely hinders economic growth. Although this might seem a rather pathological phenomenon for pedagogical economists, it has an important implication in the following sense. That is, the theory put forward in this book can explain the coexistence of exorbitant expansionary monetary policies, prominent disinflation, and stagnant economic growth in the context of this phenomenon. This is a situation that advanced countries are currently experiencing.

The remainder of this chapter is organized as follows. In Sect. 12.2, a two-period overlapping generations monetary growth model with *impure altruism* is constructed and analyzed. This is a concept developed mainly by Acemoglu (2009). In Sect. 12.3, the relationship between the competitiveness of markets and fiscal sustainability is discussed. In addition, fiscal and monetary policy relationships to inflation and economic growth are explored. Section 12.4 contains brief concluding remarks.

12.2 The Model

12.2.1 Structure of the Model

There are three strata in this economy: employers, and skilled and unskilled employees. Skilled and unskilled employees are distinguishable by whether they can contribute to progress the dexterity defined in Chap. 11. For simplicity, it is

[2] The growth rate of money and real cash balance per capita must be rigorously distinguished. The fiscal sustainability discussed above relates to the growth rate, and what causes asset crowding out is an increase in the real cash balance per capita.

assumed that there are an infinite number of unskilled workers. Each employee provides discretionary unit labor when young. This disutility is denoted as α. The lifetime utility that comes from the consumption stream (c_{1t}, c_{2t+1}) is a homothetic function (note that such a function is common with employers). Thus, the lifetime utility U is defined as:

$$U \equiv u(c_{1t}, c_{2t+1}) - \delta_t \cdot \alpha, \tag{12.1}$$

Where: δ_t is a definition function, the value of which takes unity when employed and zero when unemployed.

On the other hand, each employer hires employees to produce goods and gain profits when they are young. Assume that the same production function as formulated in Chap. 11, and:

$$y_t = F\left(\Psi\left(L_{t-1}^S, k_t\right), L_{t-1}^S + L_t^U\right) \equiv F\left(\Psi\left(L_{t-1}^S, k_t\right), L_t\right), \tag{12.2}$$

Where: L_t^S is the number of employed skilled labor force; L_t^U is that of employed unskilled labor force; L_t is, by definition, the total number of employed workers; and k_t denotes the physical capital, which is assumed to be perishable.

Although this assumption seems to be rather extreme, it implies that human capital has more endurance than physical capital because the dexterity is transmitted to descendants by education and training. In addition, an employer makes investments for the next generation, because it is assumed that every employer exercises *impure altruism*. Employers are not only concerned with their own lifetime utility but also with the utility of descendants. The inheritance is the seed of the dexterity of future skilled employees via investments on education (assume that it takes a considerable length of time for such education to be efficacious). These investments enable young employers in the next period to earn more profit by furnishing skilled employees' dexterity. There is no disutility of labor in this stratum.

In turn, the government newly issues fiat money to finance its fiscal expenditures and this, for simplicity, bears no additional utility for the private sector. The budget constraint of the government becomes:

$$M_t - M_{t-1} = p_t G_t \quad \Leftrightarrow \quad \frac{M_t}{p_t L_t} - \frac{M_{t-1}}{p_t L_t} = \frac{G_t}{p_t L_t} \Leftrightarrow g = m_t - \frac{m_{t-1}}{[1+\rho][1+\theta]} \tag{12.3}$$

Where:

$m_t \equiv \dfrac{M_t}{p_t L_t}$, $g \equiv \dfrac{G_t}{p_t L_t}$, $\rho \equiv \dfrac{p_{t+1}}{p_t} - 1$, $\theta \equiv \dfrac{L_t}{L_{t-1}} - 1.$; p_t is the current price of the goods produced in the economy; g_t is the real government expenditure per an efficient unit labor force; L_t is the total labor force measured by the efficiency unit;

ρ is the inflation rate; and θ denotes the degree of progress in dexterity nurtured by the employer's investment.[3]

12.2.2 *Agent Maximization Problems*

Employers

An employer is assumed to be impurely altruistic. From Eq. (12.1), their utility can be described as:

$$u\left(\pi_t - \phi(\theta)L_{t-1}^S - m, \frac{m}{1+\rho} + \pi_{t+1}\right), \tag{12.4}$$

$$\pi_t \equiv y_t - k_t - w_t^R\left[L_{t-1}^S + L_t^U\right] \tag{12.5}$$

Where: ϕ denotes the average adjustment cost for educating and nurturing the dexterity, defined as: $\Phi(L_t^S, L_{t-1}^S) \equiv \phi(\theta)L_{t-1}^S,\ \ \phi' > 0, \phi'' > 0$, and where Φ is the total adjustment cost, while π_t is profits in terms of the current good.

Furthermore, since unemployment prevails in the economy, the equilibrium real wage stays at the real reservation wage, for simplicity w_t^R.

The first argument in Eq. (12.4) denotes the current consumption of a young employer. This actor can consume goods that amount to profits that deduct the sum of costs for educational investment $\phi(\theta)L_{t-1}$ and the real monetary saving preparing for retirement m_t. The second argument in Eq. (12.4) is therefore *effective* future consumption. Since an employer is assumed to be an impure altruist, they feel felicity from a descendant's consumption. This effect appears in π_{t+1}. The other term, $\frac{m_t}{1+\rho}$, represents employers' own consumption during old age, financed by money carried over.

The maximization problem comprises two steps. As the first step, an employer maximizes profits with respect to $\left(k_t, L_t^U\right)$. Lifetime utility is optimized on (m,θ) as the second step. The solution of the first step is as follows. By maximizing (Eq. 12.5) with respect to $\left(k_t, L_t^U\right)$ and applying Euler's theorem:

$$\pi_t^* = \frac{\partial F}{\partial \Psi} \cdot \frac{\partial \Psi}{\partial L} \cdot L_{t-1}^S, \tag{12.6}$$

$$\frac{\partial}{\partial k} F\left(\Psi\left(\frac{k_t^*}{L_t^*}, \frac{L_{t-1}^S}{L_t^*}\right), 1\right) = 1, \tag{12.7}$$

[3] θ is the growth rate of total employed individuals in the efficiency unit. However, this rate becomes the same rate as the progress in dexterity, $\frac{L_t^S}{L_{t-1}^S}$, since the analysis is confined to the steady state where relative prices are kept constant.

$$F\left(\Psi\left(\frac{k_t^*}{L_t^*},\frac{L_{t-1}^S}{L_t^*}\right),1\right)-\frac{\partial}{\partial[L_{t-1}^S/L_t]}F\left(\Psi\left(\frac{k_t}{L_t},\frac{L_{t-1}^S}{L_t}\right),1\right)\Big|_{L_t=L_t^*}^{k_t=k_t^*}\cdot\frac{L_{t-1}^S}{L_t^*}=w_t^R. \quad (12.8)$$

Equation (12.7) implies that marginal productivity of physical capital is equal to its real price. Similarly, Eq. (12.8) means that marginal productivity of unskilled workers is equal to the equilibrium real wage. Here, from Eq. (12.7) the value of $\Psi\left(\frac{k_t^*}{L_t^*},\frac{L_{t-1}^S}{L_t^*}\right)$ is the same at any equilibrium point, so are $F\left(\Psi\left(\frac{k_t^*}{L_t^*},\frac{L_{t-1}^S}{L_t^*}\right),1\right)$ and $\frac{\partial F}{\partial \Psi}\cdot\frac{\partial \Psi}{\partial L}$. On differentiating Eq. (12.8):[4]

$$\frac{dL^*}{dw_t^R}<0. \quad (12.9)$$

Equation (12.9) implies that an employer must raise the marginal product of labor when the real reservation wage becomes dear. The unskilled worker's marginal product of labor decreases with employment level as illustrated by Fig. 12.1. Accordingly, more unskilled workers are employed when the real reservation wage decreases.

Next, the argument moves to the second step of maximization. By differentiating Eq. (12.4) with respect to m and θ:

$$\frac{\partial u}{\partial c_1}=\frac{1}{1+\rho}\cdot\frac{\partial u}{\partial c_2} \quad (12.10)$$

$$\frac{\partial u}{\partial c_1}\cdot\phi'(\theta^*)=\frac{\partial u}{\partial c_2}\cdot\frac{\partial \pi}{\partial L_t}=\frac{\partial u}{\partial c_2}\cdot\left[\frac{\partial F}{\partial \Psi}\cdot\frac{\partial \Psi}{\partial L}\right]. \quad (12.11)$$

Equation (12.10) shows that the marginal substitution rate of current good to future good is equal to its relative price (i.e. the marginal hoarding cost of money). Equation (12.11) means that the marginal investment cost in terms of utility should be equal to its marginal benefit. Combining these equations:

$$\phi'(\theta^*)=[1+\rho]\cdot\left[\frac{\partial F}{\partial \Psi}\cdot\frac{\partial \Psi}{\partial L}\right]=\frac{\frac{\partial F}{\partial \Psi}\cdot\frac{\partial \Psi}{\partial L}}{\frac{1}{1+\rho}}. \quad (12.12)$$

[4] Note that the derivative with respect to $\frac{L_{t-1}^S}{L_t}$ of the right-hand side in Equation (12.8) is: $-\frac{\partial F}{\partial \Psi}\frac{\partial \Psi}{\partial K}+\left[\frac{\partial^2 F}{\partial \Psi^2}\cdot\frac{\partial \Psi}{\partial L}+\frac{\partial F}{\partial \Psi}\cdot\frac{\partial^2 \Psi}{\partial L^2}\right]\cdot\frac{L_{t-1}^S}{L_t^*}<0$. Thus, the marginal product of unskilled employees is diminishing.

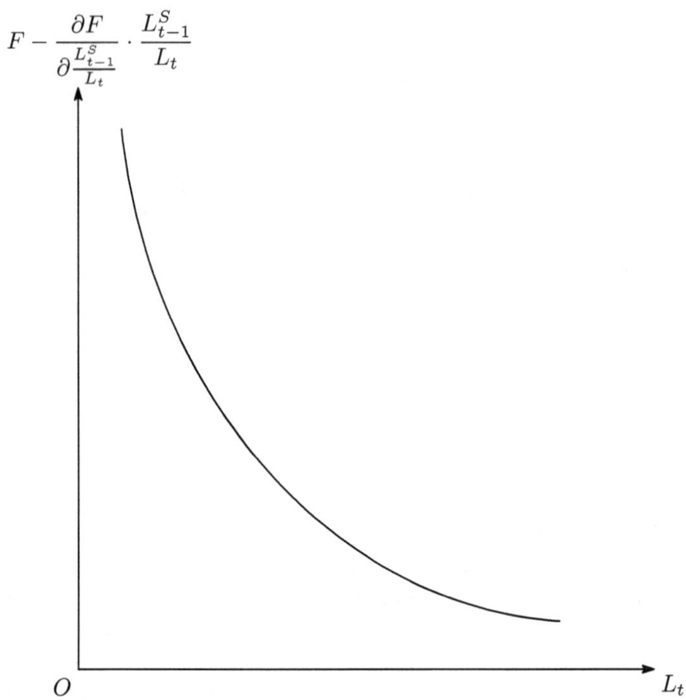

Fig. 12.1 The margina product of unskilled employee

Equation (12.12) is the investment function in this model. The right-hand side expresses the human capital marginal q, which was developed in the previous chapter and is the marginal revenue from nurturing the dexterity discounted by the rate of return for money $\frac{1}{1+\rho}$. In addition, since it is assumed that the utility function, u, is a homothetic utility function, the saving function, S^{ER}, becomes:

$$S^{ER} = s(\rho)\cdot\frac{\partial F}{\partial \Psi}\frac{\partial \Psi}{\partial L}\cdot L_{t-1}. \tag{12.13}$$

Furthermore, we assume that $s'(\rho) < 0$.

Employees Since the lifetime utility function of consumption is homothetic, the aggregate savings of employees S^{EE} is:

$$S^{ER} = s(\rho) w_t^R L_t = s(\rho)\frac{\partial F}{\partial L} L_t. \tag{12.14}$$

In addition, by using the indirect lifetime utility, IU_t (see the Mathematical Appendix in Chap. 2), the real reservation wage becomes:

$$IU_t = \frac{W_t^R}{\Lambda(p_t, p_{t+1})} = \frac{w_t^R}{\Lambda(1,\rho)} = f(\alpha) \quad \Rightarrow \quad w_t^R = f(\alpha)\cdot\Lambda(1,\rho). \tag{12.15}$$

Combining Eq. (12.15) with Eq. (12.8), the following fundamental equation concerning the dynamic motion of the equilibrium price sequence is obtained:

$$F\left(\Psi\left(\frac{k_t^*}{L_t^*}, \frac{L_{t-1}^S}{L_t^*}\right), 1\right) - \frac{\partial}{\partial[L_{t-1}^S / L_t]} F\left(\Psi\left(\frac{k_t}{L_t}, \frac{L_{t-1}^S}{L_t}\right), 1\right)\Big|_{L_t = L_t^*}^{k_t = k_t^*} \cdot \frac{L_{t-1}^S}{L_t^*} = f(\alpha)\cdot\Lambda(1,\rho^*) \tag{12.16}$$

Equation (12.16) is a variant of the fundamental equation derived in Chap. 2, and corresponds to the aggregate supply curve, which connects real NDP per capita, $\tilde{y}_t^N$, with the equilibrium inflation rate, ρ^*. Since the acceleration of inflation raises the real reservation wage, w_t^R, an employer is forced into more efficient production, which means heightening the *skill ratio*, $\frac{L_t^S}{L_t}$, by firing unskilled employees. Since $\Psi(\cdot)$ takes some constant value and $\frac{L_{t-1}^S}{L_t}$ is an increasing function of the inflation rate, ρ, from Eq. (12.16), $\frac{k_t^*}{L_t^*}$ becomes a decreasing function of ρ. Hence, the real NDP per capita, $\tilde{y}_t^N$, is:

$$\tilde{y}_t^N \equiv \frac{y_t^* - k_t}{L_t^*} = F\left(\Psi\left(\frac{k_t^*}{L_t^*}, \frac{L_{t-1}^S}{L_t^*}\right), 1\right) - \frac{k_t^*}{L_t^*}(\rho) \equiv y(\rho), \tag{12.17}$$

and an increasing function of the inflation rate as illustrated by Fig. 12.2. This is the aggregate supply function.

12.3 Market Equilibrium: The Relationship Between Market Competitiveness and the Autonomy of Capital Investment

12.3.1 The Equilibrium of the Economy

There are three markets in the model: the unskilled labor market, the goods market and money market. Using Walras' law, the equilibrium conditions for the unskilled labor market and the goods market can be concentrated. By adding (Eq. 12.13) and (Eq. 12.14), and applying Euler's theorem, the saving function per capita of the economy as a whole S_t is:

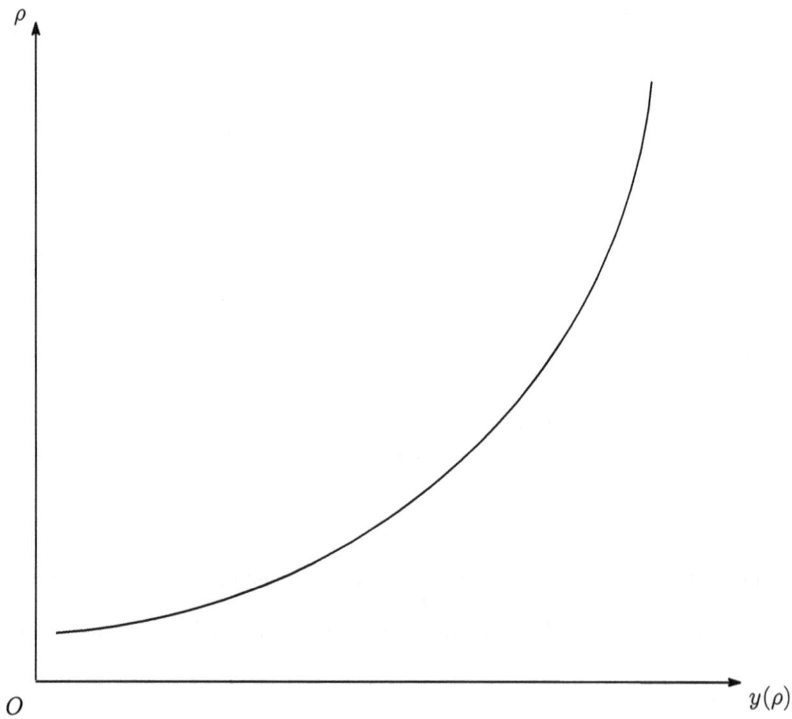

Fig. 12.2 The aggregate supply curve

$$S_t \equiv s(\rho)\left[\frac{y_t - k_t}{L_t^*}\right] \equiv s(\rho)\tilde{y}_t^N, \tag{12.18}$$

Next is the investment function, and to avoid unessential non-linearity in the investment function, it is assumed that the average adjustment cost function ϕ is an exponential function. That is:

$$\phi(\theta) = e^{\beta\theta}. \tag{12.19}$$

Equation (12.19) is illustrated by Fig. 12.3. The figure implies that not only the marginal adjustment cost increases with the growth rate, but also the adjustment cost itself is always positive even though the growth rate θ is negative. This property corresponds to the fact that costs are always incurred no matter how low the educational level. Then, from the optimality condition for the educational investment Eq. (12.12), the investment function I_t is derived as:

$$\iota \equiv \frac{I_t}{L_t^*} = \frac{1+\rho}{\beta}\cdot\left[\frac{\partial F}{\partial \Psi}\frac{\partial \Psi}{\partial L}\right]\cdot\frac{L_{t-1}}{L_t^*}. \tag{12.20}$$

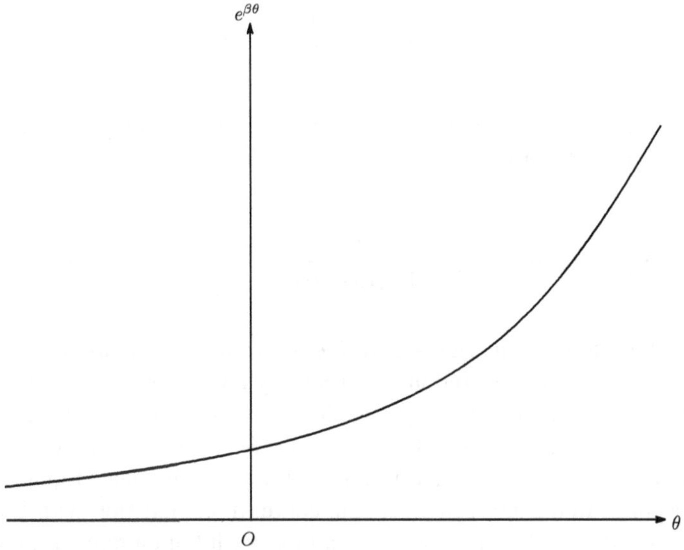

Fig. 12.3 The average adjustment cost function

Applying Euler's theorem to Eq. (12.20) and taking the definition of $\tilde{y}_t^N$ into consideration:

$$\iota(\rho) = \frac{1+\rho}{\beta} \cdot [\tilde{y}^N(\rho) - w^R(\rho)]. \tag{12.21}$$

Equation (12.21) has a clear economic implication for how inflation affects educational investment. The first effect is the reduction in opportunity cost for the investment. As inflation progresses, the rate of return for money decreases, which then stimulates educational investment. The second effect also operates in the same direction. Inflation raises the real reservation wage w^R. Since workers are assumed to be able to save their wage income only through money, the acceleration of inflation disrupts their wellbeing. Thus, they demand higher real wages, $w^R(\rho)$. However, inflation simultaneously increases real NDP per capita, $\tilde{y}^N(\rho)$, which is equal to sales per employee, and the latter effect dominates the former. Consequently, profits are heightened.[5] This stimulates investment.

To summarize, inflation stimulates education investment. This is partly because inflation lowers the opportunity cost for such investment, and partly because inflation heightens the profit rate. Furthermore, it is assumed here that unlike for the analysis in the next chapter, the growth rate of fiscal deficits per unit of labor measured in efficiency units is set at zero and $m = m_t = m_{t-1}$ holds. The government budget constraint (Eq. 12.3) is then transformed into:

[5] Note that an increase in the real reservation wage is dominated by $\tilde{y}^N(\rho)$ This assertion derives from the fact that $\frac{L_{t-1}^S}{L_t}$ is an increasing function of ρ.

$$g = [1 - \frac{1}{[1+\rho][1+\theta]}]m. \quad (12.22)$$

Equations (12.18), (12.21), and (12.22) lead to the following equilibrium condition for the good market normalized by the existing labor force in terms of efficiency unit, L_t^*:

$$s(\rho)\tilde{y}^N = \iota(\rho) + g + \frac{1}{[1+\rho][1+\theta]}m \Rightarrow s(\rho)\tilde{y}^N = \iota(\rho) + m, \quad (12.23)$$

Where: the third term of the right-hand side of the above equation in (12.23) is the expenditure of the older generation per efficiency unit of the labor force.

As far as the real cash balance per capita, m, is exogenously given, if the equilibrium inflation rate, ρ^*, is fixed, the equilibrium NDP per capita is determined so that the economy achieves equilibrium in the goods market.[6] Equation (12.23) thus corresponds to the aggregate demand curve. In conjunction with Eq. (12.23), Eqs. (12.17) and (12.12) determine the equilibrium inflation rate, ρ^*, the equilibrium employment level, L_t^*, and the equilibrium growth rate, θ^* for a given L_{t-1}.

12.3.2 Market Competitiveness and Fiscal Sustainability

Since it is apparent that the monetary growth rate under stationary equilibrium is equal to that of nominal NDP, $[1+\rho^*][1+\theta^*]$, the following theorem is obtained:

Theorem 12.1 *The growth of the monetary economy under perfect competition is sustainable in the sense that the ratio of public debts to nominal NDP (the ratio of the money stock to nominal NDP) is kept constant over time.*

The above theorem contrasts with the properties of the monetary growth model extended in the next chapter, in which the public debts-nominal NDP ratio is possibly critical for achieving economic growth. The decisive economic reason whether such a ratio is critical depends on whether employers are subject to an effective demand constraint.

When the adjustment cost function is a linear homogenous function (L_{t-1}^S, L_t), investment enables every employer to expand production steadily without facing demand constraints if markets are perfectly competitive. This is because an expansion in aggregate investment calls forth further expansion autonomously because adjustment costs and earned quasi-rent increase proportionately to accumulated human capital in equilibrium. It immediately implies that the aggregate human capital investment embodies an endogenous force of economic growth as an incessant effective demand stimulus.

[6] As discussed in Chap. 2, *confidence* in money is assumed. However, instead of using the preceding cases, without loss of generality, assume that individuals rationally believe that the current purchasing power of money, $\frac{1}{p_t}$ is unaffected by the change of current nominal money supply M_t. In this situation the government can control the real cash balance.

By contrast, consider the case that the educational investment is constrained by effective demand. In such a case, even if human capital is temporally accumulated, the actual investment expenditure never increases autonomously, and is thwarted sooner or later. Thus, investment ceases to be the driving force of economic growth in the sense that the autonomous increase in investment creates further effective demand. In other words, human capital investment does not have enough power to create new additional demand per se. Although investment enables every employer to reduce production costs, such benefits diminish and approach zero because production opportunities are limited by the level of effective demand. Since there is always a positive marginal adjustment cost for an investment, cost-reducing investments cease in the long run. Thus, other exogenous expansionary shocks, such as an acceleration in fiscal expenditure, are indispensable for sustaining economic growth. Accordingly, fiscal deficits and the public debts-nominal NDP ratio become critical, as will be proved in the next chapter.

To summarize, when goods are standardized, markets are competitive, and production and investment adjustment cost functions are linear homogeneous, the constraint of aggregate demand, to which capital investment is subject, becomes ineffective. Thus, human capital investment is empowered enough to create new demand by itself and will heighten fiscal sustainability.

12.3.3 Fiscal and Monetary Policy, Inflation, and the Economic Growth Rate

In this section, how fiscal and monetary policy affects the equilibrium economic growth rate via a change in the inflation rate is considered. There are two opposite cases where such macroeconomic policy affects economic growth. One is that an expansionary fiscal and/or monetary policy is harmful to growth. The other case is that such policies have an enhancing effect, which will be analyzed in Chap. 13. This chapter deals with the harmful case.

From the stability condition of the goods market (see Fig. 12.4), it is presumed that:

$$s'(\rho^*)\tilde{y}^f - \iota'(\rho^*) < 0 \tag{12.24}$$

This implies that an increase in the real cash balance raises the opportunity cost for educational investment as long as money is in confidence. It must be noted that a kind of *asset crowding out* occurs through an expansion of fiscal expenditure. Asset crowding out is defined as:

Definition 12.1
Asset crowding out occurs whenever an increase in the supply of an asset raises its own rate of return, and curtails the demand for other assets.

Following Eq. (12.24), the harmful case is illustrated by Fig. 12.5. Curve *AS* is the aggregate supply curve, which is expressed by Eq. (12.17). Curve *AD* is the

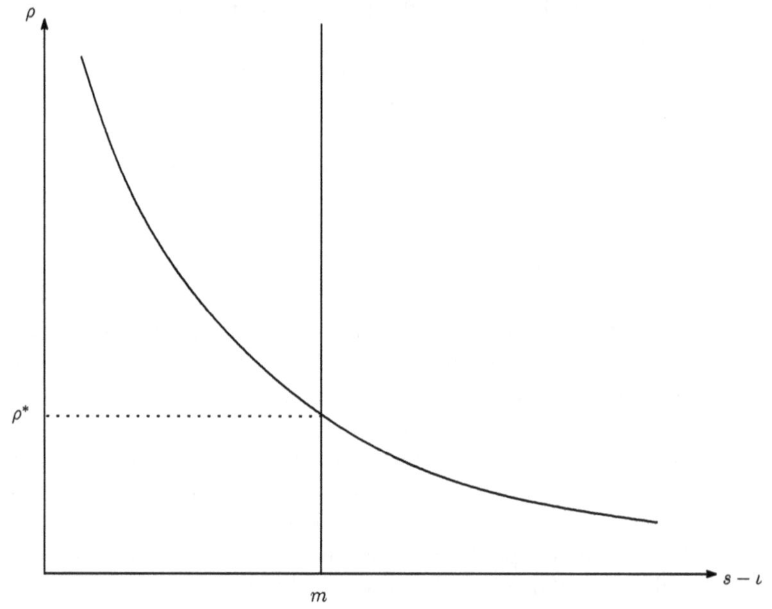

Fig. 12.4 The equilibrium of the good market

aggregate demand curve, which corresponds to Eq. (12.23). A stability condition for the economy as a whole requires that Curve *AC* should be steeper than Curve *AD*, as indicated by arrows in Fig. 12.5. Now, assume that the real cash balance is increased by an expansionary policy. Then, Curve *AD* shifts to the right, and the equilibrium point of the economy moves from Point E_0 to E_1. Thus, an expansionary policy causes disinflation and lowers real NDP per capita.

It should also be noted here that disinflation retards economic growth because it heightens the opportunity cost for investment. That is, economic growth is conversely hindered by asset crowding out. Now, this result seems rather strange because the inflation rate becomes lower despite monetary expansion. However, such a property of the model gives insights useful for understanding the current situation in most advanced economies. While the governments of such economies adopt prominent monetary expansion, disinflation advances and economic growth are retarded. The critical causes of this pathology are the deep confidence in money, which brings about asset crowding out in the sense of Definition 12.1, and the adjacent disinflation, when the condition in Eq. (12.23) is upheld.

To summarize:

Theorem 12.2

If Eq. (12.23) *and the economy is stable even under stationary expectations concerning* (ρ_t, y_t), *monetary expansion is always harmful for economic growth because disinflation advances, and the opportunity cost for educational investment becomes more expensive.*

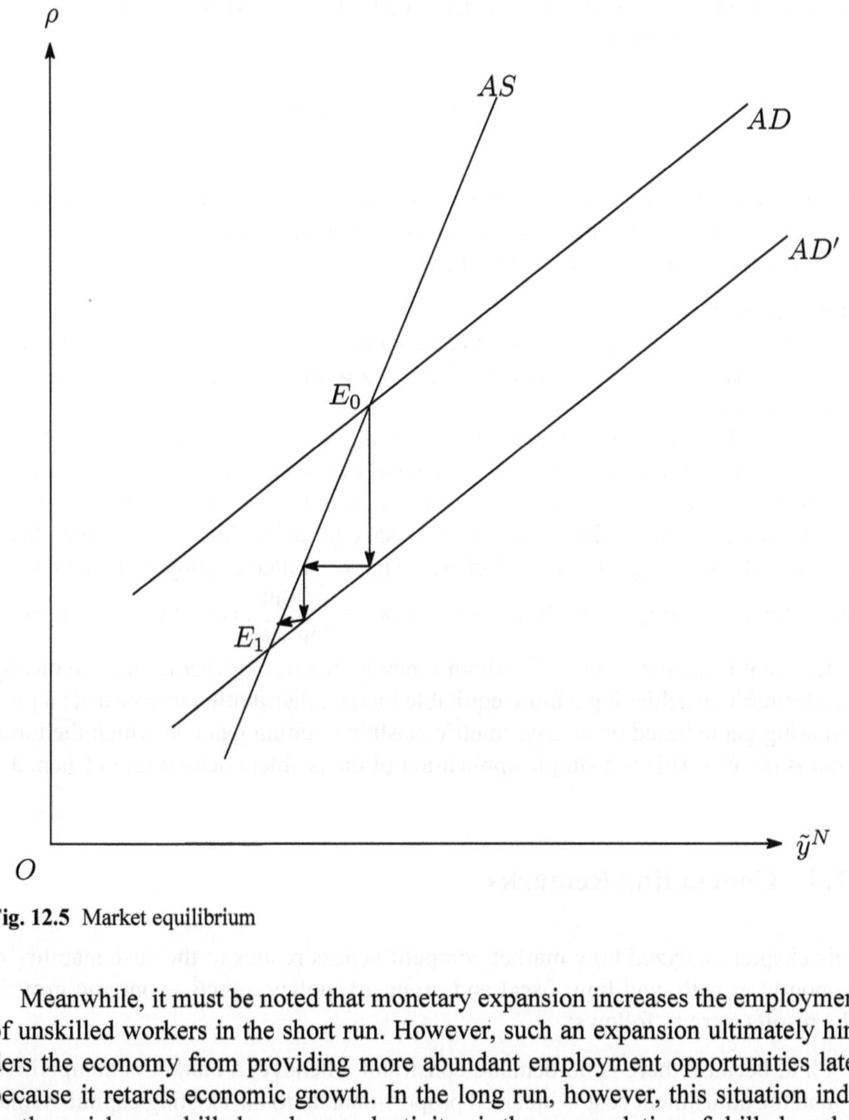

Fig. 12.5 Market equilibrium

Meanwhile, it must be noted that monetary expansion increases the employment of unskilled workers in the short run. However, such an expansion ultimately hinders the economy from providing more abundant employment opportunities later because it retards economic growth. In the long run, however, this situation indirectly enriches unskilled worker productivity via the accumulation of skilled worker dexterity.

12.3.4 Economic Welfare and the Fairness of Income Distribution

This section considers the welfare of the economy. Since the equilibrium real wage stays at the real reservation wage, there emerges no surplus on the side of employees. Hence, the analysis can be concentrated with the surplus of an employer. Since the lifetime utility of an employer is denoted by Eqs. (12.4) and (12.5), by deploying the envelope theorem:

$$\frac{dU^*}{dL_{t-1}} = \frac{\partial u}{\partial c_1} \cdot \left[\frac{\partial F}{\partial \Psi} \frac{\partial \Psi}{\partial L} \right] > 0. \tag{12.25}$$

Because the efficiency level of skilled workers, L_{t-1}, grows at the rate θ^* in equilibrium, economic growth enriches the employer stratum, and their economic welfare improves along with economic growth. Thus:

Theorem 12.3
If the government wisely manages fiscal and monetary policy in accordance with existing economic structures and heightens the growth rate, economic welfare improves dynamically.

Nevertheless, it must be noted that income disparity is problematic under the existing system. Employees, who are a large part of society, cannot share the fruits of economic growth even if they develop additional skills. As noted in Chap. 3 and 11, a profits-investment sharing system is necessary for achieving fairer income distribution while retaining the same efficiency. That is, skilled employees receive some part of the profits originating from nurtured skills, $\frac{\partial F}{\partial \Psi} \frac{\partial \Psi}{\partial L}$, in return for a part of the educational investment cost, $e^{\beta\theta}$, which is newly incurred by them. Mathematically, it is desirable in achieving a more equitable income distribution to construct a profit-sharing game based on an asymmetric Nash bargaining game at which the threat point is $(0, w^R)$. This is a simple application of the problem dealt with in Chap. 3.

12.4 Concluding Remarks

This chapter analyzed how market competitiveness relates to the sustainability of economic growth, and how fiscal and monetary policy affects economic growth. The results were as follows:

1. First, because there is no demand constraint whenever a market is competitive, and the adjustment cost is incurred proportionately to the existing capital, human capital investment creates additional effective demand in the future by itself. Such a fact implies that an economy steadily grows without unsustainable help from its government;
2. In turn, as will be shown in Chap. 13, if goods are differentiated and monopolistic competition prevails in goods markets, every employer faces an effective demand constraint. This implies that employers perceive the limit of their sales, and the incentive of the investment changes from capacity expanding to cost reducing under a given production level. Since there is a limit to cost reduction investment owing to the existence of non-negligible adjustment costs, human capital investment ceases to expand autonomously, and the economy falls into

zero growth in the long run whenever every employer faces a demand constraint. In this sense, market competitiveness plays a key role in maintaining a stable fiscal balance with moderate economic growth;

3. Inflation stimulates economic growth via two paths. One is that the opportunity cost for the educational investment is lowered by accelerating inflation, and hence enhances economic growth. The other is that the real profit rate is heightened by accelerating inflation because an increase in efficiency of production is necessitated by a more costly real wage. This owes its substance to the fact that employees confer not only the current but also future consumption when they decide whether to work. The cost of the real wage of unskilled workers makes the dexterity of skilled employees a more precious asset. As such, this effect also enhances educational investment. Thus, inflation advances economic growth;
4. However, it must be noted that inflation is not necessarily brought about by monetary expansion as the current worldwide experience suggests. That is, disinflation is prominent even under some radical stimulating monetary policies. When the real cash balance increases in line with keeping income per capita constant, the inflation rate, which is the inverse of the rate of return for money, decreases to equilibrate the goods market (equivalent to the internal loan market). This means that an expansionary monetary policy conversely lowers the inflation rate and curtails economic growth;
5. The combination of extremely expansionary monetary policies, advances in disinflation, and a slowdown of economic growth is one of the prominent features of advanced economies. It is a blind faith in the quantity theory of money that a monetary expansion always accelerates the inflation rate. The model derived in this chapter succeeds in capturing such pathology, although it is beyond the scope of the model whether an economy's fiscal sustainability is preserved under a radical and reckless fiscal-monetary policy. This problem will also be analyzed in the next chapter.

References

Acemoglu D (2009) Introduction to modern economic growth. Princeton University Press, Princeton

Dixit A, Pindyck R (1994) Investment under uncertainty. Princeton University Press, Princeton

Otaki M (2013) On the endogenous sustainability of economic growth: why is the scale of government enlarged? Theor Econ Lett 3:159–163

Otaki M, Tamura M (2013) Monetary growth theory under perfect and monopolistic competitions. Theor Econ Lett 3:216–219

Uzawa H (1969) Time preference and the Penrose effect in a two-class model of economic growth. J Polit Econ 77:628–52

Chapter 13
A Keynesian Monetary Growth Model Under Monopolistic Competition: Is Economic Growth Sustainable Without Government Help?

13.1 Introduction

Almost every developed economy experiences fiscal deficits and/or the accumulation of public debt. What do such apparently serious economic difficulties stem from? This chapter approaches this political-economic issue by applying a new type of Keynesian economic-growth model under monopolistic competition. This model is completely consistent with standard neoclassical microeconomic postulates, and presumes the common production function, which puts much importance on human capital development. The crucial factor is the potential excess production capacity that is delivered by dexterity enhancement, and/or cost-reduction investment. Whenever each employer faces a downward-sloping demand curve, the location of which is determined by effective demand in monopolistic competition, this implies that the business opportunity is ultimately limited by the effective demand economy as a whole.

Thus, it is urgently necessary for each employer to improve the dexterity of their skilled employees and aim at effective wage-cost reduction. Although such an economic motive ceaselessly works, it depends on the level of effective demand. It is certain that human capital investment can conversely stimulate effective demand as a whole. However, such empowerment gradually falls in line with the adjustment process of cost reduction. This is because opportunities for cost reduction through nurturing dexterity are limited by the level of effective demand itself.

Accordingly, unlike the perfect competition case analyzed in Chap. 12, human capital investment abdicates the role of the driving force of economic growth. That is, a monetary economy under monopolistic competition is unable to grow using its own inherent labor force. For the expansion of the effective demand that matches the aggregate production potential, the enlargement of fiscal expenditure with a non-negligible budget deficit is unavoidable. That is, governments are forced to be more active to secure stable jobs evenly for employees who are threatened by mass unemployment under the intrinsically stagnant capital investment. In summary,

M. Otaki, *Keynesian Economics and Price Theory*,
Advances in Japanese Business and Economics 7, DOI 10.1007/978-4-431-55345-8_13

economic growth in a monetary market economy under monopolistic competition is unsustainable per se, and comes to rely heavily on governmental economic activities.

It is also noteworthy that Buchanan and Wagner (1977), even if in a rather superficial and journalistic way, suggested that Keynes and his successors, including voters, underestimated the true social cost of fiscal expenditure, and that this factor exacerbated budget deficits. However, according to the model put forward in this chapter, the enlargement of government is inevitable given the genetic properties of the monetary market economy under monopolistic competition, and is not subject to irrational recognition and/or acquisitive political rent seeking.

In standard neoclassical economic-growth theory, however (Solow 1956; Swan 1956; Romer 1986), such a tragedy never occurs. This is because the concept of effective demand is not included in these theories. Incomes are determined by the amount of existing production resources, and all savings are automatically absorbed by capital investment, independently of income level. However, as shown in Chap. 2, which is mainly based on Otaki (2007, 2009), these optimistic properties of the model are not preserved in the monetary economy where money possesses an intrinsic value. The reason why money circulates beyond generations is the *confidence* in its intrinsic value held by these generations. That is, the function of the monetary economy decisively depends on the belief that the future purchasing power of money will remain stable. Since the future price level (the inverse of the purchasing power of money) affects the current price via current wage-price setting, *confidence* in the intrinsic value of money quite naturally leads to *endogenous* current price inflexibility.

Given this situation, it is rather a rare case when full-employment equilibrium is attained within a monetary economy. Unless ample money is provided via fiscal and/or monetary policy, the principle of effective demand works and incomes and savings are subject to the volume of capital investment. To summarize, the growth theory outlined here deals with the economic phenomena in a monetary economy, but the scope of the neoclassical growth theory is limited to a barter economy.

The previous chapter also analyzed a Keynesian economic-growth model. However, that model assumed perfect competition, unlike the model developed in this chapter. Since there is no demand constraint in that case, an economy achieves steady growth and high employment without accelerating government help per capita. Thus product differentiation, which is bound up with economic development, becomes a critical factor that determines the fiscal and/or, more broadly, the macroeconomic sustainability of an economy.

The remainder of this chapter is in three sections. In Sect. 13.2, using a standard overlapping generations (OLG) model in production economy, a Keynesian growth model with money and tangible/intangible assets improving labor productivity is constructed. Section 13.3 deals with some comparative statics and induces some important policy implications of this model, and Sect. 13.4 provides brief concluding remarks.

13.2 The Model

13.2.1 Structure of the Model

The deployed model basically depends on Otaki (2013). Consider a two-period OLG model with an infinite time horizon. In this economy there are three social strata: employers, skilled and unskilled employees. Each employer is dynastic and specializes in producing a differentiated good z. Employers maximize their own lifetime utility compared with the benefits for descendants that are delivered by the accumulation of tangible/intangible assets derived from the dexterity of their skilled employees. Their income is the profits of their firm when they are young. This assumption is based on *impure altruism* (Acemoglu 2009). For a discussion on the neoclassical model based on impure altruism see, for example, Andreoni (1989), Banerjee and Newman (1991, 1993), Galor and Zeira (1993), and Aghion and Bolton (1997). However, the policy implications of their research are entirely different to those derived from the model presented here.

For the model presented here, the number of skilled employees is considered to be limited, and that of unskilled employees unlimited. For simplicity, it is assumed that conversion between skilled and unskilled employees is not feasible. Both types of employee also maximize lifetime utility. They can provide unit labor only when they are young and preparing for retirement by hoarding money. It is assumed then that the disutility of labor is β. There are three kinds of market in this economy: the goods market, the labor market, and the money market. Based on Walras' law, the equilibrium condition for the money market can be skipped. In addition, assume that real government expenditure is not sufficient, and imperfect employment equilibrium prevails. Then, the labor market is in equilibrium when the equilibrium nominal wage is equalized to the nominal reservation wage, as outlined below.

Goods are differentiated within the interval $Z \equiv [0,1]$. The lifetime utility function from consumption is identical between strata and is defined as:

$$U_t \equiv u(c_{1t}, c_{2t+1}), \quad c_{it} \equiv [\int_0^1 [c_{it}(z)]^{1-\eta^{-1}} dz]^{\frac{1}{1-\eta^{-1}}}, \quad \eta > 1, \tag{13.1}$$

Where: c_{it} is the aggregate consumption level of an individual who belongs to the i-th generation during period t; and $u(\cdot)$ is a linear homogenous and concave utility function of lifetime consumption.

The demand function $D_t(z)$ for good $z \in Z$ then becomes:

$$D_t(z) = \left[\frac{p_t(z)}{p_t}\right]^{-\eta} \tilde{y}_t^N, \quad p_t \equiv \left[\int_0^1 [p_t(z)]^{1-\eta} dz\right]^{\frac{1}{1-\eta}} \tag{13.2}$$

Where: $p_t(z)$ denotes the price of good z during period t, p_t is the price index derived from instantaneous utility maximization, and $\tilde{y}_t^N$ is the real effective demand deflated by p_t, which is equal to real Net Domestic Product (NDP).

Furthermore, since the lifetime utility function is homothetic, the aggregate saving function, S_t, becomes:

$$S_t = s(\rho)\tilde{y}_t^N. \tag{13.3}$$

Where: ρ is the inflation rate.

All of the above concern common properties across strata. Next, the peculiar decision process of each stratum is revealed.

13.2.2 Employees

An employee faces the decision problem whether they participate or not. As discussed above, in any imperfect employment equilibrium, the real reservation wage is equalized to the disutility of labor, and thus any employee is indifferent to whether to work. The indirect lifetime utility, IU_t, derived from consumption is expressed by:

$$IU_t = \frac{W_t}{\Lambda(p_t, p_{t+1})}, \tag{13.4}$$

Where: Λ is a linear homogenous function, which corresponds to a lifetime price index.

Using Eq. (13.4), we can show that the nominal reservation wage, W_t^R, satisfies the following equation[1]:

$$\frac{W_t^R}{\Lambda(p_t, p_{t+1})} = \beta \quad \Rightarrow W_t^R = \Lambda(p_t, p_{t+1})\beta. \tag{13.5}$$

13.2.3 Employers

Assume that the gain obtained from the development of skilled employees' dexterity is equivalent to the same amount of future consumption, although the former is attributed to the next generation. In addition, assume savings per employer are so abundant that there is no necessity for external borrowing. Since the short-run profit maximization problem does not affect descendant utility as shown in Chap. 12, the discussion begins with this problem.

Short-Run Profit Maximization Assume the same type production function as that deployed in Chaps. 11 and 12. That is:

$$y_t = F\left(\Psi\left(k_t, L_{t-1}^S\right), L_t\right), \tag{13.6}$$

[1] For simplicity, it is assumed that the disutility of labor increases proportionately to the level of dexterity that an employee possesses.

Where: (k_t, L_{t-1}^S, L_t) is deployed physical capital, which entirely depletes during one period, number of skilled employees, and total employment during period t, respectively; and F and Ψ are linear homogenous functions.

Real NDP, $\tilde{y}_t^N$, can be written as:

$$\tilde{y}_t^N = F\left(\Psi\left(\frac{k_t}{L_t}, \frac{L_{t-1}^S}{L_t}\right), 1\right)L_t - k_t \tag{13.7}$$

Since F and Ψ are linear homogenous functions, cost minimization behavior implies:

$$\frac{\partial F}{\partial \Psi}\frac{\partial \Psi}{\partial k}\left(\Psi\left(\frac{k_t}{L_t}, \frac{L_{t-1}^S}{L_t}\right), 1\right) = 1, \tag{13.8}$$

$$\lambda\left[F - \left[\frac{\partial F}{\partial \Psi}\frac{\partial \Psi}{\partial k}\cdot\frac{k_t}{L_t} + \frac{\partial F}{\partial \Psi}\frac{\partial \Psi}{\partial L}\cdot\frac{L_{t-1}^S}{L_t}\right]\right] = w_t^R, \tag{13.9}$$

Where: λ is the Lagrangean multiplier.

It should be noted that Eq. (13.8) implies that $\Psi\left(\frac{k_t}{L_t}, \frac{L_{t-1}^S}{L_t}\right)$ takes the same value when evaluated in any optimal plan. Accordingly, it is also possible to regard: $\frac{\partial F}{\partial \Psi}, \frac{\partial F}{\partial \Psi}\frac{\partial \Psi}{\partial k}$ and $\frac{\partial F}{\partial \Psi}\frac{\partial \Psi}{\partial L}$ as having the same constant value in any optimal plan.

Equations (13.7), (13.8), and (13.9) are functions of $\left(\frac{k_t}{L_t}, \frac{L_{t-1}^S}{L_t}, \lambda\right)$ for a given $\left(\tilde{y}_t^N, w_t^R\right)$. Deploying Euler's theorem, Eq. (13.9) can be rewritten as:

$$\lambda\left[F\left(\Psi\left(\frac{k_t}{L_t}, \frac{L_{t-1}^S}{L_t}\right), 1\right) - \Psi\left(\frac{k_t}{L_t}, \frac{L_{t-1}^S}{L_t}\right)\cdot\frac{\partial F}{\partial \Psi}\right] = w_t^R.$$

Thus, only λ is a function of w_t^R as:

$$\lambda = \frac{w_t^R}{\left[F\left(\Psi\left(\frac{k_t}{L_t}, \frac{L_{t-1}^S}{L_t}\right), 1\right) - \Psi\left(\frac{k_t}{L_t}, \frac{L_{t-1}^S}{L_t}\right)\cdot\frac{\partial F}{\partial \Psi}\right]}.$$

Other endogenous variable $\left(\frac{k_t}{L_t}, \frac{L_t^S}{L_t}\right)$ are independent of w_t^R. This assertion is related to the fact that Eq. (13.8) hold.

Differentiating Eq. (13.7) and applying the envelope theorem:

$$\left[F\left(\Psi\left(\frac{k_t}{L_t},\frac{L_{t-1}^S}{L_t}\right),1\right)-\Psi\left(\frac{k_t}{L_t},\frac{L_{t-1}^S}{L_t}\right)\cdot\frac{\partial F}{\partial \Psi}\right]dL_t=-\frac{\partial F}{\partial \Psi}\frac{\partial \Psi}{\partial L}dL_{t-1}^S+d\,\tilde{y}_t^N. \quad (13.10)$$

Thus, from Eq. (13.10), the demand function of total employment, L_t, becomes:

$$L_t=L(\tilde{y}_t^N,L_{t-1}^S),\qquad \frac{\partial L}{\partial \tilde{y}_t^N}>0,\qquad \frac{\partial L}{\partial L_{t-1}^S}<0. \quad (13.11)$$

Furthermore, assume that:

$$\frac{\partial^2 L}{\partial\left[\tilde{y}_t^N\right]^2}>0,\ \frac{\partial^2 L}{\partial L_{t-1}^S\partial \tilde{y}_t^N}<0,\ \frac{\partial^2 L}{\partial\left[L_{t-1}^S\right]^2}>0,\text{ and }\lim_{L_{t-1}^S\to\infty}\frac{\partial L}{\partial L_{t-1}^S}=0 \quad (13.12)$$

Equation (13.12) means that the short-run marginal cost curve is upward sloping, and that the short-run marginal cost is economized by an increase in skilled employees measured by the efficiency unit.

Based on the demand function for good z (Eqs. 13.2 and 13.5) concerning the nominal reservation wage, the current period profit maximization under a symmetric equilibrium implies:

$$p_t(z)=\frac{W_t^R}{1-\eta^{-1}}\cdot\frac{\partial L}{\partial \tilde{y}_t^N}\quad\Rightarrow\quad 1=\frac{\Lambda(1,\rho)\beta}{1-\eta^{-1}}\cdot\frac{\partial L}{\partial \tilde{y}_t^N} \quad (13.13)$$

This is a variant of the fundamental equation formulated in Chap. 2. Equation (13.13) also corresponds to the aggregate supply curve in this chapter as illustrated by Fig. 13.1. When inflation accelerates and the real reservation wage rises, the employment level is lowered. Thus, the aggregate supply curve *AS* is downward sloping.[2]

The Long Run Maximization on Human Capital Investment Under the two assumptions outlined at the beginning of this section, it is possible to separate an employer's saving decision from that for capital investment, because there is no substantive difference between money hoarding and capital investment. An employer's decision becomes: (i) how much should be saved to maximize lifetime utility, and (ii) given optimal saving, what level of savings should be allotted to capital investment.

The first-step optimization problem expressed in (13.3) has already been solved. Since, by assumption, the second-step optimization does not directly affect the first-

[2] In Chap. 12, the aggregate supply function is upward sloping. Here, the independent variable of the aggregate supply function is the real NDP *per capita* in Chap. 12, and the *level* of the real GDP in Chap. 13.

Fig. 13.1 The aggregate supply curve

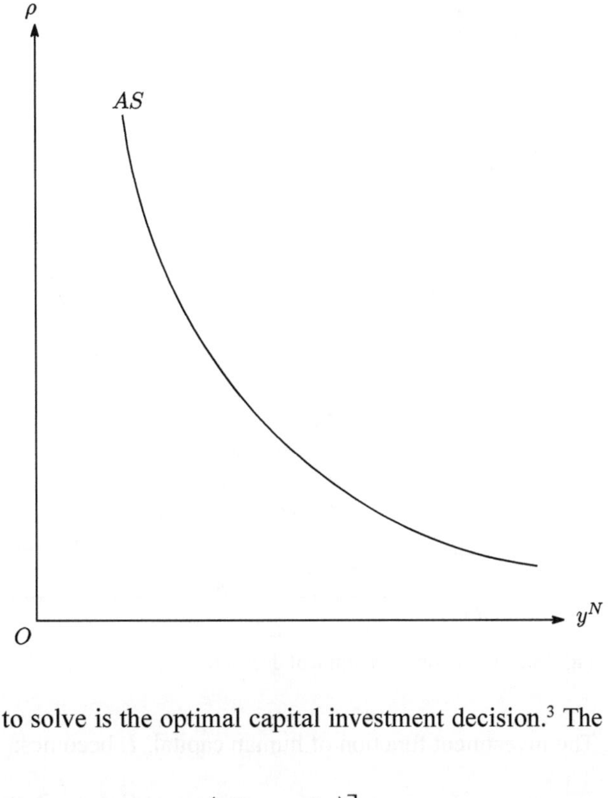

step problem, what is left to solve is the optimal capital investment decision.[3] The problem is formatted as:

$$\max_{g_t}\left[-e^{\gamma g_t}L_{t-1}^S-\rho_t\beta\cdot\Lambda(1,\rho_t)L\left(\tilde{y}_{t+1}^N,g_tL_{t-1}^S\right)\right],\quad \gamma>0, \tag{13.14}$$

Where: $e^{\gamma g_t}L_{t-1}$ is the same adjustment cost function for human capital investment as adopted in Chap. 12, and g_t is the progress rate of the dexterity embodied by skilled employees, which is defined as:

$$g_t \equiv \frac{L_t^S}{L_{t-1}^S}.$$

It must also be noted that the function is linear homogenous on $\left(L_{t-1}^S, L_t^S\right)$. The first term in Eq. (13.14) is the cost of capital investment that enhances the dexterity of skilled employees. The second term denotes the total wage cost that will be economized by capital investment.

The first-order condition for Eq. (13.14) is thus:

$$\gamma e^{\gamma g_t}=-\rho_t\cdot\Lambda(1,\rho_t)\frac{\partial}{\partial L_t}L\left(\tilde{y}_{t+1}^N,g_tL_{t-1}^S\right). \tag{13.15}$$

[3] For a more rigorous solution method, see Chap. 12.

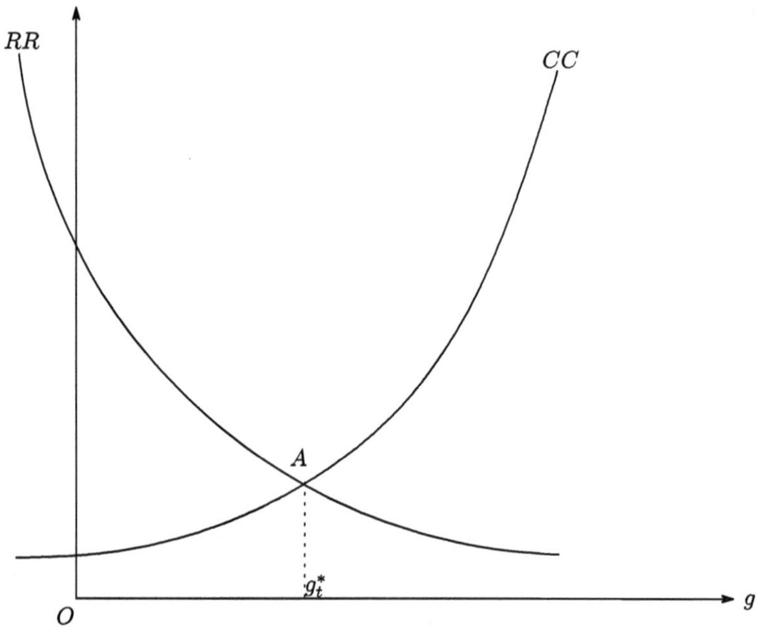

Fig. 13.2 The optimal investment decision

The investment function of human capital, I, becomes:

$$\frac{I_t}{L_{t-1}^S} = I\left(\rho_t, \tilde{y}_{t+1}^N, L_{t-1}^S\right) \equiv -\frac{\rho_t \cdot \Lambda(1,\rho_t)}{\gamma} \frac{\partial}{\partial L_{t-1}^S} L\left(\tilde{y}_{t+1}^N, g_t L_{t-1}^S\right),$$
$$\frac{\partial I}{\partial \rho} > 0, \frac{\partial I}{\partial \tilde{y}_{t+1}^N} > 0, \frac{\partial I}{\partial L_{t-1}^S} < 0 \tag{13.16}$$

Figure 13.2 illustrates the optimal decision on human capital investment. Curve *CC* corresponds to the left-hand side of Eq. (13.15), which is the marginal investment adjustment cost. The right-hand side in Eq. (13.15), which means the marginal revenue from the cost-reducing investment, is represented by Curve *RR*. The intersection, *A*, represents the optimal growth rate, g_t^*. Since marginal revenue is an increasing function of the inflation rate, ρ, Curve *RR* shifts to the right along with the acceleration of inflation, and hence human capital investment increases. The same logic is applied to the case of an increase in the real NDP, $\tilde{y}_t^N$.

For an arbitrarily fixed $(\rho_t, \tilde{y}_{t+1}^N)$, based on Eq. (13.12) the right-hand side in Eq. (13.15) converges to zero when $t \to \infty$ (see Fig. 13.3), because dexterity is deepened incessantly under the demand constraint, and hence the efficiency of the marginal investment falls without limits. This suggests that human capital investment becomes nil in the long run without the government's help under monopolistic competition.

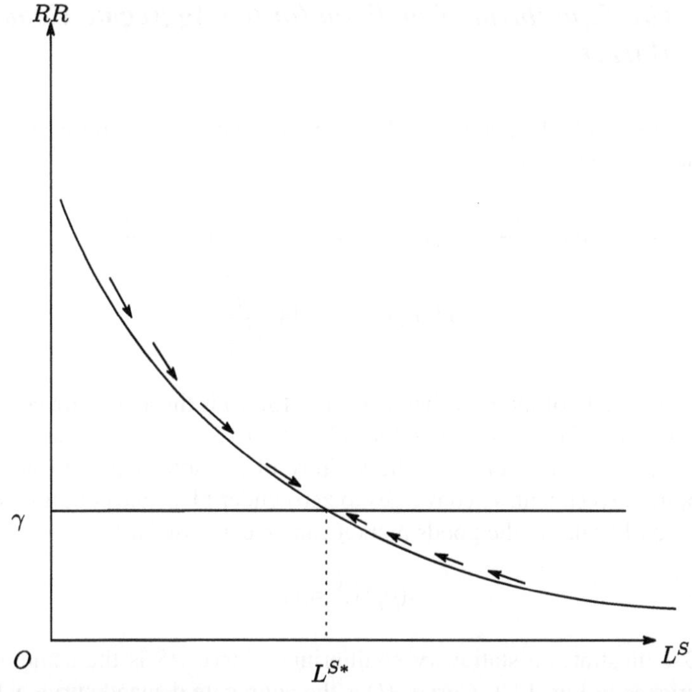

Fig. 13.3 The adjustment process

13.2.4 The Government

The government issues fiat money to finance its real expenditure, g_t. For simplicity, such expenditure is considered to be entirely wasteful and to contribute neither to an individual's utility nor the progress of labor productivity. The budget constraint can be written as:

$$g_t = \left[1 - \frac{P_{t-1}}{P_t}\right] m \tag{13.17}$$

Where: m is the real cash balance during period t, defined by $m \equiv \frac{M_t}{P_t}$. This is a measure of the burden of public debt, because an excessively high real cash balance possibly harms the *confidence* in money defined in Chap. 2. The right-hand side of Eq. (13.16) is the newly issued money that is equal to the budget deficit.

13.2.5 The Equilibrium Condition for the Aggregate Goods Market

From Eqs. (13.3), (13.16), and (13.17), the equilibrium condition for the aggregate goods market in the short run is:

$$\begin{aligned} s(\rho_t)\frac{\tilde{y}_t^N}{L_{t-1}^S} &= I\left(\rho_t, \tilde{y}_{t+1}^N, L_{t-1}^S\right) + \frac{g}{L_{t-1}^S} + \frac{P_{t-1}}{P_t}\frac{m}{L_{t-1}^S} \\ &= I\left(\rho_t, \tilde{y}_{t+1}^N, L_{t-1}^S\right) + \frac{m}{L_{t-1}^S}, \end{aligned} \tag{13.18}$$

where the third term of the right-hand side of (13.18) is the aggregate consumption of the older generation. As discussed in subsection 13.2.3 and also analyzed in the Mathematical Appendix below, at the vicinity of a stable stationary equilibrium, human capital investment, I, converges to zero under plausible conditions. Thus, a stationary equilibrium in the goods market can be expressed as:

$$s(\rho_t)\tilde{y}_t^N = m. \tag{13.19}$$

Figure 13.4 illustrates a stationary equilibrium. Curve *AS* is the same aggregate supply curve as in Fig. 13.1. Curve *AD* is the aggregate demand curve, which corresponds to Eq. (13.19). Point E_0 is a stable stationary equilibrium. It is clear from Fig. 13.4 that real NDP is constant over time as long as the real cash balance, m, is kept intact. This implies that the monetary economy cannot achieve additional growth in the long run until the real cash balance is increased by acceleration of the fiscal deficit. When the real cash balance, m, increases, Curve *AD* shifts to the right and real NDP, $\tilde{y}^{N*}$, also increases in conjunction with disinflation, which corresponds to the asset crowding-out phenomenon defined in Chap. 12 (Point E_1), as long as the rightward shift of Curve *AS* is not large. Thus:

Theorem 13.1
A monetary market economy under monopolistic competition cannot attain economic growth in the long run without accelerating fiscal deficits.

The difference between monopolistic and perfect competition is the existence of the demand constraint. As discussed in Chap. 12, employers never perceive the demand constraint, and make their investment decisions by conferring only relative prices under perfect competition. This enables autonomous human capital investment, which is free from the effective demand level. Thus, the investment becomes the driving force of economic growth in perfect competition. In contrast with the case of perfect competition, the level of effective demand limits the scale of a firm under monopolistic competition, even though production and investment adjustments are linear homogenous functions, and have potential for autonomous growth, unless the power of human capital investment is strong enough to create new effective demand and the stationary equilibrium is unstable. Otaki (2012) deals with an

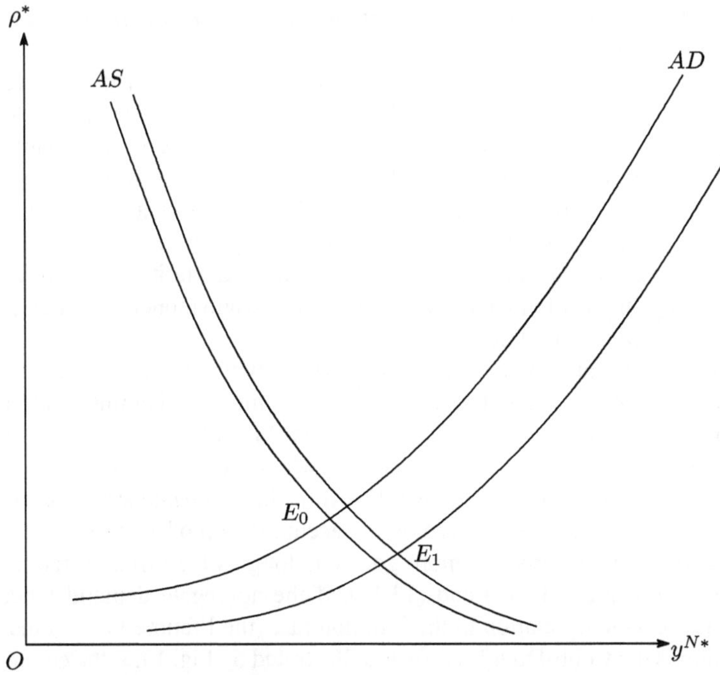

Fig. 13.4 The equilibrium of the economy

unstable growth case (endogenous growth case), although the production structure is more simplified.

In other words, as long as the stationary equilibrium is stable, capital investment, which is constrained by effective demand, is, by its nature, a cost-reducing investment via increases in employee skills. Accordingly, once an efficient production plan is realized under a given effective demand level, human capital investment that stems from such a motive becomes nil. This implies that human capital investment under monopolistic competition, unlike perfect competition, cannot enhance economic growth in the long run.

13.3 The Sustainability of Economic Growth and Fiscal Deficits

In this section, the sustainability of economic growth in the monetary market economy is discussed. Here, it must be noted that an increase in NDP does not necessarily mean an improvement in employment level. This is because the cost-reduction investment gained from nurturing the dexterity of skilled employees partially substitutes for unskilled employees. To begin with, it is necessary to define *sustainability*.

Definition 13.1 *Economic growth is sustainable only when it never reduces the level of employment.*

Although unemployment is voluntary in this model, it is not difficult to make it involuntary if the method developed by Otaki (2009) is used. Hence, at least for employees, economic growth is harmful unless the economy is sustainable. Note that even though the enhancing effect by an expansionary fiscal-monetary policy exceeds the negative effect of advancing disinflation, it is clear from Eq. (13.11) that the total employment level, L^*, does not necessary improve because unskilled employees are partly substituted by the progress in the dexterity of skilled employees. Hence, in general, whether an expansionary fiscal and monetary policy contributes to sustainability is ambiguous.

However, any progress in the educational system within a firm, which is summarized in the parameter γ, definitely endangers economic sustainability, even though this seems rather counterintuitive. It is clear from Fig. 13.3 that the dexterity possessed by skilled employees, L^{S*}, is deepened when γ takes a lower value for any fixed $(\rho^*, \tilde{y}^{N*})$. This causes a rightward shift of the aggregate supply curve, AS, because the marginal cost is lowered by the accumulation of dexterity, and an employer becomes able to produce more goods as long as the inflation rate remains unchanged. From Eqs. (13.11) and (13.13), if the aggregate demand function in Fig. 13.4 is inelastic in relation to the inflation rate (the lifetime utility function of consumption is the Cobb-Douglas form) as illustrated by Fig. 13.5, the employment

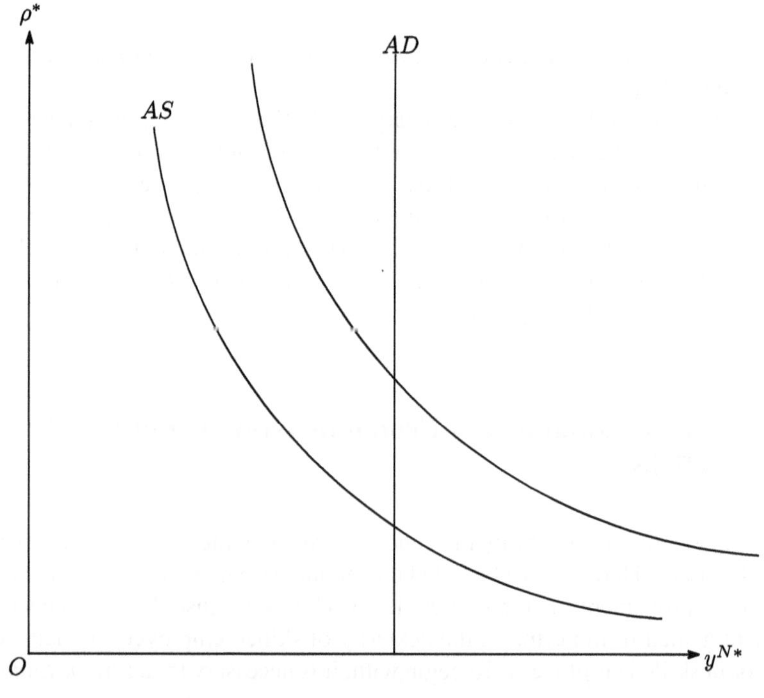

Fig. 13.5 The equilibrium of the economy (Inelastic case)

level of unskilled workers is affected. This is because the total employment level in terms of efficiency units, L^*, is decreased by the dexterity of skilled employees, L^{S*}, developing in any stationary equilibrium. Additionally, note that income disparity between skilled and unskilled employees becomes more serious.

This property of the monetary market economy is summarized by the following theorem:

Theorem 13.2 *Economic growth based on the development of the skills of limited and talented employees in a monetary market economy under monopolistic competition is unsustainable if consumption is inelastic enough to a change in the inflation rate. In addition, even if expansionary fiscal policy can temporarily stimulate the economy and boost total employment in the short run, it is possibly surpassed by the cost-reduction behavior via human capital accumulation, and in such a case, growth ultimately becomes unsustainable in the long run.*

This dismal theory explains why the scale of a government is enlarged. The short-run improvement of employment brought about by fiscal expansion becomes ineffective partly because of the advance of labor productivity enhancing human capital accumulation, and partly because of the nature of a monetary economy depicted in Theorem 13.1. Therefore, more stimulative and expensive policies are required to sustain the employment level. Such policies inevitably accumulate huge fiscal deficits, and thus the scale of government is enlarged.

13.4 Concluding Remarks

This chapter analyzed the properties of economic growth in a monetary market economy using a Keynesian growth model under monopolistic competition. The results obtained were as follows:

1. First, although the human capital investment stimulates effective demand, such an expansionary effect is possibly not strong enough to promote economic growth. This is because human capital investment aims to reduce wage costs by nurturing dexterity under the aggregate demand constraint, and hence approaches zero as the adjustment process comes to an end. This is quite contrastive with the perfect competition case, in which the capital investment increases autonomously and becomes the driving force of economic growth. As such, the monetary market economy under monopolistic competition cannot grow without some exogenous stimuli such as fiscal and monetary policies. However, such policies possibly incur non-negligible fiscal deficits;
2. Second, since there is a substitution mechanism between skilled and unskilled employees, it must be noted that an upturn in an economy does not always imply an improvement in employment. Specifically, when the aggregate savings are inelastic to the inflation rate and the dexterity of skilled employees is deepened by an endogenous progress in the educational system within a firm, progress is absorbed entirely by the development of production efficiency keeping effective

demand intact. This affects the total employment level. That is, there emerges a serious conflict between skilled and unskilled employees;

3. To dissolve such a difficulty, artificial growth-promoting policies seem to be desirable in the short run, because the dexterity of skilled employees cannot be changed. However, not only do such policies enlarge budget deficits, but once accelerated, the growth rate will possibly wither when the cost-reduction investment achieves efficient allocation. This meets the new effective demand level, at least in the long run, thereby raising the unemployment problem once again. In this sense, expansionary fiscal policy is not an ultimate cure for the problem, and thus growth in the monetary market economy under monopolistic competition is not *sustainable* unless various educational opportunities are socialized, and are open to all constituents of an economy (Dewey 1916). Some economic characteristics of socialized education are analyzed in Chap. 3. Otaki (2014) provides an example of how the socialized pedagogical skills of teachers contribute to equalizing the economic opportunities for students when capital market imperfection prevails.

Mathematical Appendix

This appendix establishes the local stability of the economy around a stationary state. On the aggregate demand curve (Eq. 13.18), the following relationship holds at the vicinity of a stationary state $(\rho^*, \tilde{y}^{N*}, L^{s*})$:

$$
\begin{aligned}
&\left[s(\rho)\tilde{y}_t^N - m\right] - \left[s(\rho^*)\tilde{y}^{N*} - m\right] = I_t \\
&= \left[L_t^S - L^{s*}\right] - \left[L_{t-1}^S - L^{s*}\right] = \left[\frac{\partial I}{\partial \rho}\frac{\partial \rho}{\partial L_{t-1}^S} + \frac{\partial I}{\partial \tilde{y}_{t+1}^N}\frac{\partial \tilde{y}_{t+1}^N}{\partial L_{t-1}^S} + \frac{\partial I}{\partial L_{t-1}^S}\right] \\
&\left[L_{t-1}^S - L^{s*}\right] + \mathrm{o}\left[\left[L_{t-1}^S - L^{s*}\right]\right].
\end{aligned}
$$

Note that $I(\cdot)$ is equal to zero at any stationary equilibrium.

If:

$$
-1 < \frac{\partial I}{\partial \rho}\frac{\partial \rho}{\partial L_{t-1}^S} + \frac{\partial I}{\partial \tilde{y}_{t+1}^N}\frac{\partial \tilde{y}_{t+1}^N}{\partial L_{t-1}^S} + \frac{\partial I}{\partial L_{t-1}^S} < 0, \tag{13.20}
$$

then also from Fig. 13.3 it is clear that $L_t^S \to L^{S*}$ when $t \to \infty$. This implies that:

$$
s(\rho)\tilde{y}_t^N \to s(\rho^*)\tilde{y}^{N*}, I_t \to 0.
$$

Thus $s(\rho)\frac{\tilde{y}_t^N}{L_t^S}+I_t \to s(\rho^*)\frac{\tilde{y}^{N*}}{L^{S*}}$, when: $t \to \infty$.

That is, Eq. (13.20) is the local stability condition of a stationary equilibrium. The condition in Eq. (13.20) implies that although the indirect effects of a change in the dexterity via the inflation rate, ρ and real NDP, $\tilde{y}^{N*}$, exist, the direct effect is that the efficiency of cost-reduction measures declines along with progress in developing dexterity, $\frac{\partial I}{\partial L_t^S}$, dominating the aforementioned effects.

References

Acemoglu D (2009) Introduction to modern economic growth. Princeton University Press, Princeton

Aghion P, Bolton P (1997) A theory of trickle-down growth and development. Rev Econ Stud 64:151–172

Andreoni J (1989) Giving with impure altruism: applications to charity and Ricardian equivalence. J Polit Econ 97:1447–1458

Banerjee AV, Newman A (1991) Risk bearing and the theory of income distribution. Rev Econ Stud 58:211–235

Banerjee AV, Newman A (1993) Occupational choice and the process of development. J Polit Econ 101:274–298

Buchanan JM, Wagner RE (1997) Democracy in deficit: the political legacy of Lord Keynes. Liberty Fund, INC, Indianapolis

Dewey J (1916) Democracy and education. Macmillan, London

Galor O, Zeira J (1993) Income distribution and macroeconomics. Rev Econ Stud 60:35–52

Romer PM (1986) Increasing returns and long-run growth. J Polit Econ 94:1002–1037

Otaki M (2007) The dynamically extended Keynesian cross and the welfare-improving fiscal policy. Econ Lett 96:23–29

Otaki M (2009) A welfare economics foundation for the full-employment policy. Econ Lett 102:1–3

Otaki M (2012) A keynesian endogenous growth theory with a rigorous microeconomic foundation. Theor Econ Lett 2:369–372

Otaki M (2013) On the endogenous sustainability of economic growth: why is the scale of government enlarged? Theor Econ Lett 3:159–163

Otaki M (2014) Efficacy in education and intergenerational wellbeing. Theor Econ Lett 4:183–189

Solow RM (1956) A contribution to the theory of economic growth. Q J Econ 70:65–94

Swan TW (1956) Economic growth and capital accumulation. Econ Rec 32:334–361

Part V
Critiques of the Existing Monetary Theories

Chapter 14
A Critique of Lucas' Theory

14.1 Introduction

Lucas (1972) puts forward two main propositions. One is that money is neutral under perfect information. The other is that some tradeoff between the output level and the inflation rate emerges when information is imperfect. The first proposition can be checked by a deterministic model, since the assumption of perfect information is theoretically equivalent to declaring the use of a deterministic model. For analyzing the second proposition, stochastic modeling is useful because imperfect knowledge concerning an individual's environment can be represented only by probability theory. The basic logic that sustains the neutrality of money is analyzed using a deterministic model in Sect. 14.2. In this section, it is shown that Lucas' proposition concerning the neutrality of money depends not only on the specific money-supply rule as pointed out by Otani (1985), but also on a rational belief in the intrinsic value of money. If the concept of *confidence* in money is introduced as formulated in Chap. 2 instead of the quantity theoretic belief that was adopted in Lucas' original work, it is possible to show that money becomes non-neutral even though the money-supply rule obeys Lucas' original formulation.

Section 14.3 deals with the stochastic version of this model. Since the subjective cumulative density function (CDF) defined with a given equilibrium price function must be congruent with the objective CDF, the fixed-point problem should be solved in a functional space, a point on which Lucas' procedure is quite ambiguous. This is a very important problem for Lucas' assertion, because he assumes the following inference problems: individuals receive information on their economic environment as a noisy signal via the equilibrium price, and try to extract the necessary information from such a signal to decide their behavior. The first-stage inference depends on the shape of the subjective equilibrium-price function. However, the resultant objective (or realized) equilibrium-price function does not necessarily coincide with the initial subjective equilibrium-price function. Lucas (1972) omitted to check whether the subjective CDF with some specified equilibrium-price function coincides with the objective CDF. As such, the objective equilibrium function must be a fixed point of the transformation of an subjective CDF, paired with the equilibrium-price

M. Otaki, *Keynesian Economics and Price Theory*,
Advances in Japanese Business and Economics 7, DOI 10.1007/978-4-431-55345-8_14

function. Thus, a more precise analysis for the existence of a rational expectations equilibrium (REE) is needed than the one Lucas (1972) performs. Section 14.3 is devoted to this purpose, and Sect. 14.4 contains brief concluding remarks.

14.2 Lucas' Theory in the Deterministic Case

14.2.1 Why Is Neutrality Upheld Under a Perfect Information Scheme?

In this section, Lucas' (1972) model is rewritten as a deterministic model, and the genetic properties of his theory analyzed. One of the most prominent features of Lucas' theory is that money is neutral under a perfect information scheme. Since his model is based on the same two-period overlapping generations model as Keynesian theory, it is important to consider why the neutrality is upheld.

The critical assumptions that sustain Lucas' proposition are twofold: (i) an extraneous belief that the equilibrium-price level increases proportionately with the quantity of money; and (ii) the peculiar money-supply rule that implies that additional money is supplied proportionately to money carried over from the previous period. These two assumptions are expressed as:

$$p_t = \kappa M_t, \tag{14.1}$$

$$M_{t+1} = x_t M_t, \tag{14.2}$$

Where:$(p_t,\ M_t)$ are the equilibrium price and the nominal stock of money during period t, respectively; and x_t denotes the growth rate of money.

When every individual is informed of the money-supply rule, which appears in Eq. (14.2), the current and future budget constraint of an individual is:

$$\begin{gathered} p_t c_t + M_t \le p_t h_t,\ p_{t+1} c_{t+1} \le M_{t+1} \\ \Rightarrow p_t c_t + \frac{p_{t+1} c_{t+1}}{x_t} \le p_t h_t . \end{gathered} \tag{14.3}$$

Where: h_t is hours worked.

Furthermore, a unit of current good is assumed to be produced by a unit working hour. Substituting Eq. (14.1) into Eq. (14.3) gives:

$$c_t + c_{t+1} \le h_t . \tag{14.4}$$

Equation (14.4) immediately leads to the neutrality of money. This equation implies that when an individual weaves the money-supply rule in Eq. (14.2) into their rational extraneous belief in Eq. (14.1), the relative price of a future good to a current good (i.e. the inflation rate) is fixed at unity and becomes independent of the nominal money supply, M_t. Since an individual determines (c_t, c_{t+1}, h_t) subject to the constraint (14.4), it is clear that the nominal money supply, M_t, does not affect these real variables, and thus neutrality is upheld. In addition, from Eq. (14.1), an increase in the nominal money supply heightens the equilibrium-price level proportionately.

Otani (1985) revealed that if the money-supply rule in Eq. (14.2) is violated, so is neutrality. In the next section, the problem of the belief in the future price while the money-supply rule is kept intact is considered.

14.2.2 "Confidence in Money" in the Lucas Model

As discussed in Chap. 2, the quantity theoretic rational belief represented by Eq. (14.1) is based on disbelief in the intrinsic value of money. That is, individuals extraneously believe that the value of money depreciates with its quantity. Instead, an alternative rational belief that individuals are confident in the intrinsic value of money can be postulated. According to Otaki (2012), this belief is defined as:

$$\frac{dp_{t+1}}{dx} = 0, \frac{dp_{t+j+1}}{p_{t+j+1}} - \frac{dp_{t+j}}{p_{t+j}} = \frac{dx}{x}, 1 \leq j. \tag{14.5}$$

The economic meaning of Eq. (14.5) is as follows. The rate of return for money initially increases in conjunction with an acceleration of the growth rate of money because individuals are confident in the value of money (the left-hand side equation in Eq. 14.5). This increased rate of return is kept intact thereafter because there is no environmental change in the economy (the right-hand side equation in Eq. 14.5). Under such a belief, money is non-neutral even in the Lucas model.

The model proposed in this section is almost unchanged from Lucas' original paper except for the belief concerning the dynamics of the value of money. Define the utility function of an individual who is born at the beginning of period t, U_t, as:

$$U_t \equiv u(c_t, n_t) + V(c_{t+1}), \tag{14.6}$$

Where: n_t is hours worked when young; and $u(\cdot)$ and $V(\cdot)$ are continuously twice differentiable concave functions. In addition, assume:

$$u_{cn} + u_{cc} < 0, u_{cn} + u_{nn} < 0, c_{t+1}V'' + V' > 0. \tag{14.7}$$

As will be shown later, the assumptions in Eq. (14.7) imply that leisure and current consumption are mutually superior goods.

When the transformation rate between leisure and good production is unity, the budget constraint becomes:

$$c_t + \frac{p_{t+1}}{xp_t} c_{t+1} \leq n_t. \tag{14.8}$$

An individual maximizes Eq. (14.6) on (c_t, c_{t+1}, n_t), subject to Eq. (14.8). The first-order condition then is:

$$-\frac{u_c}{u_n} = 1, \frac{u_c}{V'} = \frac{xp_t}{p_{t+1}}, \tag{14.9}$$

$$n_t^* = c_t^* + \frac{p_{t+1}}{xp_t} c_{t+1}^*. \tag{14.10}$$

The REE in this model is defined as the pair of Eqs. (14.5), (14.9), (14.10), and the market-clearing condition:

$$n_t^* - c_t^* = \frac{M_t}{p_t^*}. \tag{14.11}$$

Here, there are five independent equations, and the endogenous variables are $(c_t^*, c_{t+1}^*, n_t^*, p_t^*, p_{t+1}^*)$. Thus, the model is completely closed. Then, from Eqs. (14.10) and (14.11):

$$M_t = \frac{p_{t+1}^*}{x} c_{t+1}^* \Rightarrow \frac{dc_{t+1}^*}{c_{t+1}^*} = \frac{dx}{x} > 0. \tag{14.12}$$

Equation (14.12) implies that future consumption increases along with the acceleration of monetary growth.

For the preparation of comparative statics, differentiate the left-hand equation in Eq. (14.9). Then:

$$-\frac{u_{cc}u_{nn} - [u_{cn}]^2}{u_{cn} + u_{cc}} V' dn_t^* - u_c V'' dc_{t+1} = [V']^2 \left[\frac{xdp_t^* + p_t^* dx}{p_{t+1}^*} \right]. \tag{14.13}$$

By the concavity of the utility function and assumptions in Eq. (14.7), the sign of the first term of the left-hand side of Eq. (14.13) is positive. In addition to Eq. (14.13), when Eq. (14.10) is differentiated:

$$\begin{bmatrix} -\frac{u_{cc}u_{nn} - [u_{cn}]^2}{u_{cn} + u_{cc}} V' & -\frac{x[V']^2}{p_{t+1}^*} \\ 1 - \frac{dc_t^*}{dn_t^*} & \frac{p_{t+1}^*}{x[p_t^*]^2} \end{bmatrix} \begin{bmatrix} \frac{dn_t^*}{dx} \\ \frac{dp_t^*}{dx} \end{bmatrix} = \begin{bmatrix} u_c V'' \frac{dc_{t+1}^*}{dx} + \frac{[V']^2 p_t^*}{p_{t+1}^*} \\ 0 \end{bmatrix} \tag{14.14}$$

Using the assumption in Eq. (14.7) and the results of Eq. (14.12), elementary calculus leads to:

$$\frac{dn_t^*}{dx} > 0, -1 < \frac{xdp_t^*}{p_t^* dx} < 0. \tag{14.15}$$

Since rational belief in the value of money obeys Eq. (14.5), the real cash balance, $\frac{M_{t+j}}{\overset{*}{p}_{t+j}}$, and the rate of return for money, $\frac{x\overset{*}{p}_{t+j}}{\overset{*}{p}_{t+j+1}}$, are constant over time; the equilibrium of this model is the *stationary* REE.

To summarize, if the rational belief in Eq. (14.1) (the quantity theoretic belief) is interchanged by another rational belief in Eq. (14.5) (the confidence in money), money becomes non-neutral in the Lucas model even though the money-supply rule remains Eq. (14.2). This is because as long as money is confident, any acceleration in the growth rate of money supply heightens the rate of return on money, and, as a result, future consumption is stimulated instead of current consumption by the mechanism of intertemporal substitution. Moreover, since leisure time and current consumption are mutually superior goods, hours worked and output levels increase simultaneously.

14.3 Lucas' Theory in the Stochastic Case

14.3.1 What Are the Problems?

The previous section analyzed the basic structure of the Lucas (1972) model using a deterministic approach. In this section, a difficulty in Lucas' paper (pointed out by Grammond) is considered concerning whether there is legitimacy in transforming the joint CDF that includes market equilibrium information into a CDF that includes only the state of nature in the model. From this, it appears that the Lucas (1983) formulation is hardly tenable in the light of Grammond's critique. That is, any transformed joint CDF of environment/equilibrium price cannot be free from the form of the equilibrium-price function, which can be given arbitrarily.

The essence of the Lucas (1972) model is a signal extraction problem, which is compatible with the market equilibrium condition. The model, however, contains a very difficult problem. That is, the functional form of the equilibrium price inseparably connects with the results of the signal extraction. In other words, whenever individuals try to extract the relevant information on their environment via the market mechanism, they must have exact knowledge on the objective equilibrium-price function.

Structurally, Lucas' model relies on two-stage statistical inference as illustrated in Fig. 14.1. The first stage is to extract information concerning the realized economic environment (i.e. the increased rate of money supply and the population of young individuals) via an arbitrarily fixed equilibrium-price function, even though it is affected by noise. In the second stage, individuals infer the true state of nature using the extracted noisy information. The most difficult problem lies in the feedback of individual economic behavior to the equilibrium-price function. Individuals maximize their utility using the extracted information under some fixed subjective equilibrium-price function, and thus the extracted information determines the realized equilibrium-price. Succinctly, the form of an initial subjective equilibrium-

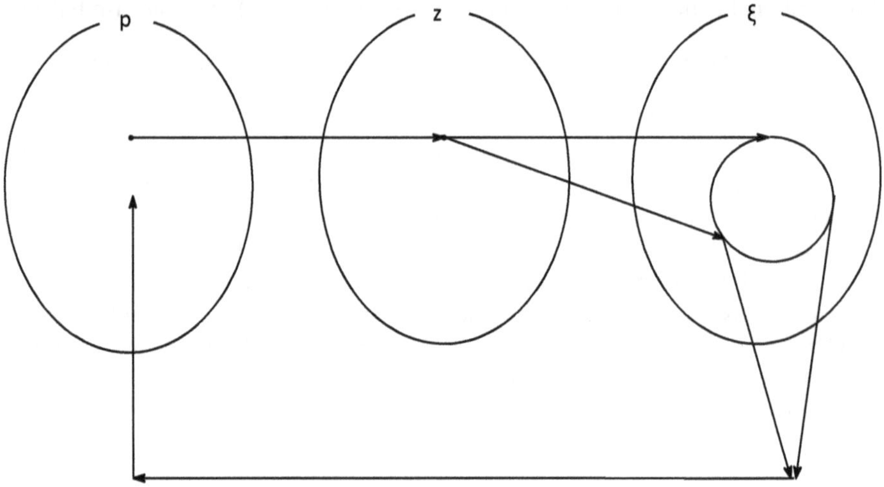

Fig. 14.1 The two stage inference and feedback to the price

price function affects that of the resultant objective equilibrium-price function. Accordingly, the objective equilibrium-price function should be a fixed point of such mapping that weaves the change in the CDF in accordance with the change in the equilibrium-price function, as long as an economy achieves REE.

The main purpose of this section is to consider whether Lucas (1972) succeeds in finding the REE that preserves such a property. It will be shown that the subjective joint CDF, which is made up of only exogenously given environmental variables, varies along with a change in the form of the equilibrium-price function as in Grammond's assertion, and so is the conditional CDF of these variables. In this sense, the form of the functional equation, which is proposed as the REE by Lucas (1972), is imprecise.

14.3.2 The Unsolvable Fixed-Point Problem

The original formulation by Lucas (1972) of the maximization problem compatible with REE is formatted as:

$$h\left(\frac{mx}{\theta p}\right)\frac{1}{p}=\int V'\left(\frac{mxx'}{\theta p'}\right)\frac{x'}{p'}\,dF(x',p'\mid m,p), \tag{14.16}$$

Where: the left-hand side of Eq. (14.17) denotes the marginal utility derived from current consumption, and the right-hand side is that from future consumption; x is the increased rate of money; θ denotes the population of the young individuals; and m denotes money carried over from the previous period.

The variables attached by the symbol' represent the future random variable. That is, Eq. (14.17) is a compounded Euler equation that includes the market-clearing condition in Lucas' (1972) model. Each individual maximizes their lifetime utility using the currently available information (*m, p*). Lucas specifies the equilibrium-price function as:

$$p = m\phi(z), \quad z \equiv \frac{x}{\theta}. \tag{14.17}$$

Substituting Eq. (14.18) into (14.17), Lucas insists that the following functional equation is obtained:

$$h\left(\frac{z}{\phi(z)}\right)\frac{z}{\phi(z)} = \int V'\left(\frac{x}{\xi}\cdot\frac{\theta'}{\theta}\cdot\frac{z'}{\phi(z')}\right)\frac{x}{\xi}\cdot\frac{\theta'}{\theta}\cdot\frac{z'}{\phi(z')}\, dG(\xi, x', \theta' \mid z), \tag{14.18}$$

Where: ξ is the current additional money supply, and is unknowable to individuals (Lucas 1972).

Here, ξ, should be strictly distinguished from x, which means the realized value of ξ. The imperfect informational structure of the model, which is the backbone of Lucas (1972), urgently requires such awareness.

The main issue is whether the transformation from Eq. (14.16) to (14.18) is feasible independently of the functional form of Eq. (14.17). Since x' and θ' are assumed to follow *i.i.d.* processes, the problem reduces to whether the conditional CDF, G, can be defined independently of the form of the tentatively fixed equilibrium-price function in Eq. (14.17), as expressed by Eq. (14.18). In considering this problem, it should be noted that an individual can infer the realized value z only through the realized equilibrium price, p, and hence Eq. (12.18) should be rewritten as:

$$G(\xi, x', \theta' \mid \phi(z)).$$

This provides a negative answer to Lucas' (1972) model and formally validates Grammond's critique. That is:

Theorem 14.1
The conditional cumulative density function $G(\xi, x', \theta' \mid \phi(z))$ *can never be invariant with the form of the arbitrarily fixed equilibrium-price function* $\phi(\cdot)$.

Proof
Since (x', θ') are *i.i.d.* processes independent of ξ, focus should be directed towards the relationship between the joint density function, $j(\xi, z, \cdot)$, of the CDF, $J(\xi, z, \cdot)$, which represents the true state of the economic environment, and the joint density function $g(\xi, p, \cdot)$ of the CDF, $G(\xi, p, \cdot)$, which is endogenously determined by the equilibrium-price function. These two density functions should become coincident by the transformation below:

$$p = \phi(z), \; \xi = \xi.$$

By definition and the formula for the transformation of the probability density function, $g(\xi, p, \cdot)$ is transformed into:

$$g(\xi, p, \cdot) \Rightarrow \phi'(z) g(\xi, \phi(z), \cdot),$$
$$\phi'(z) g(\xi, \phi(z), \cdot) = j(\xi, z, \cdot) \quad (14.19)$$

Thus:

$$g(\xi, \phi(z), \cdot) = \frac{1}{\phi'(z)} \cdot j(\xi, z, \cdot). \quad (14.20)$$

It must be accepted that the term $g(\xi, \phi(z), \cdot)$ in Eq. (14.20) is a probability density function before proceeding to the next step. Integrating both sides of Eq. (14.20) gives:

$$\int g(\xi, \phi(z), x', \theta') d\xi \, d\phi(z) \, dx' d\theta'$$
$$= \int \frac{j(\xi, z, x', \theta')}{\phi'(z)} d\xi \, d\phi(z) \, dx' d\theta'$$
$$= \int j(\xi, z, x', \theta') d\xi \, dz \, dx' d\theta' = 1$$

The range of the integration is all domains of (ξ, z, x', θ'). Thus, $g(\xi, \phi(z), \cdot)$ in Eq. (14.20) is a probability density function. Hence, Eq. (14.20) implies that the conditional density function of ξ on the equilibrium price, $\phi(z)$, is:

$$g(\xi, \cdot | \phi(z)) = \frac{j(\xi, \cdot | z)}{\phi'(z)}, \quad (14.21)$$

Equation (14.21) completes the proof.

This proof shows that the transformation between joint distribution functions depends on the shape of ϕ as Grammond suggests. That is, besides the exogenously given distribution, J, a tentatively fixed shape of the equilibrium function, $\phi(\cdot)$, intrinsically affects the resultant equilibrium-price function. Lucas substantively alleges that the following functional equation corresponds to the market equilibrium condition:

$$h\left(\frac{x}{\theta \phi(z)}\right) \frac{x}{\theta \phi(z)} = \int V'\left(\frac{x}{\xi} \cdot \frac{\theta'}{\theta} \cdot \frac{z'}{\phi(z')}\right) \frac{x}{\xi} \cdot \frac{\theta'}{\theta} \cdot \frac{z'}{\phi(z')} dJ(\xi, x', \theta' | z). \quad (14.22)$$

However, if the initial-condition effect for searching a fixed point is accepted as discussed, from the condition in Eq. (14.21), the correct form of the functional equation is:

$$h\left(\frac{x}{\theta\phi(z)}\right)\frac{x}{\theta\phi(z)}$$
$$=\frac{1}{\phi'(z)}\int V'\left(\frac{x}{\xi}\cdot\frac{\theta'}{\theta}\cdot\frac{z'}{\phi(z')}\right)\frac{x}{\xi}\cdot\frac{\theta'}{\theta}\cdot\frac{z'}{\phi(z')}\,dJ(\xi,x',\theta'\mid z). \tag{14.23}$$

This equation differs from Eq. (14.22) at the point where the inverse of the equilibrium-price function is multiplied in the right-hand side of the equation, and is unable to apply the simple contraction mapping method that Lucas uses for showing the unique existence of the market equilibrium. Thus, Grammond's critique is valid, and Lucas' (1972) transformation must be modified. In other words, Lucas abbreviates the procedure for searching for the fixed point of the objective CDF, G. This implies that that the initially given function, G, cannot possibly correspond to the subjective CDF, J, as in Lucas' original formulation.

14.3.3 The Problem of Second-Stage Inference

As mentioned above, Lucas' theory includes two-stage statistical inference: infer z from the equilibrium price, p; then infer the current interest of money, x, from the inferred z. In the previous section, it was shown that the procedure in the first-stage inference is invalid. As a result, Lucas' theory must be re-interpreted as follows. Individuals directly receive a noisy signal, z, by some means (not via the equilibrium price), and infer the true state of the economy. Then, the difficulty of the first-stage inference as shown in the previous subsection is avoidable.

If such an interpretation is admissible, the functional equation that represents the market equilibrium is not Eq. (14.23) but (14.22). However, as Otaki (2013) points out, there is still a difficulty in proving the existence of the market equilibrium: this relates to the distinction of the random variable, ξ, and its realized value, x. It must be noted that the current increased rate of money is unknown and should be treated as a random variable, ξ, when the maximization problem of an individual is dealt with. Nevertheless, since in the economy as a whole this value is already realized, x must be used in such a case. Although Lucas initially covers this distinction, he makes $\xi = x$ when he induces the functional equation. In this case, Eq. (14.23) becomes:

$$h\left(\frac{z}{\phi(z)}\right)\frac{z}{\theta\phi(z)}=\int V'\left(\frac{\theta'}{\theta}\cdot\frac{z'}{\phi(z')}\right)\frac{\theta'}{\theta}\cdot\frac{z'}{\phi(z')}\,dJ(\xi,x',\theta'\mid z). \tag{14.24}$$

Using the method of contraction mapping in Banach space under certain assumptions, Lucas proves the unique existence of the equilibrium function, $\phi(z)$. However, this procedure is also imprecise. This can be shown as follows: by rearranging terms in Eq. (14.22):

$$h\left(\frac{x}{\theta\phi(z)}\right)\frac{x}{\theta\phi(z)}=\int V'\left(\frac{z\theta'}{\xi}\cdot\frac{z'}{\phi(z')}\right)\frac{z\theta'}{\xi}\cdot\frac{z'}{\phi(z')}dJ(\xi,x',\theta'\mid z). \quad (14.25)$$

Define Ψ as:

$$\Psi(z)\equiv h\left(\frac{z}{\phi(z)}\right)\frac{z}{\phi(z)}. \quad (14.26)$$

Furthermore, denote:

$$G_1(x)\equiv[h(x)x]^{-1}, G_2(x)\equiv V'(x)x. \quad (14.27)$$

Then, substituting Eqs. (14.26) and (14.27) into Eq. (14.25), the following functional equation on $\Psi(z)$ is obtained:

$$\Psi(z)=\int G_2\left(\frac{z\theta'}{\xi}G_1(\Psi(z'))\right)dJ(\xi,x',\theta'\mid z). \quad (14.28)$$

In this formulation the family of solutions is confined to bounded and continuous functions. It is easy to show that if the supreme norm to such a family is adopted, the generated space B becomes a Banach space. Define the operator $T_f : B \to B$ as:

$$T_f \equiv \ln\int G_2\left(\frac{z\theta'}{\xi}G_1\left(e^{f(z')}\right)\right)dJ(\xi,x',\theta'\mid z) \quad (14.29)$$

Where: $\ln\Psi(z)$ is the fixed point of the operator.

By using the contraction mapping method in this way, Lucas intended to prove the unique existence of $\ln\Psi(z)$.

For the convenience of proof, define $w(\cdot)$ as:

$$w(z,z',\theta',\xi)\equiv\frac{G_2\left(\frac{z\theta'}{\xi}G_1\left(e^{g(z')}\right)\right)}{\int G_2\left(\frac{z\theta'}{\xi}G_1\left(e^{g(z')}\right)\right)dJ(\xi,x',\theta'\mid z)}$$

Since $\int w(\cdot)dJ(\xi,x',\theta'\mid z)=1$, and:

$$\|T_f-T_g\|=\sup_z\left|\ln\int w(z,z',\theta',\xi)\frac{G_2\left(\frac{z\theta'}{\xi}G_1\left(e^{f(z')}\right)\right)}{G_2\left(\frac{z\theta'}{\xi}G_1\left(e^{g(z')}\right)\right)}dJ(\xi,x',\theta'\mid z)\right|$$

$$\leq \sup_z\sup_{z',\theta',\xi}\left|\ln G_2\left(\frac{z\theta'}{\xi}G_1\left(e^{f(z')}\right)\right)-\ln G_2\left(\frac{z\theta'}{\xi}G_1\left(e^{f(z')}\right)\right)\right| \quad (14.30)$$

and $\left(z', \frac{\theta'}{\xi}\right)$ becomes the function of z. These relationships can be denoted as:

$$z' = \omega(z), \frac{\theta'}{\xi} = \chi(z).$$

Substituting these functions into Eq. (14.30) gives:

$$\| T_f - T_g \| \le \sup_z | \ln G_2\left(z\chi(z) G_1\left(e^{f(\omega(z))}\right)\right) - \ln G_2\left(z\chi(z) G_1\left(e^{g(\omega(z))}\right)\right)| \tag{14.31}$$

Define:

$$z^* \equiv \arg\sup_z | \ln G_2\left(z\chi(z) G_1\left(e^{f(\omega(z))}\right)\right) - \ln G_2\left(z\chi(z) G_1\left(e^{g(\omega(z))}\right)\right)|$$

$x_1 \equiv f\left(\omega\left(z^*\right)\right)$, $x_2 \equiv g\left(\omega\left(z^*\right)\right)$, and assume that:

$$0 < \frac{xG_1'}{G_1} < 1, 0 < \frac{xG_2'}{G_2} \le 1 - a < 1. \tag{14.32}$$

The following inequality is obtained by applying the mean value theorem to Eq. (14.31):

$$\| T_f - T_g \| \le [1-a] | x_1 - x_2 | \le [1-a] \| f(\omega(z)) - g(\omega(z)) \|$$

In general, $\omega(z) \ne z$, the above inequality never means that T_f is a contraction mapping; thus, Lucas' proof is incomplete, and some additional assumptions besides Eq. (14.31) are necessary to complete the job.

The origin of the problem is the fact that z' depends on z. Accordingly, when considering Eq. (14.32), assume that $G_2(\cdot)$ is multiplicatively separable. That is, assume that $G_2(\cdot)$ satisfies:

$$G_2(xy) = G_2(x) \cdot G_2(y). \tag{14.33}$$

Equation (14.31) becomes:

$$\| T_f - T_g \| \le \sup_z | \ln G_2\left(G_1\left(e^{f(z)}\right)\right) - \ln G_2\left(G_1\left(e^{g(z)}\right)\right)| \le [1-a] | f(z) - g(z) |$$

Then, under the assumptions in Eq. (14.33), T_f is a contraction mapping. This is a sufficient condition for completing Lucas' proof. It appears that it is quite difficult to find an alternative sufficient condition, although such a condition possibly exists.

However, as shown in the Mathematical Appendix, based on Small (2007) the function that satisfies Eq. (14.33) is limited to power functions. That is:

$$G(x) = x^{\beta} \Leftrightarrow V(x) = \frac{x^{\beta}}{\beta}.$$

Furthermore, the assumption in Eq. (14.32) requires $0 < \beta < 1$. Thus, although Lucas' assertion seems to be upheld by broad classes of the utility function, when the calculation is performed it is seen that his assertion is only valid within a rather restrictive class, even though the difficulty in the inference problem is skipped. This situation genetically stems from the relationship between the equilibrium-price function and CDFs, and assumes that a noisy signal concerning the state of the economy, z, can be directly observed.

14.4 Concluding Remarks

This chapter examined whether Lucas' (1972) signal extraction problem with general equilibrium is properly formatted. The results obtained were as follows:

1. First, the neutrality of money under certainty is upheld by the following assumptions concerning the brief on the intrinsic value of money and the money-supply rule. That is, when individuals express disbelief in the intrinsic value of money and consider that its value decreases proportionately with its quantity, money becomes neutral under the money-supply rule that Lucas assumes. Otherwise, if individuals are confident of the value of money, as defined in Chap. 2, an increase in the growth rate of money heightens the rate of return for money, thereby increasing hours worked and future consumption. Thus, money is non-neutral whenever individuals are confident of the value of money in the deterministic version of Lucas' model where information is complete;
2. Second, this analysis clarifies that fact that Lucas' original paper contains two basic weaknesses. One is that he substantively skips solving the fixed problem of the subjective CDF, which is inseparable from the specification of an initially endowed subjective equilibrium-price function. The objective CDF is obtained as a fixed point of the subjective CDF in the REE. In this sense, unlike his assertion, what he attempts to do is to search for a unique equilibrium-price function under the assumption that individuals can directly obtain the realized noisy signal, z, without the help of the information that an equilibrium price conveys;
3. The third point is that even though the abovementioned limitation is admitted, his proof of existence is still incomplete. This stems from the confusion that the realized value of the growth rate of money is unknowable to individuals and should be treated as a random variable when the maximization problem is considered, while it becomes a real number when the macroeconomic environment is depicted;

4. As this distinction should be made, an additional condition is required for completing the existence proof. This chapter succeeded in providing a sufficient condition. Nevertheless, such a condition is quite restrictive with respect to the class of the utility function.

14.5 Mathematical Appendix

This appendix aims to sketch the proof that the solution of the functional equation $G(xy) = G(x) \cdot G(y)$ is limited to power function $G(x) = x^{\gamma}$.

14.5.1 The First Step

Fact
The solution of the functional equation:

$$f(x+y) = f(x) + f(y) \tag{14.34}$$

is limited to:

$$f(x) = \gamma x, \tag{14.35}$$

Where: γ is an arbitrary constant.

14.5.2 The Second Step

Theorem 14.2
The solution of the functional equation

$$f(x+y) = f(x) \cdot f(y), \tag{14.36}$$

is limited to:

$$f(x) = \gamma^{x}, \tag{14.37}$$

where: γ is an arbitrary positive constant.

Proof
Define: $h(x) \equiv \log f(x)$. Then, by Eq. (14.36):

$$h(x) + h(y) = \log f(x) \cdot f(y) = \log f(x+y) = h(x+y). \tag{14.38}$$

Thus, h satisfies the functional Eq. (14.34). Hence, using Fact:

$$h(x) \equiv \log f(x) = \alpha x \Rightarrow f(x) = \gamma^{x}.$$

14.5.3 The Final Step

Theorem 14.3
The solution of the functional equation:

$$f(x \cdot y) = f(x) \cdot f(y), \tag{14.39}$$

is limited to:

$$f(x) = x^{\gamma}, \tag{14.40}$$

where: γ is an arbitrary constant.

Proof
Define:
$u \equiv \log x, v \equiv \log y, f(x) \equiv h(\log x)$. Then from Eq. (14.39):

$$h(\log x) \cdot h(\log y) = h(\log x \cdot y) = h(\log x + \log y) \Leftrightarrow h(u + v) = h(u) \cdot h(v).$$

This is the same functional equation as Eq. (14.36). Applying Theorem 14.3 thus gives:

$$f(x) \equiv h(u) = \alpha^{u} = \alpha^{\log x} = x^{\gamma}.$$

References

Lucas RE Jr (1972) Expectations and the neutrality of money. J Econ Theory 4:103–124
Lucas RE Jr (1983) Corrigendum to expectations and the neutrality of money. J Econ Theory 31:196–199
Otaki M (2012) The role of money: credible asset or numeraire? Theor Econ Lett 2:365–368
Otaki M (2013) A study on Lucas' expectations and the neutrality of money-II'. Theor Econ Lett 3:168–170
Otani K (1985) Rational expectations and the non-neutrality of money. Weltwirtschaftliches Arch 121:207–216
Small C (2007) Functional equations and how to solve them. Springer + Business Media, New York

Chapter 15
Does the Search Model Succeed in Describing a Monetary Economy?

15.1 Introduction

This chapter explores the function of money in the search model. There exist two main functions of money: the transaction demand for clearing, and the demand for a store of value. Kiyotaki and Wright (1989) succeed in describing these functions using a search model. This model critically depends on the difficulty of the *double coincidence of wants*, which stems from differences in individual preferences.

However, this difficulty also exists in the overlapping generations (OLG) models developed by Samuelson (1958) and Lucas (1972) before research on the search model progressed. In the first half of this chapter, the gist of the Kiyotaki and Wright (1989) model is presented, and the advantages of search theory-based monetary theory for an OLG model are considered. The second half is devoted to analyzing the properties of Kiyotaki and Wright (1991), which is also regarded as a seminal work on the search money model. These writers insist that money can circulate, without possessing the property of store of value, simply by adding a new position of a so-called "money trader" into Diamond's (1981) search model.

However, if money is perishable while differentiated goods are durable, some advantage exists on the side of the goods market. Namely, the visiting opportunities of exchange in a barter economy are more frequent than those in a monetary economy. This leads to the following conjecture: unless money possesses both of the above properties (a store of value and a medium of exchange), it is unable to circulate. Based on Kiyotaki and Wright (1991), the validity of this conjecture may be ascertained. In addition, we show that unlike Kiyotaki and Wright (1989), money never circulates genetically in Kiyotaki and Wright (1991) because they fail to introduce the advantage of money hoarding (i.e. as a measure to overcome the difficulty of the double coincidence of wants).

This chapter is organized as follows. In Sect. 15.2, a simple model based on Kiyotaki and Wright (1989) is constructed, and its properties analyzed in comparison with the OLG model. Section 15.3 is devoted to considering whether money can circulate only as a transaction medium, based on Kiyotaki and Wright (1991). The

M. Otaki, *Keynesian Economics and Price Theory*,
Advances in Japanese Business and Economics 7, DOI 10.1007/978-4-431-55345-8_15

discussion shows that money does not circulate at least until being attached by its function as a store of value. Furthermore, even if the aforementioned necessary conditions are satisfied, money cannot circulate in the Kiyotaki and Wright (1991) model, because there is no prerogative for hoarding money in their model. Section 15.4 contains brief concluding remarks.

15.2 The Simplified Kiyotaki–Wright (1989) Model

15.2.1 The Structure of the Model

In this section, the Kiyotaki–Wright (1989) model is simplified to clarify its properties. These properties succeed in representing the difficulty of the double coincidence of wants in the search model as follows. It is presumed that there are three types of individuals: type 1; type 2; and type 3. Type 1 feels utility only from the consumption of a good that type 3 produces, and in turn produces a good that only type 2 wants to consume. Let this preference-production relationship be denoted as $(3, 2)^1$. Then, the other relationships, which Kiyotaki and Wright (1989) presume, can be written $(1, 3)^2$ (type 2) and $(2, 1)^3$ (type 3).

In this vein, the double coincidence of wants can be defined as:

Definition 15.1
The double coincidence of wants is attained only when there exists a pair that satisfies $(x, y)^i$ and $(y, x)^i$ for some i, j.

Such a match is defined by the following symbol:

$$\left\{(x,y)^i,(y,x)^j\right\}.$$

It is clear from the abovementioned assumptions that Kiyotaki and Wright (1989) succeed in representing the difficulty of the double coincidence of wants.

The equilibrium concept of their model is to allot a consistent ratio of holding good x of type i individuals, p_{xi} (x, $i = 1, 2, 3$). The original model deals with a rather complex case. However, if it is assumed that:

$$p_{21} = p_{32} = p_{13} = 1, \tag{15.1}$$

It is possible to see that exchange never occurs, and that an individual is unable to enjoy consumption. Since there is no opportunity for exchange, the ratios in Eq. (15.1) are self-enforcing.

Next, a monetary economy model, in which all individuals are confident in the intrinsic value of money, and believe that it can be converted to any kind of good whenever they wish, is outlined. Such a situation can be described as:

$$\left\{(m,x)^i,(x,m)^j\right\}, \quad \forall x,i,j, \quad i \neq j.$$

If money circulates, and a monetary economy is sustainable, there is a chain of matches such as:

$$\left\{(x,m)^i,(m,x)^j\right\},\left\{(y,m)^j,(m,y)^k\right\},\left\{(z,m)^k,(m,z)^i\right\} \tag{15.2}$$

It is clear then that:

$$\left\{(1,m)^2,(m,1)^1\right\},\left\{(3,m)^1,(m,3)^3\right\},\left\{(2,m)^3,(m,2)^2\right\} \tag{15.3}$$

satisfies this condition. Thus, the acute existence of money dissolves the difficulty of the double coincidence of wants, and enables every individual to enjoy their consumption.

Whenever Eq. (15.3) constitutes the equilibrium of the Kiyotaki and Wright (1989) model, there should be a consistent (time-invariant) and *incentive compatible* ratio of individuals who have each type of commodity and money. The incentive compatibility of their model means that the lifetime utility of type i obtained from the money-holding position, V_{mi}, exceeds that obtained from the commodity-holding position, V_{pi}, in which no consumption opportunity exists. Their model thus assumes that each type of individual exists in equal amounts, and hence they encounter each type of individual with the same probability $\frac{1}{3}$. They also assume that it takes one period to change their position and the utility discount rate is β.

Based on these assumptions, it is possible to show that the pair of probabilities:

$$p_{12} = p_{23} = p_{31} = p_{im} = \frac{1}{2}, \tag{15.4}$$

is one of the equilibrium points in the sense of Kiyotaki and Wright (1989), where p_{im} is the ratio of type i money holders to the same type of individuals.

First, the allotted probabilities in Eq. (15.4) are proven to be consistent (time-invariant). Consider the inflow into the money holders (the outflow from the commodity holders) of type i. This becomes $\frac{1}{3}\times\frac{1}{2}\times\frac{1}{2}=\frac{1}{12}$. The probability (equivalent to the frequency under the law of large numbers) of the outflow from the money holders (the inflow into the commodity holders) of the same type of individuals is also $\frac{1}{3}\times\frac{1}{2}\times\frac{1}{2}=\frac{1}{12}$.

Thus, the inflow and outflow are equilibrated. Hence, the probabilities in (15.4) are time-invariant. Second, the incentive-compatibility condition:

$$V_{mi} > V_{pi}, \forall i, \tag{15.5}$$

is upheld, and V_{pi} thus satisfies the following equation:

$$V_{pi} = b\left[V_{pi} + V_{pi} + \frac{1}{2}\left[V_{mi} + V_{pi}\right]\right], \quad b \equiv \frac{\beta}{3}. \tag{15.6}$$

The first and second terms in Eq. (15.6) are the obtained utility when a type i producer encounters those who do not genetically match them. For example, this corresponds to the case that a commodity holder of type 1 encounters type 1 and 3 individuals. The third term represents the expected lifetime utility when a producer encounters the type that they can potentially match. For example, a commodity holder of type 1 encounters a type 2 individual.

Rearranging Eq. (15.6) gives:

$$V_{mi} = \frac{1-2.5b}{0.5b} V_{pi}. \tag{15.7}$$

Since $0 < b < \frac{1}{3}$, it is clear from Eq. (15.7) that:

$$V_{mi} > V_{pi}, \forall i. \tag{15.8}$$

This inequality proves that the probabilities in Eq. (15.4) satisfy the incentive-compatibility condition for sustaining a monetary economy. Consequently, it is proven that the pairs of matches in Eq. (15.3) and their probabilities assigned in Eq. (15.4) constitute one of the equilibrium points. This is so because in the moneyless economy where probabilities are assigned by Eq. (15.1), and in the preference/production structure $(3, 2)^1$, $(1, 3)^2$, $(2, 1)^3$, no individual enjoys consumption and the introduction of money to the economy apparently improves economic welfare.

In addition to this point, in the monetary economy:

$$V_{mi} = b\left[V_{mi} + V_{mi} + \frac{1}{2}\left[u + V_{pi} + V_{mi}\right]\right], \tag{15.9}$$

holds and u denotes the utility derived from consumption. Substituting Eq. (15.7) into Eq. (15.8) and rearranging the terms gives:

$$V_{mi} = \sum_{j=1}^{\infty} \left[\frac{0.5b}{1-2.5b}\right]^{2j-1} \cdot u. \tag{15.10}$$

Here, it should be noted that the lifetime utility term V_{mi} entirely comprises the instantaneous utility during odd-number periods. This is because any type of money holder moves towards the producer side (commodity holder) during at least one period.

15.2.2 *What Is the Substantial Contribution of the Search Model to Monetary Theory?*

Kiyotaki and Wright (1989) assert that they succeeded in describing the role of money as a medium of transaction to overcome the difficulty of the double coincidence of wants. Indeed, they have achieved this. However, there is another important point that should be considered in evaluating their substantial contribution. Although they seem to emphasize money as the transaction medium entity, it should be noted that such a function is inseparable from the other function of money as a store of value. As analyzed in the next section, if money ceases to be a store of value, it never circulates. The intuitive reason for this situation is as follows. When money is nearly perishable, there is not enough time to wait for the arrival of the chance for exchange, and at its limit money becomes worthless, and therefore, by definition, never circulates. Thus, these two functions of money (transaction medium and store of value) are genetically inseparable.

When this inseparability in the functions of money is admitted, it is possible to see that an OLG model with money possesses the same properties. For the purpose of economizing notations, it is assumed that individuals enjoy consumption only when they grow old and retire. Denote the *n*-th generation's preference/production structure without money as $(1_{n+1}, 1_n)^n$. This symbol means that a new generation wants one unit of a future good. Nevertheless, the production opportunity is concentrated in the first half of their life and bears one unit of the current good. However, the older generation, born in the previous period, coexists with the younger. Their preference/production structure is $(1_n, 1_{n-1})^{n-1}$. According to Definition 15.1, it is clear that there exists a difficulty of double coincidence of wants between the coexisting n−1th and n th generations. No one enjoys consumption forever. This is the same structure as the former part of Kiyotaki and Wright (1989) analyzed above.

Consider that money is injected into the economy, and all individuals believe in the intrinsic value of money. Then, the preference/production structures change into:

$$(1_{n+1}, 1_n)^n \Rightarrow (m, 1_n)^n, (1_n, 1_{n-1})^{n-1} \Rightarrow (1_n, m)^{n-1}, \quad \forall n \geq 1. \tag{15.11}$$

Equation (15.11) implies that the introduction of money creates a sequence of the *match*. That is:

$$\left\{(m, 1_n)^n, (1_n, m)^{n-1}\right\}, \quad \forall n \geq 1. \tag{15.12}$$

Equation (15.12) implies that the very existence of money dissolves the difficulty. Money serves not merely as a store of value (younger individuals save their money preparing for consumption) but also as a medium of transaction (older individuals buy goods from the young in exchange for their hoarding money).

Consequently, search theory does not exceed the OLG model in the sense that both acknowledge money to be both a transaction medium and a store of value for overcoming the difficulty of the double coincidence of wants. If both theories describe the same distinct features of a monetary economy, superiority should be judged from tractability in analyzing phenomena peculiar to a monetary economy. As the contents of this book suggest, the OLG model can provide definitive answers to various problems in a monetary economy. However, there is still difficulty in analyzing how a change in the nominal money supply affects the economy when the search model is deployed.

15.3 The Kiyotaki–Wright (1991) Model and Its Properties

15.3.1 Structure of the Model

In this section, we consider the other contribution of the Kiyotaki–Wright theory to monetary economics. The model developed in this book entirely depends on Kiyotaki and Wright (1991). The individual actors are classified into three: producers; commodity traders; and money traders. A producer possesses nothing and is searching for an opportunity for production. A commodity trader has already finished production and is searching for a counterpart of exchange. This counterpart is a commodity trader or a money trader. To become a money trader, it is necessary to become a commodity trader in advance. A money trader seeks a commodity trader for consumption. Money is assumed to be accepted with probability one by any trader, whereas a similar situation never exists as a guarantee in barter trade.

15.3.2 Assumptions

The assumptions of the model can now be stated:

1. A unit good produced by each producer is differentiated in the interval $z \in [0, 1]$. The good z is more preferable when z approaches 0. Namely, the utility derived from the consumption of a unit good z, $u(z)$, is a decreasing function of z;
2. There are three positions that an individual may occupy: a "producer", a "commodity trader", and/or a "money trader". Producers are in the process of searching for an opportunity for production. If they encounter a beneficial production opportunity, they produce a unit of good and wait to exchange this for other types of good, because the model excludes the possibility of self-consumption. An individual in such a position is called a commodity trader. Commodity traders face two opportunities. When they encounter other types of commodity trader who have a good that meets their preference, they exchange goods and go back to being a producer. Otherwise, when they encounter a money trader, who has a unit of fiat money, they sell goods in exchange for money and become a money trader. Money traders are only searching for the opportunity to purchase their favorite goods. When they succeed in this transaction, they consume it and return to being a producer. However, money is nearly perishable, and they can stay in this position within the utmost time length ε;
3. The opportunity of production follows a Poisson process with mean α. Further, the opportunity of exchange also follows the Poisson process with mean β; and
4. $F(C)$is the cumulative distribution function of the production cost C. If C is located above x, the producer waits for the next chance.

15.3.3 Analysis of the Model

In this section the Kiyotaki–Wright (1991) model is explained, and it is proven that money never circulates without the role of a store of value, contrary to their assertion. Let the expected lifetime utility of a producer, commodity trader, and money trader be denoted as V_p, V_c, and V_m, respectively. In this case, it is easy to show that:

$$rV_p = \alpha \int_0^x \left[V_c - V_p - u(C) \right] dF(C). \tag{15.13}$$

and that:

$$rV_c = \beta \left[1-m\right] \int_0^x \left\{ u(z) - \left[V_c - V_p \right] \right\} dz + \beta\, m y \left[V_m - V_c \right]. \tag{15.14}$$

Where: m is the ratio of money traders to total traders and is given exogenously; x denotes the upper bound of the good at which a commodity trader accepts an exchange; and y is the upper bound of the good that a money trader accepts in exchange for money.

Here Eqs. (15.13) and (15.14) have the following economic meaning. The left-hand side of each equation represents the returns from maintaining a position. The right-hand side is the gains obtained by changing position, which includes realized utility from consumption and/or the implicit capital gain from upgrading a position. To equalize both sides of the equation, the values of the lifetime utility V_p, V_c, are determined. The problem for the Kiyotaki–Wright (1991) model lies in the derivation of V_m. The transition from a money trader to a producer is classified into four cases if money is not storable:

i. To match with a commodity trader and exchange money for a good;
ii. To match with a non-preferable commodity trader and get nothing;
iii. To match with a money trader and get nothing; or
iv. To match with no one.

Summing these four cases gives:

$$V_m = e^{-r\varepsilon} \left\{ \beta\varepsilon \left[\left[1-m\right] \int_0^y u(z) \mathrm{d}z + V_p \right] + \left[1 - \beta\varepsilon\right] V_p \right\} + o(\varepsilon). \tag{15.15}$$

Where: ε is the short interval within which money can serve as a medium of exchange.

The first term of the right-hand side of Eq. (15.15) corresponds to Case i, ii, and iii, and the second term corresponds to Case iv. Subtracting $e^{-r\varepsilon} V_m$ from both sides and rearranging the terms:

$$\frac{1-e^{-r\varepsilon}}{\varepsilon} V_m = e^{-r\varepsilon} \left\{ \beta \left[1-m\right] \int_0^y u(z) \mathrm{d}z + \left[\frac{V_p - V_m}{\varepsilon} \right] \right\} + o(\varepsilon). \tag{15.16}$$

Letting $\varepsilon \to 0$:

$$rV_m = \beta[1-m]\int_0^y u(z)\mathrm{d}z + \lim_{\varepsilon \to 0}\frac{V_p - V_m}{\varepsilon}. \tag{15.17}$$

In addition to Eqs. (15.13), (15.14), and (15.16), the value-matching conditions require that:

$$V_c = V_p + u(x). \tag{15.18}$$

$$V_m = V_p \tag{15.19}$$

Equation (15.19) is necessary for Eq. (15.16) or (15.17) to retain economic meaning. The reason $V_m = V_p$ is required is to prevent the return from being a money trader from diverging to negative infinity. That is, if Eq. (15.19) is not satisfied, a discontinuous jump in the value function occurs with probability one within any small interval. Economically, this implies that the loss caused by perishing money (the second term of Eq. (15.17)) is kept invariant while the gain from the trade becomes infinitesimally small (the first term of Eq. (15.17)) when the relevant interval approaches zero.

This model possesses five equations and five endogenous variables (V_p, V_c, V_m, x, y). As such, it is closed. Nevertheless, it contains a contradiction for circulating money, as expressed in the following theorem:

Theorem 15.1
In the model, $V_c > V_m$, holds, and money never circulates under Assumption 2.

Proof
From Eqs. (15.18) and (15.19):

$$V_c = V_p + u(x) > V_p = V_m.$$

Inequality $V_c > V_m$ implies that no commodity trader wishes to become a money trader. Accordingly, money never circulates without possessing the role of a store of value.

15.3.4 Money as a Store of Value

In this section, Assumption 2 is replaced and it is assumed that money is perpetually storable. Then, the transition from a money trader to a producer may be classified into four cases:

i. To match with a preferred commodity trader, exchange money for a good, and then become a producer;
ii. To match with a non-preferable commodity trader, and stay a money holder;

iii. To match with a money trader, get nothing, and stay a money trader; or
iv. To match with no one, and stay a money trader.

Consequently:

$$V_m = e^{-r\varepsilon} \left\{ \begin{array}{l} \left\{ \beta \varepsilon [1-m] \int_0^y u(z)\, dz + yV_p \right\} \\ +\beta \varepsilon \left\{ m + [1-m][1-y] \right\} V_m + [1-\beta \varepsilon] V_m \end{array} \right\} + o(\varepsilon).$$

The first term on the right-hand side corresponds to the expected utility gained in Case (i), the second term corresponds to the gain in Cases (ii) and (iii), and the third term is the gain in Case (iv). Rearranging terms and letting $\varepsilon \to 0$ gives:

$$rV_m = \beta [1-m] \left\{ \int_0^y \left[u(z) - \left[V_m - V_p \right] \right] dz \right\}. \tag{15.20}$$

Equation (15.20) is the equation that Kiyotaki and Wright (1991) actually use for the proof of the existence of a monetary economy. Interchanging the value-matching conditions $V_m = V_p$ with $V_m = V_p + u(y)$ gives:

$$V_m = V_p + u(y), V_c = V_p + u(x). \tag{15.21}$$

Equation (15.21) leads to the following lemma:

Lemma 15.1

$$y < x \tag{15.22}$$

Proof
Whenever a monetary economy is sustainable, the position of money trader should be strictly preferred to that of commodity trader. Hence:

$$V_m > V_p \tag{15.23}$$

holds.
From Eq. (15.21):

$$u(y) > u(x). \tag{15.24}$$

Equation (15.24) is equivalent to Eq. (15.22).

To prove that even though money is storable, it never circulates within Kiyotaki and Wright (1991), Eq. (15.20) must be a monotonously increasing function of y. That is, by substituting Eq. (15.21) into (15.20):

$$rV_m(y) = \beta [1-m] \left[\int_0^y \left[u(z) - u(y) \right] dz \right]. \tag{15.25}$$

Differentiating Eq. (15.25) with respect to y shows that:

$$r\frac{dV_m(y)}{dy} = -\beta[1-m]u'(y)y\left[\int_0^y [u(z)-]dz\right] > 0, \tag{15.26}$$

holds. Meanwhile, it should be noted that:

$$0 \leq y \leq x. \tag{15.27}$$

Accordingly, if once an individual becomes a money trader, the critical value y is such that:

$$y = x, \tag{15.28}$$

Equation (15.28) contradicts Lemma 15.1. Thus, there is no individual who wants money.

Consequently:

Theorem 15.2
*Money never circulates in the Kiyotaki–Wright (*1991*) model even though it is storable.*

The critical reason that money never circulates is that there is no advantage stemming from money hoarding. In other words, unlike in their previous article, Kiyotaki and Wright (1991) did not succeed in entering the difficulty of the double coincidence of wants into the model.

15.4 Concluding Remarks

This chapter has shown that money never circulates as a purely transactional medium in the search model, as suggested by Kiyotaki and Wright (1991). To sustain the monetary economy, money should also be a store of value that presumes the existence of the difficulty of the double coincidence of wants. In this sense, both functions are inseparable and are innate natures attached to money. Finally, if both functions are required in the search model, the OLG model seems far more tractable than the search model developed by Kiyotaki and Wright (1989), because money plays the same roles within the search model: the younger generation receives money as a store of value, and the older generation uses it as a transaction medium.

References

Diamond P (1982) Aggregate-demand management in search equilibrium. J Polit Econ 90:881–894
Kiyotaki N, Wright R (1989) On money as a medium of exchange. J Polit Econ 97:927–954

Kiyotaki N, Wright R (1991) A contribution to the pure theory of money. J Econ Theory 23:215–235
Lucas R Jr (1972) Expectations and the neutrality of money. J Econ Theory 4:103–124
Samuelson P (1958) An exact consumption loan model of interest with or without the contrivance of money. J Polit Econ 66:467–482

Appendix: Exchanges of Views Between Referees and the Author

Several referees provided helpful comments on the author's initial draft, in the form of referee reports. The referee comments have been summarized below. The author attempts to reply to the comments in the following way.

Reviewer 1

Comment 1
I am afraid that the fundamental equation fails to induce the correct equilibrium price sequence. For example, the author fixes the equilibrium price P_{t+1} to solve the current equilibrium price P_t. If so, he needs to fix P_{t+2} to solve P_{t+1} and so on. It seems to me that this procedure contradicts the infinite time horizon OLG model.

Reply to Comment 1
The fundamental equation is a non-linear *first-order* difference equation. Hence, if we begin by providing an initial condition that has a plausible economic meaning (we call such a condition *confidence of money*), we can obtain an exact equilibrium price sequence of REE.

Reviewer 2

Comment 1
I agree with the author that the fundamental equation determines the equilibrium inflation rate. However, even though the assumption of the confidence of money is upheld and future equilibrium prices are governed by that equation, it seems to me that how the initial (or current) price, P_t, is determined is quite ambiguous.

M. Otaki, *Keynesian Economics and Price Theory*,
Advances in Japanese Business and Economics 7, DOI 10.1007/978-4-431-55345-8

Reply to Comment 1

If the assumption of the *confidence of money* is permissible (I believe so), backward induction based on the fundamental equation solves the initial equilibrium price p_t.

Comment 2

There is an alternative procedure to overcome the indeterminacy of the absolute price level within the infinite time horizon OLG model (i.e., *fiscal theory of price level determination*). This procedure is characterized as follows.

First, the policy variable is assumed to be the rate of interest, and thus real money supply becomes an endogenous variable. Second, the integrated and intertemporal budget constraint of the government and the central bank is never violated. Accordingly, the absolute price level is determined such that the endogenous real money supply keeps the intertemporal balanced-budget condition for a given path of nominal money supply. Compared with this hypothesis, what is the advantage of the author's concept (i.e., the *confidence* of money)?

Reply to Comment 2

This problem belongs not to the consistency of logic but to the relevance of the assumptions. In general, an OLG model assumes the decentralization of decision making across generations. An individual's concern is limited to his/her lifetime. From this point of view, the concept of the *credibility of money,* which asserts that individuals believe in the stable value of money in their lifetime, is a natural presumption compared with the *fiscal theory of price level determination*, which requires information concerning an infinitely far future.

In addition, we should remember the current difficult economic conditions in Japan. Despite the exorbitant accumulation of public debt and undisciplined fiscal deficits, the price level (CPI) is quite stable. How does the *fiscal theory of price determination* explain such a reality?

Comment 3

What happens if the growth rate of nominal money supply differs from the inflation rate, which is determined by the fundamental equation?

Reply to Comment 3

Our main concern is to exhibit a stationary equilibrium that follows Keynesian theory. For this purpose, the nominal money supply growth rate is fixed to the equilibrium inflation rate determined by the fundamental equation. Otherwise, if that growth rate is above (below) the equilibrium inflation rate, full (zero) employment is ultimately achieved.

Index

M. Otaki, *Keynesian Economics and Price Theory,*
Advances in Japanese Business and Economics 7, DOI 10.1007/978-4-431-55345-8

MIX
Papier aus verantwortungsvollen Quellen
Paper from responsible sources
FSC® C105338

If you have any concerns about our products,
you can contact us on
ProductSafety@springernature.com

In case Publisher is established outside the EU,
the EU authorized representative is:
Springer Nature Customer Service Center GmbH
Europaplatz 3, 69115 Heidelberg, Germany

Printed by Libri Plureos GmbH
in Hamburg, Germany